LAW AND THE STRANGER

The Amherst Series in Law, Jurisprudence, and Social Thought

EDITED BY

Austin Sarat, Lawrence Douglas, and Martha Merrill Umphrey

Law and the Stranger

Edited by

AUSTIN SARAT

LAWRENCE DOUGLAS

MARTHA MERRILL UMPHREY

STANFORD LAW BOOKS

An imprint of Stanford University Press • Stanford, California

Stanford University Press
Stanford, California

Library of Congress Cataloging-in-Publication Data

Law and the stranger / edited by Austin Sarat, Lawrence Douglas, and Martha Merrill Umphrey.
p. cm. — (The Amherst series in law, jurisprudence, and social thought)
Includes bibliographical references and index.
ISBN 978-0-8047-7154-2 (cloth : alk. paper)
1. Aliens. 2. Emigration and immigration law—Philosophy. 3. Law—Philosophy. 4. Sociological jurisprudence. I. Sarat, Austin. II. Douglas, Lawrence. III. Umphrey, Martha Merrill. IV. Series: Amherst series in law, jurisprudence, and social thought.
K3274.L39 2010
342.08'3—dc22

2009052925

Printed in the United States of America on acid-free, archival-quality paper

Typeset at Stanford University Press in 10/14.5 Minion

For my son Ben with love and the hope that he finds a world of hospitality (AS)

Acknowledgments

The essays contained in this book were originally prepared for and presented as a seminar series at Amherst College. We are grateful to our Amherst College colleagues David Delaney, Nasser Hussain, and Adam Sitze for their intellectual companionship. We thank our students in Amherst College's Department of Law, Jurisprudence and Social Thought for their interest in the issues addressed in this book. Finally, we would like to express our appreciation for generous financial support provided by Amherst College.

Contents

Contributors

PAUL SCHIFF BERMAN is Dean and Foundation Professor of Law at the Sandra Day O'Connor College of Law at Arizona State University

LEORA BILSKY is Senior Lecturer in the Faculty of Law at Tel-Aviv University

PHENG CHEAH is Associate Professor of Rhetoric at the University of California, Berkeley

LAWRENCE DOUGLAS is James J. Grosfeld Professor of Law, Jurisprudence and Social Thought at Amherst College

AUSTIN SARAT is the William Nelson Cromwell Professor of Jurisprudence and Political Science and Professor of Law, Jurisprudence and Social Thought at Amherst College

HILARY SCHOR is Professor of English, Comparative Literature, Gender Studies, and Law at the University of Southern California

ROGERS M. SMITH is Christopher H. Browne Distinguished Professor of Political Science at the University of Pennsylvania

MARTHA MERRILL UMPHREY is Professor of Law, Jurisprudence and Social Thought at Amherst College

KENJI YOSHINO is Chief Justice Earl Warren Professor of Constitutional Law at New York University School of Law

LAW AND THE STRANGER

Negotiating (with) Strangers

AUSTIN SARAT
LAWRENCE DOUGLAS
MARTHA MERRILL UMPHREY

Law calls community into being. It constitutes the "we" it governs, hailing us as those subject to its power, naming us as the group under its jurisdiction. This performative act of naming necessarily produces an outside as well as an inside, a border whose crossing is guarded in order to maintain the identity, coherence, and integrity of the space and people within. Those wishing to enter must negotiate a complex terrain of defensive mechanisms, expectations, assumptions, and legal proscriptions. Is that, "we" ask, someone who should be allowed to enter, someone to whom we should offer hospitality? We in turn negotiate those questions with and through law, which enforces the boundary between inside and outside in both physical and epistemological ways. We know who "we" are by situating ourselves, or by being situated, in relation to that boundary.

Law and the Stranger explores ways in which law, and in particular liberal legal regimes, identifies and responds to strangers within and across their borders, both historically and in the present day. The chapters in this book analyze the ambiguous place strangers occupy in communities not their own, and each chapter, from its own perspective (whether theoretical, jurisprudential, historical, or literary), reflects on the ways in which dealing with strangers challenges the laws and communities that invite or parry them.

The inquiries here are all the more timely because questions about how nations, peoples, and communities ought to negotiate with strangers have emerged as an increasingly pressing issue in the early twenty-first century, a time of intensified global conflict and global interconnection both economically and technologically. While Barack Obama may be moving away from the by-now familiar invocation of a "war on terror," it remains the case that the geopolitics of the United States and Western Europe are inextricably connected to battles, both military and cultural, being fought in other lands. And, as the recent global economic crisis has all too clearly emphasized, the interdependence of nations with each other and with global institutions means that vulnerabilities apparent in one nation's economy reverberate around the world in waves that can bring smaller nations to their knees.

In such a context, conflicts (whether literal or metaphoric) among states, religions, classes, ethnicities, religions, and cultural groups seem to impose themselves on liberal legal regimes in ways that can put their liberalism under pressure. How have and should liberal states confer recognition on those who knock on the door and ask for entry? What complications arise when those perceived as strangers are inside the polity rather than outside supplicants? What, if anything, is owed to strangers without regard to their moral, political, or economic worth?

To the extent that extending hospitality is a legal project, a bestowing of recognition according to conditions created by law, we might say that strangers are made through law, rather than born through accidents of geography. What kind of legal subject is constituted by these processes of recognition? How does the legal recognition of a stranger come to constitute both stranger and self?

What Is a Stranger?

Georg Simmel, one of the most insightful commentators on the social identity of the stranger, argued that strangers are not, as common sense might have it, those who are not known, but are instead those who have been encountered but not fully assimilated into the community. Simmel describes strangers as potential wanderers, people within a community who have not belonged to it from the start and who import qualities that do not stem from the community itself. Such people are, he writes, "a synthesis of nearness and distance." Under auspicious circumstances, that ambiguous position within a group can confer a distinct kind of power on the stranger in relation to the rest of the community.

Dwelling, however temporarily, with others, strangers approach new communities with what Simmel describes as an attitude of "objectivity" because the stranger is not "radically committed to the unique ingredients and particular tendencies of the group." Strangers such as these can engender a particular kind of intimacy dependent upon their remove from the enveloping everyday world of common custom and culture. They can be entrusted with community members' confidences and confessions that cannot otherwise be spoken. The stranger's objectivity accords him or her a bird's-eye view, unburdened by "habit, piety, and precedent."[1]

Focusing specifically on cultural narratives of the stranger, Bonnie Honig builds on this insight in *Democracy and the Foreigner*, arguing that fantasies of foreignness point to not just fear of corruption but also its cure. Honig argues that narratives that imagine foreigners specifically as founders rather than enemies point to a deep impulse toward renewal. "Sometimes," she notes, "the figure of the foreigner serves as a device that allows regimes to import from outside (and then, often, to export back to the outside) some specific and much-needed but also potentially dangerous virtue, talent, perspective, practice, gift, or quality that they cannot provide for themselves (or they cannot admit they have)."[2] In Honig's view, our capacity to imagine foreigners as founders creates the possibility of what she calls "democratic cosmopolitanism," an ideal that "seeks out friends and partners even (or especially) among strangers and foreigners."[3] Such strangers become objects of desire, sometimes mythologized, who continually help to refound the national community.[4]

Yet both Simmel and Honig note that even those strangers we seem to welcome are also dangerous presences, easily transmuted into scapegoats when communities feel threatened. As Rene Girard observed, scapegoating and sacrificial violence restore equilibrium to a community threatened by internally generated violence.[5] Simmel ties this possibility to the greater distance and objectivity of the stranger, which enables those within a community under attack to claim that they were provoked from outside the community, not from within.[6] Honig reverses the logic of Simmel's proposition insofar as she argues that a scapegoat need not be in the first instance a foreigner; rather, a scapegoat is one cast as a foreigner, and as such, cast out of a community. Scapegoating, she argues, is "a social practice that finds or produces the object it needs."[7]

Simmel suggests that a stranger's dual remoteness and nearness has a further effect: in giving a community a sense of the more abstracted nature of the relation between it and those beyond its geographic or cultural borders, the stranger's ambiguous presence highlights the general qualities shared by all individuals. "The stranger is close to us, insofar as we feel between him and ourselves common features of a national, social, occupational, or generally human, nature. He is far from us, insofar as these common features extend beyond him or us, and connect us only because they connect a great many people."[8] If the stranger is not "one of us," the connections we perceive with him or her nevertheless point to a thin but powerful basis for reciprocal recognition even across the sometimes high barriers of group identification, of the kind necessary for a regime of human rights.[9]

Strangers and Hospitality

"I have always depended upon the kindness of strangers," purrs Blanche DuBois in Tennessee Williams's *A Streetcar Named Desire*. Blanche's imposition on strangers is cast as an ethical problem in Williams's play, but some scholars have noted that beyond the ethical there is, or ought to be, a legal dimension to the extension of hospitality to strangers. The foundation of these claims is Immanuel Kant's argument that strangers have what he calls a "cosmopolitan right . . . not to be treated in a hostile manner by another upon his arrival on the other's territory." This right, Kant suggests, is "a right to *visit,* to which all human beings have a claim, to present oneself to society by virtue of the right of common possession of the earth."[10] This argument posits a thin but broad basis for a right—one need not recognize in the stranger even Simmel's "common features of a national, social, occupational, or generally human, nature"—and that right is at best minimal: not to be treated with hostility upon arrival. Yet it is a universal right, one that subtends much of the present era's theorizations concerning proper exercises of law in a globalizing world.

Distinguishing between the foreigner and the barbarian (of which more below), Jacques Derrida extends Kant's analysis in arguing that what he calls "conditional hospitality" involves reciprocal obligations, passed down across generations, based on a logic of minimal familiarity. That, in turn, "presupposes . . . that it is possible for them [the foreigners] to be called by their names, to have names, to be subjects in law, to be questioned and to be liable, to have crimes imputed to them, to be held responsible, to be equipped with nameable identities, and proper names."[11] This capacity to be named by and before the law makes the stranger legible to the law. As Derrida describes it:

> [T]his foreigner, then, is someone with whom to receive him, you begin by asking his name; you enjoin him to state and to guarantee his identity, as you would a witness before a court. This is someone to whom you put a question and address a demand, the first demand, the minimal demand being: "What is your name?" or then "In telling me what your name is, in responding to this request, you are responding on your own behalf, you are responsible before the law and before your hosts, you are a subject in law."[12]

Although the question "What is your name?" may require a translated response, its very asking not only invites but interpolates a good-faith respondent into the law, which for Derrida confers a right to hospitality on the stranger and engenders reciprocal responsibilities.

In Derrida's view, however, that right is contingent; the host must necessarily choose the guest. There is, Derrida says, no hospitality without sovereignty over one's home; and "since there is also no hospitality without finitude, sovereignty can only be exercised by filtering, choosing, and thus by excluding and doing violence."[13] Hence Derrida, unlike Kant, sees the conferral of hospitality and legal recognition as always already bound up with the violence of law.

Border Patrol: Law's Negotiations with Strangers

In a world of nation-states, modern law organizes these general conceptualizations of the stranger along the axis of citizen/alien. As Rogers Smith reminds us in his chapter in this book, conditions of exclusion and conditional entry vary from culture to culture and era to era, but immigration restrictions and border patrols are constant features of the modern nation state.[14] Border crossings can be dangerous business; now, in our tightly controlled world borders are in some places likely to be walls made of concrete, metal, and barbed wire; guards are ready with weapons and ever-searching gazes; and noncitizens are subject to passport controls and biometric scans, and sometimes redirected to small, windowless interrogation rooms.[15]

Beyond those concrete borders, though, liberal legal regimes by their very nature grapple continuously with the question of how to negotiate with strangers standing at their points of entry: those who wish to gain access to the privileges of citizenship, those who request entry on a contingent basis for economic or other reasons, and those who remain outside the physical or legal boundaries of the sovereign state but who are nevertheless interwoven in some way with it. As Seyla Benhabib puts it:

> Sovereignty entails the right of a people to control its borders as well as define the procedures for admitting "aliens" into its territory and society; yet in a liberal democratic polity, such sovereignty claims must always be constrained by human rights, which individuals are entitled to, not by virtue of being citizens or members of a polity, but insofar as they are simply human beings.[16]

If one agrees with Benhabib that there is, descriptively, a set of universal rights,[17] then one must ask, normatively speaking, how liberal legal regimes should accommodate strangers who claim the right of hospitality.

Embracing the concept of "human rights" in their most abstract form, one that empties humans of their specificity in order to confer universal rights upon abstract legal subjects, does not, Will Kymlicka suggests, in the end resolve some of the most important issues emerging from cultural difference.[18] Rather, negotiations across borders require a thicker understanding of both the subjects in negotiation and the ethical relations at stake. Contemporary scholars have framed their analysis of this problematic in a number of ways. Some emphasize differences across groups and identities and call for a politics of recognition that accords dignity and respect—and sometimes legal recognition—to those differences. The literature in this area emphasizes the dialogic nature of identity production and urges attention to, in particular, cultural diversity.[19]

According of substantive rights through mutual recognition, argues Axel Honneth, confers both self-respect (the capacity to assert claims as a morally responsible agent) and self-esteem (the capacity to be distinguished as an individual according to qualities that are valued).[20] A liberal polity, these scholars suggest, has the moral responsibility to engage in a politics of equal recognition of this sort, particularly in an increasingly multicultural world. This type of analysis informs the work of the kind done in this book by Paul Berman and Leora Bilsky, both of whom are concerned to create discursive legal spaces open enough that conflicts between states and communities can be articulated and adjudicated in a way that respects national and cultural differences.

Other scholars emphasize the ways in which identities hybridize when individuals and groups interact, producing a cosmopolitanism that can transcend the we/they binary. As Benhabib puts it:

> I think of cultures as complex human practices of signification and representation, of organization and attribution, which are internally driven by conflicting narratives. Cultures are formed through complex dialogues with other cultures. In most cultures that have attained some degree of internal differentiation, the dialogue with the other(s) is internal rather than extrinsic to the culture itself.[21]

Julia Kristeva suggests that one who chooses cosmopolitanism is one who, "against origins and starting from them, [has] chosen a transnational or international position situated at the crossing of boundaries."[22]

Indeed, scholars of cosmopolitism problematize the very idea of the border or boundary in ways that cut against some multiculturalists' assumptions about the authenticity and containability of differing cultures. As Homi Bhabha observes, "The boundary is Janus-faced and the problem of outside/inside must always itself be a process of hybridity, incorporating new 'people' in relation to a body politic." Indeed, Bhabha argues, "The 'other' is never outside or beyond us; it emerges forcefully, within cultural discourse, when we *think* we speak most intimately and indigenously 'between ourselves.'"[23] One can see this dynamic at play most clearly in the chapters by Hilary Schor and Kenji Yoshino, below, both of which turn to the literary to trace internal contradictions in narratives about the relation between strangers and law. Theorizing cosmopolitanism enables a self-reflexivity that destabilizes the citizen/alien binary. To the extent that we are capable of such self-reflexivity, our task is to recognize our own internal foreignness in order to discover and abjure what Kristeva calls "the violence of the desire to be different."[24]

The Stranger and the Barbarian

Of course, not all polities are liberal, and not all liberal polities adhere to principles of liberalism and human rights at every turn. When apparently endangered either by threats of external violence or fears of economic disruption, even liberal legal regimes can exert a fierce sovereign power that discriminates and repulses those desiring to enter. The tension inhering in dialogues between those inside and outside a polity, whether literalized in an exchange at an actual border or built into the gritty details of any law governing immigration, informs a community's identity, which, as Benedict Anderson tells us, is imagined as both limited and sovereign.[25] In his controversial work *The Clash of*

Civilizations, for example, Samuel Huntington argues that "we know who we are only when we know who we are not and often only when we know whom we are against."[26] The first part of this claim seems relatively uncontroversial. As Robert Cover argued, the stories we tell about our selves, our origins, and our moral and ethical commitments, and that inform the law of any given *nomos*, help to differentiate us from groups we perceive to hold different commitments.[27] Identity is in that sense profoundly relational. Huntington's further claim, however—that we know who we are "often only" by identifying our *enemies*—extends that proposition in undifferentiated ways, and places violence rather than respect at the heart of the self-other relation.

This conception of the we/they relation harkens back to the problematic of scapegoating and reminds us of Honig's claim that scapegoating is a social practice that finds or produces the object it needs. The move to classify the other as "enemy" rather than "stranger" as a means of self-knowledge and self-recognition implies the possibility that strangers can be *manufactured* in order to define and strengthen a community's identity. What is law's role in that process? That role might be best perceived by examining a limit case, one in which a community reimagines a member or encounters another who, rather than being forcibly excluded or forbidden from entering for reasons of policy, is thought *incapable* of meaningful entry into "civilized" community quite without regard to policy or expedience. This kind of epistemic violence need not be written into any legal regulation (though often enough across the history of colonialism, for example, it was). For reasons of language, of custom, of religion, of climate, of physiology, even of being, some borders appear unbreachable.

To assert a divide between potential recognition and necessary nonrecognition is to invoke the venerable conceptual distinction between the stranger and the barbarian. The word "barbarian" has its origins in ancient Greece: the Greeks caricatured those who lived outside their city-states after what they heard as the guttural, untranslatable "bar-bar" of their speech. From its inception, then, the word signified both linguistic opacity and lack of interest in overcoming that opacity. In Derrida's terms, barbarians are those who cannot have a name, and therefore cannot be interpolated into the law. Strangers can be offered hospitality and brought into the fold; barbarians cannot, and are therefore always already excluded from the reciprocal relations of conditional hospitality.[28]

Uday Singh Mehta asserts that the term "barbarian" took on a distinctly modern character only during the Enlightenment, when philosophers and politicians began to conceive of barbarism as the direct converse of "civilization."[29] Moreover, Hannah Arendt locates the origins of totalitarianism in this kind of "race thinking" and argues that its logic ultimately generated, after World War I, stateless populations that were no longer accorded the rights of man.[30] Having lost their homes and political status, refugees found it impossible to find a new place in a world in which humanity was, finally, completely organized and "civilized." Like scapegoats, the stateless no longer belonged to any community whatsoever, with the result that they lost the very right to have rights.[31] And like savages, stateless people were, and are, thrown back into a state of nature in which they live and die without leaving a trace.[32]

One can see the effects of this kind of displacement in Pheng Cheah's chapter on migrant workers in a global economy. Perhaps the best example of contemporary legal attempts to constitute a class of stateless "barbarians," nameless, untranslatable, and unrecognizable to law, is the post 9/11 Bush administration strategy of holding "alien enemy combatants" at the U.S. naval base at Guantanamo Bay, Cuba. As Amy Kaplan has made clear, since the United States brokered a lease agreement with the Cuban government in 1903 (made perpetual in 1934), Guantanamo Bay has served as a "transitional political space," one with an indeterminate relation to law grounded in the harsh history of U.S. imperialism.[33]

In 2002, exerting what it asserted was plenary executive authority, the Bush administration began to use Guantanamo as a detention center for several hundred men captured abroad, mostly in Afghanistan during the early days of combat, detaining them indefinitely and incommunicado. In a series of cases beginning in 2004, the Bush administration argued that because Cuba, not the United States, is under the lease agreement the "ultimate sovereign" governing Guantanamo Bay, U.S. courts lacked jurisdiction to issue the "Great Writ" of habeas corpus to force the government to articulate a reason for holding prisoners in Guantanamo.[34] In conjuring the new legal category "enemy combatant" in order to exempt those persons from many of the protections of international law and international treaties, the Bush administration attempted effectively to render stateless those it detained in a place unmoored from any sovereign law. Its inhabitants erased as legal subjects, Guantanamo became, to those who endorsed this strategy, synonymous with a black hole that no legal light could penetrate.

Refusing this rendering of foreign nationals as barbarians, both the Supreme Court and the Obama administration have recognized those in Guantanamo as strangers owed some hospitality by U.S. courts, giving name to them in law by asserting the expansiveness of habeas corpus at least in places over which the United States has de facto sovereignty.[35] The Court's decisions rest on a reading of the legal history of habeas corpus rather than an analysis of the universality of human rights, and as such are limited in their reach. Yet the decisions can stand for the proposition forwarded by Arendt, that the right to have rights can be guaranteed by humanity itself—indeed only by humanity itself (that is, no longer by nature or history, as the great Enlightenment political philosophers imagined)—through government.[36] In granting the minimal recognition of habeas corpus, the Supreme Court's extension of the reach of U.S. sovereignty in effect allows the detainees to name themselves before the law: it accords them conditional hospitality, which in turn engages the minimal reciprocity of recognition by right.[37]

As Kristeva suggests, "Strangely, the foreigner lives within us: he is the hidden face of our identity, the space that wrecks our abode, the time in which understanding and affinity founder."[38] Thus the struggle between the Bush administration and the courts is a struggle, in the end, over the very definition of "Americanness." Debates about the rights that the United States will accord strangers-turned-barbarians have made us agonizingly self-conscious of the tensions in our own moral and legal commitment to the ideal of the rule of law. We have watched ourselves as we have responded to revelations of torture and abuse, to assertions about the need for indefinite detainment, and to the countermoves various institutions have made as they resist those revelations and assertions. As a number of the chapters in this book suggest, that self-consciousness can point in the direction of a greater justice, both now and in the future.

Overview of the Chapters

In the chapters that follow, our contributors examine sites of encounter and estrangement within and across the borders of nation-states, situating "strangers" in the delicately ambiguous space wherein legal recognition and the rendering of hospitality is negotiated. We begin with two chapters that explicitly address relations of hospitality, exploring how legislation and court decisions conjure strangers in particular ways that can either emphasize or de-emphasize the divide between citizen and alien.

Pheng Cheah's "Necessary Strangers: Law's Hospitality in the Age of Transnational Migrancy" explores the ways in which global capitalism, and the circulation of workers across borders, creates what he calls "necessary strangers." Cheah both takes up and critiques Kant's ideas on neighborliness and hospitality as a way of framing his analysis of globalization's effects. Kant argues that conditional hospitality of the sort discussed above flows from sovereignty and nation states, and that law's relation to the stranger is governed by a dynamic of attraction and repulsion that can be overcome only by the unconditional hospitality afforded through commerce and world trade. Cheah counters this claim of Kant's with two examples illustrating the ways in which contemporary globalization intensifies rather than ameliorates the tension one already finds in law between the attraction and repulsion of the stranger: the legal construction of female migrant domestic workers in Southeast Singapore and migrant sex workers moving from mainland China to Hong Kong.

Foreign domestic workers and sex workers—that is, low-status workers—are fundamentally disposable in the world market, Cheah argues, and law is implicated in global capitalism's modalities of inclusion and exclusion. One can see this hostility, he suggests, in Singapore's imposition of levies and security bonds on families who hire foreign domestic workers. Cheah also analyses Fruit Chan's 2000 film *Durian Durian*, in which a mainland Chinese sex worker travels to Hong Kong and then back to the mainland. Though the protagonist can find refuge in ties of friendship, Cheah notes that her work disqualifies her from the law's hospitality, rendering her permanently dislocated from both work and home. Moreover, Cheah argues, human rights law and international equality movements, which might ameliorate some of the more oppressive conditions of this conditional hospitality, are limited in vision, scope, and implementation. Both examples suggest that even in the world of global commerce, because law necessarily involves coercion, its hospitality can never be unconditional; global capitalism has made such workers into permanent strangers.

In "The Strangers in Ourselves: The Rights of Suspect Citizens in the Age of Terrorism," Rogers M. Smith traces an opposing tendency in U.S. legal history. Smith argues that courts and legislators have, over the course of the last two hundred years, treated citizens and aliens in the United States with relative equality: when the rights of aliens have been curtailed, so too have the rights of at least some citizens, and vice versa. That is, American political leaders have not generally sought support by expanding the rights of citizens at the expense of the rights of aliens (as opposed to denying rights along lines of race or ethnicity). For example, during World War II, all those of Japanese descent, whether citizens or noncitizen immigrants, were forced into internment camps. More recently, post-9/11, concern over threats from aliens and immigrants has had the effect of curtailing the rights of citizens as well.

Smith provides a history of this relative equality between citizens and aliens, focusing in particular on a recent confluence of, on the one hand, legislation aimed at limiting immigration that had the effect of curtailing various forms of public assistance more generally and, on the other, Bush-era legislation emerging out of the "war on terror" that weakened the boundary between citizen and alien, in relation to increasing the police powers of the state. That blurring, Smith argues, creates the danger that constitutional safeguards that do not apply abroad will also be eroded in the United States as well. The category of "unlawful enemy combatant," emerging out of the World War II–era case *Ex Parte Quirin*, applied to combatants of any nationality, citizen or noncitizen. Smith reviews several Bush-era cases that, even as they constrained the government from stripping prisoners of habeas protections, depended on the same kind of logic. He concludes that, in these contexts, the relative equation of citizens and noncitizens vis-à-vis rights denials is deliberate. The United States under the Bush administration viewed more of its citizens as "cultural strangers."

The next two chapters focus specifically on the problem of jurisdictional conflict and the jurisprudence of negotiating with strangers. In "Strangers Within: The Barghouti and the Bishara Criminal Trials," Leora Bilsky examines two terror trials in Israel. In these trials, the same acts of violence were considered, on one side, a legitimate part of political resistance and, on the other side, terrifying criminal acts. How, she asks, ought the criminal law of a sovereign state confront this kind of radical difference? In such trials judges take on an explicitly political role in adjudicating the boundary between inside and outside, one that threatens their courts' legitimacy, particularly if the court itself is perceived as allied with one of the adversarial parties.

Drawing on constitutional law and its relatively expansive view of judicial discretion, Bilsky suggests that certain legal reforms are necessary in the area of criminal law in order to confront directly the politics of boundary-drawing in political trials. In making this claim, she analyzes the trials of Azmi Bishara, an Israeli citizen and member of the Knesset, and Marwan Barghouti, an elected member of the Palestinian parliament. Both were indicted for making speeches that incited terror attacks, and both in different ways argued against the Israeli criminal courts' jurisdiction as a means of justifying their acts and contesting their unequal treatment. In each case, jurisdictional rules precluded such arguments.

Invoking the work of Alexander Bickel and other constitutional scholars, Bilsky proposes two reforms of criminal trials that would enlarge the space for such arguments in terror cases. First, she endorses the "abuse of process" defense, barring prosecution when there is "substantial harm to the sense of fairness and justice," as a way for courts to address the issue of unequal treatment of strangers directly. Second, she argues, Israeli courts ought to move in the direction of jury trials and embrace the possibility of jury nullification, whose secrecy makes possible an indirect corrective to the systematically unequal treatment of Arabs.

Paul Schiff Berman, in "Conflict of Laws and the Legal Negotiation of Difference," moves from the arena of criminal law to a more general critique of territory-based modes of adjudication. The existence of multiple normative communities in an era of globalization, Berman notes, requires that law constantly negotiate the "permeable and ever-shifting divide" between the familiar and the strange. Drawing on the works of Hannah Arendt and Iris Marion Young, and employing an expansive understanding of "law" to explore conflicts not just among sovereign nations but also among normative communities, Berman advocates what he calls a "cosmopolitan pluralist vision" of conflict of laws that both recognizes the multiple affiliations people hold and can enable the crafting of hybrid rules that blend laws across normative boundaries.

A number of cases, particularly those involving the Internet, prove Berman's point that territory-based modes of adjudication make little sense between sovereign states. Rather than accepting the sometimes nonsensical outcomes in those cases, Berman suggests that we might do better by adopting some concepts from conflict of laws jurisprudence—jurisdiction, choice of law, and judgment recognition—as means of negotiating with strangers in a globalized world. Such doctrines, properly understood, can generate an international and transnational process of community definition and norm creation, or, at the very least, open up a discursive space in which conflicts among normative communities can be adjudicated in a principled and substantive way. Ultimately, Berman argues, we should aspire to "unassimilable otherness," a state that allows communication across difference rather than annihilation of difference.

The final two chapters engage the question of negotiating with strangers through a literary lens, emphasizing the political and discursive estrangement of groups internal to particular communities. In "Who's the Stranger? Jews, Women, and Bastards in *Daniel Deronda*," Hilary M. Schor reads George Eliot's 1876 *Daniel Deronda* as a novel of strangers—Jews and women, disenfranchised aliens in England—who are both outside the law's full dispensation of rights and estranged by their own consciousness. Eliot wrote *Daniel Deronda* at a historical moment in England when Parliament was debating the emancipation of Jews (as well as other groups), a national conversation that raised difficult questions about the meaning one could attach to "England" as a nation. This general anxiety about the internal cohesiveness of community, and the identification of strangers within it, resonated across the social landscape; and as a backstory it informs the novel's complex intertwined plots, one involving Daniel Deronda's embrace of strangeness as he adopts his newly discovered Jewish identity, the other implicating Gwendolyn Harleth's increasing estrangement from herself as a woman and wife.

Schor argues that law in *Daniel Deronda* appears both implicitly, in persistent references to parliamentary debate at moments when the rights and privileges of Jews, women, and bastards are at issue, and explicitly in assertions that a "stranger" to the law, one without certain legal privileges, can still exert herself to become a kind of legal subject who makes and keeps promises. As the novel ends, after accepting her loss of social position with the death of a miscreant husband she had once promised another woman never to marry, a chastened Gwendolyn realizes her estrangement from herself and her community; and it is that felt estrangement, Schor suggests, that signals the first step in working toward a future of full rights and privileges for women. Indeed the very form of the novel, particularly its discontinuous time frame, signals the possibility of a future emancipation beyond the bounds of the text. Legal rights, Schor's reading of Eliot suggests, are only one part of that process, which begins with the first glimmerings of self-consciousness and understanding that one is a stranger even in the community in which one lives.

Kenji Yoshino also attends to the question of literary form in the final chapter, "Of Stranger Spaces." As a law and literature scholar concerned with the treatment of racial minorities, Yoshino takes up the genre of utopian literature, whose fanciful qualities allow us to reimagine our own world, and relates it to the "fancy" in some genres of legal rhetoric. While utopias offer us a useful picture of estrangement from the real worlds we inhabit, and engender a productive self-consciousness in their readers, Yoshino argues that they fail as both art and governance plans because the worlds they conjure are at best illiberal and antilegal.

He contrasts the illiberalism of utopias with the antitotalitarian gestures of "heterotopias," a concept first forwarded by Michel Foucault, to describe countersites in the real world that represent, contest, and invert other real-world sites in acts of imagination. In heterotopias, Yoshino argues, the world can be reimagined without being literally revised or enacted. This reimagining is a form of estrangement that we can see easily enough in literature, but can also be located within the world of legal discourse.

We might think that imagination has little place in law insofar as our primary concern is with wielding violence appropriately, and so we tend to exclude flights of fancy from legal reasoning on ethical grounds. And yet, Yoshino argues, legal actors often do engage in flights of fancy in heterotopic legal genres. He flags three in particular—dissents, hortatory laws (specifically the Universal Declaration of Human Rights), and dicta—locating in their rhetorical freedom the impulse to imagine a better world. Focusing specifically on the trope of colorblindness, Yoshino offers as examples of legal heterotopia Harlan's dissent in *Plessy*, the hortatory quality of the rhetoric in *Brown*, and O'Connor's dicta in *Grutter*. In each, he argues, we can see the ways in which poetry and imagination, grounded in the real, make possible a productive estrangement from the present and conjure another, more just, world.

Taken together, the chapters that follow understand encounters with strangers to be part of an ongoing and reiterative process of negotiation in a globalizing world. That process has no teleology; it is not imagined as leading to a world of sameness and unity of the sort Kant imagined. Rather, *Law and the Stranger* suggests that law is both productive of those encounters and a medium through which we negotiate the tensions that emerge from them. If those tensions can produce a self-consciousness within and about law's role in constituting the border between inside and outside, perhaps they can in the end prove productive, pointing in the direction of a less hostile and more hospitable world.

Notes

1. Georg Simmel, "The Stranger," in *The Sociology of Georg Simmel,* ed. Kurt H. Wolff (New York: Free Press, 1950), 404.

2. Bonnie Honig, *Democracy and the Foreigner* (Princeton: Princeton University Press, 2001), 3.

3. Ibid., 13.

4. One can see echoes of this dynamic in some of the press coverage and popular response to Barack Obama's 2008 presidential candidacy. *New York Times* columnist David Brooks, asking why Obama did not have a greater lead in the polls three months before the general election, wrote: "Obama has been a sojourner. He opened his book 'Dreams From My Father' with a quotation from Chronicles: 'For we are strangers before thee, and sojourners, as were all our fathers.' There is a sense that because of his unique background and temperament, Obama lives apart. He put one foot in the institutions he rose through on his journey but never fully engaged." David Brooks, *New York Times,* August 5, 2008, http://www.nytimes.com/2008/08/05/opinion/05brooks.html. Moreover, Obama took on the role of the cosmopolitan candidate who eschewed a racialized identity politics in favor of assertions of commonality across political and cultural lines. One can also see the trope of the sojourner again and again in films concerning law across a variety of genres: Judge Dan Haywood wanders Nuremberg as an interested/disinterested stranger while presiding over the trial of Nazi judges in *Judgment at Nuremberg*; Ranse Stoddard brings his law books to Shinbone in order to import a different legal order to the Old West in *The Man Who Shot Liberty Valance.* See *Judgment at Nuremberg,* DVD, directed by Stanley Kramer (1961; Santa Monica, CA: MGM Home Entertainment, 2004); *The Man Who Shot Liberty Valance,* DVD, directed by John Ford (1962; Hollywood, CA: Paramount, 2005).

5. Rene Girard, *Violence and the Sacred,* trans. Patrick Gregory (Baltimore, MD: Johns Hopkins University Press, 1977).

6. Simmel, "The Stranger," 405.

7. Honig, *Democracy and the Foreigner*, 34.

8. Simmel, "The Stranger," 406.

9. However conceived, "human rights" comprise the minimum quantum of those qualities we imagine connect us all, but defining the scope of human rights is a notoriously contentious enterprise. Minimally, John Rawls offers the following list: "the right to life (to the means of subsistence and security); to liberty (to freedom from slavery, serfdom, and forced occupation, and to a sufficient measure of liberty of conscience to ensure freedom of religion and thought); to property (personal property); and to formal equality as pressed by the rules of natural justice (that is, that similar cases be treated similarly)." Rawls, *The Law of Peoples* (Cambridge: Harvard University Press, 1999), 65.

10. Immanuel Kant, *Toward Perpetual Peace and Other Writings on Politics, Peace, and History*, ed. Pauline Kleingeld, trans. David L. Colclasure (New Haven: Yale University Press, 2006), 82.

11. Jacques Derrida, *Of Hospitality*, trans. Rachel Bowlby (Stanford: Stanford University Press, 2000), 23.

12. Ibid., 27.

13. Ibid., 55.

14. The United States, for example, first began to regulate immigration with the Naturalization Act of 1790, which restricted naturalization to "free white persons" of "good moral character" and required the applicant to have lived in the country for two years prior to becoming naturalized. While the passage of the Fourteenth Amendment ensured citizenship for people of African descent, Congress continued to employ race-based criteria for citizenship in excluding potential immigrants from various parts of Asia with the 1882 Chinese Exclusion Act and the Immigration Act of 1924. The Immigration and Nationality Act of 1952 (INA, or the McCarran-Walter Act) discontinued race-based quotas in favor of those based on nationality. The complex layers of contemporary immigration law include proliferating categorical distinctions between, for example, immigrant and nonimmigrant visitors, documented and undocumented workers, and immigrants and refugees. Indeed, as Linda Bosniak documents, the idea of citizenship itself is not an either/or concept; rather it is composed of "distinct discourses designating a range of institutions and experiences and social practices." See Linda Bosniak, *The Citizen and the Alien* (Princeton: Princeton University Press, 2006), 3. See also Ian F. Haney-Lopez, *White by Law: The Legal Construction of Race* (New York: New York University Press, 1996); Lucy Salyer, *Law Harsh as Tigers: Chinese Immigrants and the Shaping of Modern Immigration Law* (Chapel Hill: University of North Carolina Press, 1995).

15. A number of controversial border fences are currently under construction. On the barrier that Israel is erecting between Jerusalem and the West Bank, see Yossi Klein

Halevi, "Fenced In," *New Republic* (November 10, 2003), 18–19. On the U.S.-Mexican border fence, see Peter Andreas, *Border Games: Policing the US-Mexico Divide* (Ithaca, NY: Cornell University Press, 2000).

16. Seyla Benhabib, *The Claims of Culture: Equality and Diversity in the Global Era* (Princeton: Princeton University Press, 2002), 152.

17. Of course there are critics sympathetic to Benhabib who disavow the language of human rights, or at least its overemphasis. See, for example, Bhikhu Parek, "Finding a Proper Place for Human Rights," in *Displacement, Asylum, Migration*, ed. Kate Tunstall (Oxford: Oxford University Press, 2006): 17–43; and Slavoj Zizek, "Against the Ideology of Human Rights," in *Displacement, Asylum, Migration*, ed. Kate Tunstall (Oxford: Oxford University Press, 2006), 56–85.

18. Consider, for example, language rights, recognizing nonmajoritarian religious practices, and so forth. See Will Kymlicka, *Multicultural Citizenship: A Liberal Theory of Rights* (Oxford: Clarendon Press, 1995), 4; see generally Kymlicka and Wayne Norman, *Citizenship in Diverse Societies* (Oxford: Oxford University Press, 2000).

19. The claim here is that both group and individual identity comes from recognition (or its absence) by another; and that people or groups can suffer if they are mirrored back in a confining or demeaning way. Charles Taylor, "The Politics of Recognition," in *Multiculturalism: A Critical Reader*, ed. David Theo Goldberg (Cambridge, MA: Basil Blackwell, 1994), 75–76.

20. See, generally, Axel Honneth, *The Struggle for Recognition: The Moral Grammar of Social Conflict*, trans. Joel Anderson (Cambridge: Polity Press, 1995). See also Iris Marion Young, *Justice and the Politics of Difference* (Princeton: Princeton University Press, 1990).

21. Benhabib, *The Claims of Culture*, ix. See also Benhabib, *Another Cosmopolitanism* (Oxford: Oxford University Press, 2006).

22. Julia Kristeva, *Nations without Nationalism*, trans. Leon S. Roudiez (New York: Columbia University Press , 1993), 23.

23. Homi K. Bhabha, *Nation and Narration* (London: Routledge, 1990), 4. On cosmopolitanism, see also Kwame Anthony Appiah, *Cosmopolitanism: Ethics in a World of Strangers* (New York: W. W. Norton, 2006); Pheng Cheah, *Inhuman Conditions: On Cosmopolitanism and Human Rights* (Cambridge, MA: Harvard University Press, 2006); and Cheah and Bruce Robbins, eds., *Cosmopolitics: Thinking and Feeling beyond the Nation* (Minneapolis: University of Minnesota, 1998).

24. Kristeva, *Nations without Nationalism*, 45. Etienne Balibar offers yet a third way to conceptualize emerging relations in a globalizing Europe, rejecting both the idea that citizenship is now being reconstituted on the supranational level and that we are seeing a dissolution of the notions of "community" and "people" in a cosmopolitical society. The basic problems, he argues, "result from an open process of immanent transforma-

tion of national identity, national sovereignty, and national membership" that he calls the "transnationalization of the political." Balibar, *We, the People of Europe? Reflections on Transnational Citizenship* (Princeton: Princeton University Press, 2004), vii.

25. Benedict Anderson, *Imagined Communities: Reflections on the Origins and Spread of Nationalism* (London: Verso, 1991), 6–7.

26. Samuel Huntington, *The Clash of Civilizations and the Remaking of World Order* (New York: Simon and Schuster, 1996), 21.

27. Robert Cover, "Nomos and Narrative," in *Narrative, Violence, and the Law*, ed. Martha Minow, Michael Ryan, and Austin Sarat (Ann Arbor: University of Michigan Press, 1992), 95.

28. On the distinction between stranger and barbarian, see also Simmel, "The Stranger," 407. J. M. Coetzee's masterful novel *Waiting for the Barbarians* is, among other things, a meditation on the problematics of linguistic division and translation across the categories of stranger and barbarian, and on the ways in which desire both can and cannot breach that divide within ostensibly liberal societies and subjectivities. Coetzee, *Waiting for the Barbarians* (New York: Penguin, 1980).

29. Uday Singh Mehta, *Liberalism and Empire: A Study in Nineteenth-Century British Liberal Thought* (Chicago: University of Chicago Press, 1999), 99. In the nineteenth century, for example, J. S. Mill equated barbarians with "savages" who were for him a distinct, noncommunal category of being unfit for self-government.

30. Hannah Arendt, *The Origins of Totalitarianism* (New York: Harcourt Brace Jovanovich, 1973), 268.

31. Arendt defines the right to have rights as the right to live in a place where one is judged by one's actions and opinions, and the right to belong to some kind of community. Ibid.

32. Ibid., 300. Linda Kerber has argued that Arendt's analysis of statelessness is in the contemporary era best understood as a condition that changes over time, revealing shifting domestic values and power relations across international boundaries. Kerber, "Toward a History of Statelessness," *American Quarterly* 57, no. 3 (2005): 731.

33. Amy Kaplan, "Where Is Guantanamo?" *American Quarterly* 57, no. 3 (2005): 832–33.

34. *Rasul v. Bush*, 124 S.Ct. 2693 (2004); *Hamdi v. Rumsfeld*, 542 U.S. 507 (2004); *Hamdan v. Rumsfeld*, 548 U.S. 557 (2006); *Boumediene v. Bush*, 128 S.Ct. 2229 (2008).

35. On this point, see *Rasul* and *Boumediene*.

36. Arendt, *Origins of Totalitarianism*, 298.

37. It does not, on the Court's terms, require the leap of faith that Derrida assimilates to the idea of "absolute hospitality," which requires a host to open his or her house not only to foreigners but to the "absolute, unknown, anonymous other" without asking for either name or reciprocity of relation. Nothing commands such hospitality, and it

is by definition unregulable. Indeed, Derrida argues, "The law of absolute hospitality commands a break with hospitality by right, with law or justice as rights." Only absolute hospitality can be accorded to the stateless; once communities or nations attempt to interpolate the stateless into law, they cease to be stateless by definition. Derrida, *Of Hospitality*, 27.

38. Julia Kristeva, *Strangers to Ourselves*, trans. Leon Roudiez (New York: Columbia University Press, 1991), 1.

Necessary Strangers: Law's Hospitality in the Age of Transnational Migrancy

PHENG CHEAH

A recent newspaper article on security and the decline of great cities in the North Atlantic region provides a convenient illustration of what I will call in this essay "the aporia of law as hospitality to the stranger." In this article, entitled "Flight to Safety," the author, Joel Kotkin, argues that the decline in population in great cities such as London, Paris, Hamburg, Milan, and Frankfurt, can largely be attributed to the increasingly poor standards of security in these cities. On the U.S. side, the shifting of financial services firms from New York to suburbs and smaller cities as a result of September 11 is mentioned as another example. Such a trend, Kotkin suggests, is not new. "Many of the earliest cities of antiquity—in places as dispersed as Mesopotamia, China, India and Mesoamerica—shrank and ultimately disappeared after being overrun by more violent but often far less civilized peoples."[1] The Roman Empire, however, is the case from antiquity that is closest to home, the historical exemplar that is most consanguine to America and the North Atlantic fraternity of nation-states.

> The best-known example of security-driven collapse is Rome. The Roman Empire was a confederation of cities. By the second century, people, products and ideas were traveling quickly from urban center to urban center over secure sea lanes and 51,000 miles of paved roads stretching from Jerusalem to Boulogne, which connected scores of cities in between. Europe would not again see such secure and well-peopled cities until well into the 19th century. . . . This archipelago of cities did not fall in one cataclysmic crash, but as a result of repeated assaults by brigands and stateless hordes over hundreds of years. The attacks led to a gradual withdrawal of the Roman presence, first from the outermost empire, such as Britain, and a gradual shift of population from beleaguered cities to the rural hinterlands. By the seventh century, virtually all the empire's great cities—large provincial centers such as Trier, on the German frontier, Marseilles and Roman Londinium—had either been abandoned or

> had shrunk to shadows of themselves. Rome itself, a behemoth of almost a million people in the second century, was reduced to a pitiful ruin populated by less than a tenth of that number.[2]

What these telling historical examples teach us, Kotkin stresses, is the need of great cities and therefore the states that they are part of to protect and secure themselves from and against foreigners, especially those nomadic, stateless, and barbaric hordes who despised urban civilization. Such foreigners are the precursors of today's terrorists. What is interesting for present purposes is that a large part of this task of security devolves on the law, especially immigration law. Western cities have become insecure and vulnerable to terrorism because of "trendy multiculturalism" and "overly permissive immigration policies."

> Unfettered in their own enclave, Muslim extremists in Brooklyn helped organize the first attack on the World Trade Center in the early 1990s . . . . In Europe, multiculturalism has been elevated to a kind of social dogma, exacerbating the separation between Muslim immigrants and the host society. . . . If cities are to survive, they will need to face this latest threat to urban survival with something more than liberal platitudes, displays of pluck and determination. They will have to face up to the need for sometimes harsh measures, such as tighter immigration laws, preventive detention and widespread surveillance of suspected terrorists. They will also need to institute measures that encourage immigrants to assimilate, such as fostering greater economic opportunity for newcomers or enforcing immersion in the national language and political institutions.[3]

Yet, despite Kotkin's obvious right-wing xenophobia, he is nevertheless forced to acknowledge that the use of law to exclude and monitor foreigners is starkly at odds with the very open-mindedness that we often take to exemplify the spirit of the rule of law. As Kotkin puts it:

> The kinds of policies needed to secure their safety may pose a serious dilemma for great cities that have been built on the values of openness, freedom of movement, privacy, tolerance and due process. Yet to survive, these same cities may now need to shift their primary focus to protecting their people, their commerce and their future against those who seek to undermine and even, ultimately, destroy them.

We can rephrase the dilemma as follows: is not the law, the lawfulness that is law's defining feature and that distinguishes a lawful condition from a state of nature, synonymous with welcome, receptiveness, and hospitality to the stranger as other? Is not law hospitality itself as opposed to the hostility of nature? For the places that Kotkin describes are *great cities* (*civitates*) precisely because they are, by definition, no longer part of nature. They are sites of *civilization* and *civility*, communities with the lawful political organization of a state.[4] Yet, how and why is it that this hospitality—and the law is hospitality itself—repeatedly and interminably shades into and becomes contaminated by that condition of hostility from which it differentiated itself in the first place?

We know the conventional answer to these questions. Despite the axiomatic equation of the rule of law with openness, the openness of the law cannot be unconditional because the state-society organizational complex that is the source of law and that law is supposed to regulatively permeate in turn has to protect "itself" from external threats, whether this "self" is named "the state," "the people," "society," or "the nation." The conditional character of law's hospitality is a direct consequence of the territorial limits of state sovereignty and jurisdiction. In this context, what is foreign is also *potentially* a threat to the survival of the self. Hence, it must be determined, subjected to detention and quarantine, surveillance, regulation, or even not allowed entry. Or the foreign can be permitted to enter, but if it is determined to be dangerous as long as it is allowed to remain foreign, it must be rendered appropriate to the *corps propre* of the host through assimilation or integration. In other words, an unconditional openness is potentially self-destructive. What could be destroyed is precisely the host that is able to give hospitality to the stranger. Hence, hospitality cannot be unconditional if it is to continue to be hospitable. In this regard, right-wing arguments concerning security and the preventive war against terrorism are only the most extreme manifestations of the conditional character of law's hospitality toward the stranger.

Following this logic, globalization can be regarded as the age of the universal hospitality of the law. Insofar as conditionality is understood in terms of limitations to the extensiveness of nation-state sovereignty, globalization can elevate the conditional hospitality of the law toward the stranger into a hospitality that is universal in extension insofar as the global spread of legal mechanisms required for a global mode of production and world trade will gradually lead to the global institutionalization of the rule of law. If the entire world is bound together by universally accepted legal codes and standards, then all states and their individual members would subsist in a civil condition. The body of the sovereign host would now extend throughout the world and be identical to humanity. Hospitality would therefore no longer need to be conditional, since any potential or virtual *external* threat to the host would be removed with the annihilation of all externality to law. Since any threat would be internal to the body of the host, its removal will no longer involve legalized paramilitary tactics and sanctions such as surveillance, denial of entry, and deportation.

In the spirit of Hannah Arendt's reflections on the decline of the nation-state, we can understand the various emergent sovereignties and legal regimes beyond the nation-state that have developed after World War II and especially after the end of the Cold War, such as regimes of public international law emanating from the United Nations and bilateral and multilateral treaties and agreements, the International Criminal Court, the International Court of Justice, transnational human rights instruments, and the international civil society of NGOs as progressive attempts at eroding the conditionality of law's hospitality to the stranger.[5] They do not annul existing state sovereignty but instead constitute a supplementary transnational jurisdiction that can correct the deficiencies of state jurisdiction and check the abuse of the coercive legal power of sovereign states in relation to powerless strangers such as stateless peoples, exiles, and refugees. This transnational jurisdiction obeys and seeks to implement a higher law of hospitality—the right of humanity as a universal host. While this higher law of hospitality does not yet have the executive power for enforcement because humanity qua universal host is not yet fully actualized and sovereign, it is nevertheless posited as an ultimate end or telos. Even if it is not explicitly named as such, this higher law of hospitality informs most contemporary theorizing about the normative and political implications of globalization such as the influential work of Saskia Sassen, or Habermas's reflections on global democracy.[6] It is especially noticeable in Michael Hardt's and Antonio Negri's argument that as a result of global migration, "the cities of the earth will become at once great deposits of cooperating humanity and locomotives for circulation, temporary residences and networks of the mass distribution of living humanity."[7] In *Empire*, the higher law of hospitality takes the form of a political demand for "global citizenship," a demand that "the existent fact of capitalist production be recognized juridically and that all workers be given the full rights of citizenship."[8]

The equation of transnational legal regimes with unconditional hospitality is problematic in at least two ways. First, the suggestion that globalization is the material condition of progress toward unconditional hospitality does not sufficiently account for the ways in which the transnational connections formed by capitalist globalization necessarily exclude certain categories of foreigners and strangers even as it simultaneously incorporates them into the circuits of global capitalist accumulation out of an equal necessity. These strangers are necessary strangers to the functioning of global capitalism. But their incorporation into its circuits has to be partial. But second and more important, insofar as law or right necessarily involves coercion because it is an instrument designed to secure the integrity of a collective body qua host, the hospitality it embodies and institutionalizes cannot by definition be unconditional. This chapter explores the role of law in the interminable processes of incorporation/exclusion of global capitalism in order to draw out some of their general theoretical implications for understanding the aporetic character of law's hospitality toward the stranger. I begin with a reading of Kant's account of cosmopolitan right as a philosophical template for the understanding of law as universal hospitality. Kant's account is important because it shows the aspirations of right—law in the strict sense of juridical institutions—to unconditional hospitality even as it points out that right is always inadequate to law in a higher sense, the moral law that lifts us up into the unconditioned realm of moral freedom. The inability of right to achieve an unconditional openness is clearly seen in various movements of repulsion and attraction that characterize Kant's discussion of its different modalities. Kant, however, regards world trade as a means of overcoming or at least mitigating the limited hospitality of right because it leads to a cosmopolitan world federation. In the final two sections of the paper, I examine two different cases of the legal incorporation/exclusion of strangers in high-growth East and Southeast Asia—the abuse of foreign female domestic workers in Singapore, and the treatment of sex-workers from Mainland China in Hong Kong—in order to argue that far from generating an unconditional hospitality, economic globalization generates various legal regimes that exemplify the structurally compromised and contaminated character of right as a form of hospitality. If right can always lead only to a conditional form of hospitality, should we not think of the unconditional beyond the figure of the law to which Kant still confined morality qua the moral law?

1. The Neighborliness of the Law: Kant on the Cosmopolitan Right of Hospitality

The fact that hospitality is the implicit essence and truth of the law can be seen in the fact that Kant's philosophy of law, the *Doctrine of Right* (*Der Rechtslehre*), ends with a section on cosmopolitan right (*das Weltbürgerrecht*).[9] All forms of right exist as necessary conditions for the end of perpetual peace, and cosmopolitan right is the highest stage of right.

> Since the (narrower or wider) community [*Gemeinschaft*] of the nations [*den Völkern*] of the earth has now gone so far that a violation of right on *one* place of the earth is felt in *all*, the idea of cosmopolitan right is no fantastic or exaggerated way of representing right; it is, instead, a supplement to the unwritten code of the right of a state and the right of nations necessary for the sake of any public rights of human beings and so for perpetual peace[.][10]

Cosmopolitan right is defined as the right of the stranger or foreigner (*Fremdling*) to hospitality (*Hospitalität*) or hospitableness (*Wirtbarkeit*) (*TPP*, 328/213). Kant's discourse on law is at heart a discourse on neighborliness and the other as neighbor. The preamble of Section II of *Toward Perpetual Peace* distinguishes between the state of nature and a lawful condition (*gesetzlicher Zustand*) in terms of war and peace, in terms of relations with enemies and neighbors (322/203). The state of nature is a state/condition of war (*ein Zustand des Krieges*) because one is under the constant threat of hostility (*Feindseligkeit*), since the other is an enemy (*Feind*) who can always potentially threaten my security (*Sicherheit*). In contradistinction, a lawful condition is a condition of peace because it turns the other into a neighbor (*Nachbar*) who can give me an assurance (*Sicherheit*) of peace because he will treat me as a neighbor and not an enemy. What lawfulness establishes is therefore neighborliness, relations between neighbors. Such relations simultaneously give rise to assurances, expectations, and promises of security that will surely be fulfilled.

Kant explains the meaning of neighborliness in a footnote. The reason why relations of neighborliness lead to assurances of security is that two people become neighbors only by entering into "a condition of *being under* civil laws [*im bürgerlich-gesetzlichen Zustande sind*]" (ibid.). One therefore becomes a neighbor of and to another by mutually submitting to a third party, a superior power (*Gewalt*) external to the first two parties that can regulate their relations. My assurance of security to my neighbor may come from me (and vice versa), but it needs the mediation of a third party—namely, the law—to make sure that my assurance is backed up by external sanctions. Now, although a lawful condition is the basis of peace, law also necessarily involves violence. This is already implied by the semantic ambiguity of the word *Gewalt*, which can variously be translated as (legitimate) *power*, *force*, but also *violence*, an example of the last being Walter Benjamin's *Zur Kritik der Gewalt*.[11] In Kant's text, this violence of the law arises not only because, as Robert Cover has forcefully shown, the execution of the law requires violence since it is the impositional inscription of an ideal image or norm onto material reality. In Kant's view, the violence of the law follows directly from the very physics of human relations. Kant immediately adds to his definition of law as neighborliness the following remark on the right to compel neighborliness from the other or to repel the other:

> But a human being [*Der Mensch*] (or a nation [*das Volk*]) in a mere state of nature denies me this assurance [*Sicherheit*] [of peace] and already wrongs me just by being near [*neben*] me in this condition, even if not actively (*facto*) yet by the lawlessness of his condition (*statu iniusto*), by which he constantly threatens me; and I can coerce [*nötigen*—compel/necessitate] him either to enter with me into a condition of being under civil laws [*einen gemeinschaftlich-gesetzlichen Zustand*] or to leave my neighborhood [*Nachbarschaft*]. (Ibid.)

The legitimate violence of the law is manifested in this right either to compel the other to enter into a condition of lawful community—that is, to compel the other to be a neighbor—or to expel the other from my neighborhood. But from where does this right to compel and expel issue? It arises from the fact that human beings are always *physically* in relations where they can externally and mutually affect or influence one another. At the very heart of law as hospitality is a physics or logistics of human relations. "Hence the postulate on which all the following articles are based is that all men who can mutually affect one another [*auf einander wechselseitig einfließen konnen*] must belong to a civil constitution" (ibid.). "For if only one of these were in a relation of physically affecting another [*im Verhältnisse des physischen Einflusses auf den andern*] and were yet in a state of nature, the condition of war would be bound up with this" (ibid.). In such a situation, anyone remaining in a state of nature will drag everyone else he or she is in contact with into a state of war. Hence, the function of law is to transform the merely physical fact of the power of mutual affection/influence into conditions of mutual security. The other who is physically close to me and who can affect me and whom I can tolerate and keep in closest proximity is my neighbor. Keeping the other in close proximity can involve coercion. In contradistinction, the other whom I cannot tolerate in close proximity must be banished from my neighborhood and from lawful relations so that he can no longer affect me adversely and contaminate the lawful condition in which I exist. This other in a state of nature is prima facie my enemy because he already wrongs me simply by existing in the wrongful state of nature. Accordingly, this state of nature must be kept in permanent quarantine from my lawful condition.

In Kant's view, these movements and forces of attraction and repulsion are fundamental to law. For law always involves the force of necessitation and compulsion. In the Second Critique, Kant notes that this cobelonging of law and compulsion follows directly from the ontological constitution of human beings as finite creatures with sensuous inclinations who do not always follow the rules of reason.

> [F]or a being in whom reason quite alone is not the determining ground of the will, this rule is an *imperative*, that is, a rule indicated by an "ought" [*ein Sollen*], which expresses objective necessitation to the action and signifies that if reason completely determined the will the action would without fail take place in accordance with this rule.[12]

The practical law of moral reason is a special kind of imperative. It is categorical in nature, something we must and ought to follow unconditionally because it applies to all rational beings. It is important to note that although Kant characterizes morality in terms of law (*Gesetz*), he rigorously distinguishes the sphere of legality and right from that of morality. The fact that we experience morality as a law or categorical imperative indicates that we as finite beings experience it as the compulsion of reason. However, the unconditionality of the moral law also points to an unconditioned realm of freedom where we are no longer compelled because the moral law is the exercise of our self-determination through reason and thus enables us to transcend the blind necessity of the realm of nature where we are conditioned by our sensuous needs and inclinations. The unconditionality of the moral law implies an infinite openness not only to all human beings but to all rational beings.

In contradistinction, law's compulsive and coercive character remains at work in the sphere of right or legality proper since law in the narrow sense is required to regulate the collective or social life of finite human beings. The fact that human collective existence necessarily involves coercion is best seen in Kant's idea of the unsocial sociability of human beings (*die ungesellige Geselligkeit der Menschen*). Kant defines unsocial sociability as the

> tendency to come together in society, coupled, however, with a continual resistance which constantly threatens to break this society up. This predisposition [*Anlage*] is obviously rooted in human nature. Man has an inclination to live in society [*vergesellschaften*], since he feels in this state more like a man, that is, he feels able to develop his natural predispositions [*Naturanlagen*]. But he also has a great tendency to live as an individual [*vereinzelnen*], to isolate himself, since he also encounters in himself the unsocial characteristic of wanting to direct everything in accordance with his own ideas [*Sinne*]. He therefore expects resistance all around, just as he knows of himself that he is in turn inclined to offer resistance to others. It is this very resistance which awakens all man's powers [*Kräfte*] and induces him to overcome his tendency to laziness. Through his desire for honour, domination [*Herrsucht*] and possession [*Habsucht*], it drives him to seek status among his fellows, whom he cannot *bear* yet cannot *bear to leave.*[13]

Hence, human society is "a *pathologically* enforced union into a society [*eine pathologisch-abgedrungene Zusammeneinstimmung zu einer Gesellschaft*]."[14] Here, we see in embryonic form the movements and forces of compulsory attraction and repulsion/expulsion of the other that are at work in the law. Law's function is precisely to regulate the various tensions of unsocial sociability in the hope that gradual historical progress will transform a society formed from pathological impulses into "a moral whole." As we will see, the same physics and logistics of human relations are at work in the different levels of right. This is why Kant repeatedly characterizes relations to the other in the three forms of right using spatial metaphors of distance and proximity. It is also important to note that in Kant's view, legality can only ever approach morality asymptotically, as the latter's simulacrum. This means that although hospitality is the essence of right, right, even cosmopolitan right, can never achieve the unconditional openness that characterizes moral freedom.

We have so far been following Kant's thoughts on the other as neighbor and enemy. But where is the stranger or foreigner in this dichotomous landscape?

Contrary to the colloquial English understanding that opposes the stranger to the familiar neighbor, Kant regards the stranger as a type of neighbor, as a species of the genus "neighbor." Through an extended analogy, the transition of relations between individuals from a state of nature to a lawful condition, from relations of enmity to relations of neighborliness, serves as a template for the relations between states at the level of international law and relations between individuals and states at the level of cosmopolitan right. In other words, human relations are composed of three different modes or levels of mutual physical influence/affection that ought to be governed by three different types of right. In order to be legitimate, a civil constitution must be in accord with these three kinds of right. They are: the right of citizens within a state in relation to each other, the right of nations in relation to each other at the level of interstate relations, and finally, and most important for present purposes, "*the right of citizens of the world* [*Weltbürgerrecht*], insofar as individuals [*Menschen*] and states, standing in the relation of externally affecting one another [*in äußerem auf einander einfließendem Verhältnis stehend*], are to be regarded as citizens of a universal state of mankind [*als Bürger eines allgemeinen Menschenstaats*] (*ius cosmopoliticum*)" (ibid.). These three forms of right therefore create and govern three types of neighbors: the fellow citizen or compeer as an equal member of the same state; the fellow nation-state as a member of the fraternal confederation of nation-states; and the fellow cosmopolitan or world citizen as a member of a universal state of mankind. The stranger or foreigner who is owed hospitality is the neighbor at the level of cosmopolitan right. He or she exists in a substrate of neighborly relations between individuals and foreign states as well as between individuals from different states.

Each level of right and each of the three types of relations to neighbors involves the same movements of compulsory attraction and repulsion/expulsion. At the level of international right, Kant emphasizes once again that in a natural condition where they are independent of external laws, states already wrong one another just by existing next to one another (*Nebenandersein*) (326/209). The physical adjacency or merely contingent contiguity of states to each other in a condition of nature is itself a violation of right. This merely accidental next-ness or nearness must be transformed into a meaningful or lawful proximity—that is, neighborliness. For the sake of its security (*Sicherheit*), a given state can and ought to require other states to enter into a constitution that is analogous to a civil constitution. This will bring about the desired neighborliness. The neighbor at the level of international right is therefore formed by a kind of incorporation into a confederation or league. At the level of cosmopolitan right, however, the neighbor is not constituted through incorporation but only through a much more limited or conditional form of tie. For this third type of neighbor is a stranger/foreigner, and he or she can only be brought closer to a certain degree. A certain distance must be kept and, therefore, a certain force of repulsion must be at work in cosmopolitan right. Let us look more closely at this.

Given that cosmopolitan right is more extensive in its reach than the two other forms of right, one might expect it to be less conditional and to place the neighbors that it creates in the closest proximity. Yet, Kant begins his definition of cosmopolitan right with a massive limitation and condition: "Cosmopolitan right shall be limited [*eingeschränkt*] to the conditions [*Bedingungen*] of universal hospitality" (328/213):

> *Hospitality* (hospitableness) means the right of a foreigner [*eines Fremdlings*] not to be treated with hostility because he has arrived on the land of another. The other can turn him away, if this can be done without destroying him, but as long as he behaves peaceably where he is [*auf seinem Platz*—in his place], he cannot be treated with hostility. What he can claim is not the *right to be a guest* [*Gastrecht*] (for this a special beneficent pact would be required, making him a member of the household for a certain time), but the *right to visit* [*Besuchsrecht*]; this right, to present oneself for society, belongs to all human beings by virtue of the right of possession in common of the earth's surface on which, as a sphere, they cannot disperse infinitely [*Unendliche zerstreuen*] but must finally put up with being near one another [*sondern endlich sich doch neben einander dulden zu mussen*] [.] (328–29/213–14)

The movements of attraction and repulsion are especially striking in this passage. In the first place, the spherical nature of the earth means that there is a physical, earthly, or terrestrial law of attraction that brings the other near to me. There is an a priori natural community before historical forms of society insofar as we have a communal right to possess the earth's surface.[15] This is why the right to hospitality is also a natural right. Since we cannot disperse infinitely—that is, without end or limit, since there are limitations to how separate we can be—we must tolerate being next to each other. Nature helps us in this because while some parts of the earth are inhospitable to human life, nature enables us to traverse over these unpopulated parts so that we can be near each other. This natural community would be the basis and condition of *possibility* of historical consensual forms of human society (*Gesellschaft*).

But at the same time, the other remains a foreigner or stranger. He cannot coincide with me either spatially or temporally, he cannot be the same as me. He cannot be a member of my household. The right to hospitality is not the right to be a guest (because to be a guest requires a consensual pact that allows the other to be for, a limited period of time, similar to me) but only a right to visit and to present oneself for society. But in this putting off or pushing away of the other, in this keeping of the other at bay, one also cannot annihilate the other. The other must be kept at a respectful distance, at a conserving or preserving distance so that he can continually present himself for society. The presentation of the other for society is important because sociability, as Kant points out in the Third Critique, is what distinguishes humanity from animality. Kant explicitly contrasts this balanced proximity of the foreigner or stranger, the delicate distance of hospitality, to the inhospitality of both piracy and colonization. The former annihilates the respectful distance that must be maintained with the other by treating the approaching other as an object for plunder. Colonization is even worse, since the doctrine of *terra nullius* effectively annihilates and effaces the other by literally counting the inhabitants of other lands as nothing (*die Einwohner rechneten sie für nichts*) (329/214–15).

Conversely, countries can rightfully place conditions on hospitality to visiting strangers with imperialist designs. China and Japan have given them access (*Zugang*), but not entry (*Eingang*). In the Japanese case, only the Dutch can have access, and they are excluded (*ausschließen*), like prisoners, from any community with natives (330/216). But even so, Kant does not say that imperialists are lawless, and that such others should be cast out of the neighborhood and treated as enemies in a state of nature, that all commerce (*Verkehr*) should be banned. They remain strangers or visitors—that is, neighbors who ought to be treated with some hospitality however restricted it is because they come for commerce.

Let us sum up Kant's views on law and the stranger. First, the stranger cannot be too close. There are degrees of proximity that can be intolerable and, hence, hospitality can and should justifiably be restricted, limited, and conditional. Second, the stranger is necessary to the law for at least two reasons.

The appearance of the stranger before me is a test for the lawfulness of the law, since any legitimate constitution must respect cosmopolitan right and show hospitality. Indeed, cosmopolitan right is the highest level of lawfulness that one can achieve. But more important, insofar as law or right is an instrument for achieving or bringing out humanity, my intercourse or exchange with the stranger as governed by cosmopolitan right also fosters the unity of humanity as a collective empirical subject. Third, one can also surmise, although Kant does not explicitly say so, that the other remains a stranger and foreigner because of the existence of the territorial state. The spatial dynamics of distance and nearness, the movements of attraction and repulsion are direct consequences of the fact that human relations remain constricted by the institutional form of the nation-state. We can infer as much from Kant's comments on colonization as well as his suggestion that the majesty of the state, its desire for self-aggrandization, is a direct cause of war. The limitations of state sovereignty thus reinforce the distinction between the unconditionality of moral freedom and the universality of right. The right to hospitality may be a universal right grounded in nature and reason. But it remains conditional and restricted because human relations are hampered by the limited sovereignty of territorial states.

But although the universality of right can never be fully adequate to the unconditionality of the moral law, it can attempt to approximate it in the simulacral form of the cosmopolitan federation. What is interesting for present purposes is that Kant grants this power of approximation to world trade. He argues that there is a countering force that progressively compensates for and supplements the restrictions imposed by the territorial state, thereby enabling a stronger form of hospitality. This is the power of commerce. In the first place, commerce motivates us to move across inhospitable areas of the earth. It leads to the annulment of natural inhospitality. Indeed, the right to hospitality is itself defined in terms of safeguarding the conditions that make commerce possible. "But this right to hospitality [*Hospitalitätsrecht*]—that is, the authorization of a foreign newcomer [*der fremden Ankömmlinge*]—does not extend beyond the conditions which make it possible to seek commerce with the old inhabitants [*die Bedingungen der Möglichkeit, einer Verkehr mit den Einwohnen zu versuchen*]" (329/214). *The Doctrine of Right* is even more explicit about this equation of hospitality with the possibility of commerce. The original communal right to the land that follows from the spherical nature of the earth is not a right to possess the land for use or a right to own property in it. It is only "a community of possible physical interaction [*der physischen möglichen Wechselwirkung*] (*commercium*), that is, in a thoroughgoing relation of each to all the others of offering to engage in commerce with any other [*in einem durchgängigen Verhältnisse, eines zu allen anderen, sich zum Verkehr untereinander anzubieten*] and each has a right to make this attempt without the other being authorized to behave toward it as an enemy because it has made this attempt" (*MM*, 489/476).

The equation of hospitality with the mere possibility of commerce appears to restrict the right to hospitality. In fact, it gives hospitality the built-in potential of approximating the unconditional. For commerce, Kant argues, is a second assurance that grounds the law's assurance of peace. It is nature's way of guaranteeing or assuring that the assurance of peace that comes with increasing lawfulness will necessarily be achieved. Consequently, it can soften the restrictions that the rigid divisions of sovereign nation-states impose on cosmopolitan right. Commerce brings people together and makes them want to be neighbors. The discovery of salt and iron leads to trade. They are "perhaps the first articles, everywhere in demand, of a trade [*eines Handelsverkehrs*] among various peoples, by which they are brought into a peaceable relation to each other and so into understanding, community, and peaceable relations with one another, even with the most distant [*in ein friedliches Verhältnis gegen einander, uns so, selbst mit Entfernteren, in Einverständnis, Gemeinschaft und friedliches Verhältnis unter einander gebracht werden*]" (*TPP*, 333/221). The spirit of commerce (*Handelsgeist*), which is antipathetic to war, unites the world into a peaceful whole by working through the self-interests of nation-states. It supplements cosmopolitan right by providing the security against violence and war that the concept of cosmopolitan right in itself is not able to provide, thereby gradually leading us to perpetual peace (336/226). Commerce is nature's way of making us more lawful, more hospitable, and ultimately more humane. It can remove some of the impediments posed by the territorial state to hospitality. In his celebration of commerce as a fundamental human trait and a humanizing force, Kant is not too far off from Adam Smith: "[E]very man . . . lives by exchanging, or becomes in some measure a merchant, and the society itself grows to be what is properly a commercial society."[16]

Kant's account of law's hospitality to the stranger is therefore marked by two different tendencies. On the one hand, Kant brings out the tension between attraction and repulsion of the stranger in the relation of hospitality, a tension that always restricts and compromises hospitality and makes it conditional. On the other hand, insofar as this restriction of hospitality is connected to the political form of the territorial sovereign state, Kant also gestures toward a more open form of hospitality (perpetual peace), which he locates in emergent forms of transnational right, and whose actualization he links to commerce and world trade. In this respect, Kant lays the philosophical blueprint for the widespread understanding that ties the development and spread of the rule of law and transnational human rights to the globalization of market structures through world trade and the transnationalization of production. This view is not only advanced by neoliberal justifications of globalization. Saskia Sassen, for example, has argued that the transnationalization of the legitimation process through the use of international covenants by governments to formulate national policy has led to the emergence of new subjects who are able to make political claims. "This is a move away from statism—the absolute right of states to represent their people in international law and international relations—toward a conceptual and operational opening for the emergence of other subjects of, and actors in, international law. The international human rights regime has been a key mechanism for making subjects out of those hitherto invisible in international law—first nation people, immigrants, and refugees, women."[17] This denationalization of state sovereignty is, however, inextricably tied to the transnational commercial-legal scaffolding necessary for the circulation of global capital. The emergence of these new subjects of human rights goes hand in hand with protecting the rights of global capital. In Sassen's own words, "[D]eregulation is a vehicle through which a growing number of states are furthering economic globalization and guaranteeing the rights of global capital, an essential ingredient of the former."[18]

One could, however, suggest the very opposite, that far from leading to a resolution of the tension between the law's attraction and repulsion of the stranger and, therefore, to a more open hospitality, contemporary globalization exacerbates this tension. In the next two sections, I examine two cases of transnational economic migration in which the law must include the stranger and also simultaneously exclude her: the legal construction of the female migrant domestic worker in Southeast Asia and the migrant sex-worker from Mainland

China to Hong Kong. These cases illustrate two points: first, that the interaction brought about by global circuits of migrant labor do not lead to greater hospitality in the Kantian sense, nor to a simplification of class antagonisms into a worldwide struggle between property owners and workers as Marx envisaged it. Instead, such circuits intensify and multiply the lines of inclusion/exclusion of foreigners and strangers by incorporating and organizing them into an international division of labor under which workers who have low-status occupations and come predominantly from poorer countries are more disposable than others, sometimes even when the migrant worker belongs to the same ethnocultural group or national body, such as in the case of migrant sex-workers from the mainland to Hong Kong. Second, the law plays a fundamental role in these technologies of exclusion/inclusion. Far from being a mere instrument, something that is superstructural or epiphenomenal to global capitalism, law is instead infrastructural. The hierarchies of global capitalism are articulated, generated, and sustained by various legal technologies, which are important sites of struggle against the coercion and subjectification of strangers in an era of global migration.

2. Strangers in the Home: The Global Trade in Domestic Workers

The material conditions for the accelerated deployment of foreign guest workers in Southeast Asia arise directly from a broader structural change in the system of capital accumulation that we now understand under the related rubrics of "the new international division of labor" and "flexible" or "disorganized global capitalism."[19] This change led to dramatic economic growth in East and Southeast Asia: the pre-1997 "economic miracle" of the East Asian newly industrialized economies (NIEs) of South Korea, Taiwan, Hong Kong, and Singapore, and the repetition of the same pattern of hyperdevelopment among the tiger economies of Southeast Asia (Malaysia and Thailand). At the same time, however, the regime of flexible accumulation also created a regional divide within Southeast Asia between high-growth and low-growth countries that were either able or unable to adapt to the regime of flexible accumulation and harness foreign capital flows for their development. This is the direct condition of the acceleration of labor migration in Southeast Asia. For as countries such as Singapore and Malaysia undergo a transformation in their workforce because of rapid industrialization, they experience a shortage of low-skilled manual labor and begin to import migrant labor from their less developed neighbors to perform what are sometimes called the 3D jobs, "dirty, dangerous, and demanding." On the other hand, the Philippines actively exports workers overseas because of the inability of its economy to absorb the labor of its citizens, so much so that the Marcos regime regarded the export of labor as a matter of "national interest" and embarked on its aggressive labor export policy, citing the alleviation of chronic unemployment and the relief of the balance of payments deficit as the two key economic benefits.[20]

This transnational trade in labor is crucial to the current conjuncture of global capitalism and is actively sanctioned by international economic bodies. The World Bank's *World Development Report, 1991* observed that labor migration could aid in curbing unemployment and reducing the worldwide disparity in income. Migrants returning from more advanced countries also contributed to the diffusion of technology.[21] The 1995 report, entitled *Workers in an Integrating World*, described migration as "an important economic and social safety valve" that allowed "labor to relocate to areas where it was more scarce" and stressed the efficiency gains it created, particularly in the form of higher wages for migrant workers, foreign exchange remittances to sending countries, the possible stimulation of capital investment, and lower production costs in receiving countries.[22] This means that economic globalization and the forms of national development it promotes in the postcolonial world are inseparable from a practical discourse of hospitality toward migrant workers. What hospitality does the law of labor-receiving countries show toward these necessary strangers? Let us consider the case of Singapore, which is arguably the most successful example of a high-growth country under the regime of flexible accumulation.

The project of cultivating human capital on which Singaporean hyperdevelopment has been based is governed by a discourse of hospitality that is based on cost-benefit calculations. As part of its ongoing ambitions to upgrade to a non–labor intensive, knowledge-based economy and to become the high-technology and financial center for Asia and the primary Asian hub of transnational capital investments in high–value added manufacture and services, the Singaporean state has formulated a complex foreign labor policy to facilitate the upgrading of its 'indigenous' human resources.[23] On the one hand, the most generous hospitality is practiced to facilitate the gathering of "global talent." On the other, a severely restricted form of hospitality is offered to lower-end migrant workers. As an example of generous hospitality, the state has set up a recruiting agency entitled "Contact Singapore," with a global network of offices in cities such as Boston, Chicago, London, Sydney, Chennai, Hong Kong, and Shanghai.[24] Contact Singapore's motto is "Singapore: Your World of Possibilities." It has launched an international print and web ad campaign that features examples of global talent who have been attracted to Singapore. One ad quotes Richard Tomlin, an English banker who is the vice-chairman of UBS Warburg in Asia, saying, "Like Singapore, I believe people are the greatest assets." The state hopes that some of this "foreign talent" will become integrated, develop loyalties to Singapore, and settle there. But even those highly skilled expatriates who do not stay permanently will make a lasting contribution by transferring skills and professional expertise to the local population, thereby improving the quality of Singapore's human capital in the long term. In the words of its deputy prime minister: "[F]or this nation to keep growing, a continued inflow of talent is essential. Without this inflow, Singapore cannot be a cosmopolitan society, or support the diverse activities and services which make us relevant to the world. . . . Hence, our systematic policy is to attract a broad spectrum of foreign talent, ranging from skilled workers to professionals, from all round the world. Some will come to work for a time, before moving on. But we hope a fair proportion will eventually sink roots and make this their home and nation."[25] To attract such talent to linger or settle permanently, the government has launched an aggressive campaign to market Singapore as a city with a thriving cosmopolitan culture and creative lifestyle.[26]

A different kind of hospitality is afforded to low-skilled or unskilled foreign workers needed to fill menial jobs that are crucial to the economy and the reproduction of social life but are shunned by the local workforce as it is upgraded to meet the needs of a progressively capital-intensive economy. Foreign domestic workers (FDWs) are a significant component of this lower tier of migrant labor. To augment the professional and skilled worker sector, the Singapore government encouraged educated middle-class women to join the workforce even as it sought to reverse the declining birth and marriage rates of such women. The Singapore state thus made accessible a pool of live-in foreign domestic helpers who could take care of household chores and child-care needs.[27] Hence, another kind of cosmopolitanism coexists with the high-end cosmopolitanism of talented professionals as its bipolar opposite: the underclass foreign domestic helpers who are the disavowed support of the aspiring global city. As part of the reproductive sphere, these migrant workers are crucial to the sustaining of social and civil life. But they are not recognized as "foreign talent." They are merely "foreign workers" to be used and discarded rather than integrated into the social fabric of the city-state. Indeed, these two poles of cosmopolitan labor have distinctly different legal statuses. Members of the higher tier hold "employment passes" and enjoy liberal benefits and conditions of employment designed to induce them to take up permanent residence and even citizenship, whereas those in the lower tier merely hold temporary "work permits" that must be renewed every two years for a maximum stay of eight years and are subject to stringent legal restrictions.

These two modalities of hospitality certainly exceed Kant's understanding of the right to hospitality as a right to visitation. They involve the right to be a guest, and in the case of desirable foreign professionals, also a possible right of abode. But as biopolitical technologies (Foucault) for the cultivation of human capital, the right to hospitality in question is regulated by laws that determine both the limits of hospitality and the targeted recipients of different forms of hospitality according to cost-benefit calculations. Such hospitality is therefore conditional, and this conditionality has negative consequences for FDWs. Foucault's concept of biopower was formulated to explain the productive regulation of the population as a resource during the rise of industrial capitalism in Europe, where it is precisely a matter of tethering individual bodies and the population to processes of production and to society by making the socioeconomic system hospitable to the people so that they could be utilized as resources. He could not envisage that postindustrial hyperdevelopment outside the North Atlantic would require a revolving pool of temporary labor consisting of foreign bodies that are emphatically barred from becoming part of the permanent population. Such bodies do not need to be cultivated and augmented in the same way as those belonging to the permanent labor force. They do not need to be subjectified as members of the population because their presence is only temporary. Their absorption into the permanent workforce is to be vigorously prohibited because it is not of any value to the receiving country. When exhausted, their forces can always be replenished through substitution by other temporary migrants. As Noeleen Heyzer and Vivienne Wee observe, "[B]ecause of their transient immigration status, foreign domestic workers (FDWs) are treated by the receiving governments as needed but undesirable aliens who have to be controlled stringently, with only their labour to be extracted and the rest of them as persons to be restricted."[28]

This is, therefore, a form of labor whose constitution requires only a very limited form of hospitality. It involves discipline and regulation, but without either increasing/enhancing their bodily forces through concerted training or any subjectification. FDWs can never hope to become citizens of Singapore. Their only subjective incentive to be attached to the Singaporean economic machine as host is financial remuneration. The limited hospitality of this biopolitical formation leads to the widespread dehumanization of FDWs. Its legal technologies simultaneously include and exclude, attract and repel the FDW. The Singapore state indirectly deploys the labor power of FDWs, but refuses to treat such employment as a genuine labor relation that deserves legal protection. Terms of employment are never only a matter of consensual agreement between two private parties. Since labor is connected to the basic needs of human beings who are members of the population, work conditions are subject to government regulation and protection—for instance, the establishment of maximum hours of the work week, minimum pay, paid leave, sick leave, and so forth. The Singapore state's refusal to provide fuller regulation of the working conditions of FDWs stems from the fact that unskilled migrant workers are always already viewed disadvantageously in comparison to highly skilled migrants and the local population. They are beings with a lesser status, on which the state does not need to expend resources and care. Although the Ministry of Manpower acknowledges the important economic and social contributions of FDWs to Singaporean society, these are not enough to warrant their full integration into the Singaporean population.[29] In response to a question about the state's foreign labor policy, an official of the ministry drew a telling contrast between the compatibility of high-end migrant workers with the local population and the incompatibility of FDWs: "[It] is a question of 'how do you judiciously manage the growing population [of FDWs]. . . . They [professional and educated migrant workers] don't create social problems. They don't fall down from a height. You don't have the problem of housing them. You don't have the problem of them not being able to assimilate and integrate into our local population. They are more global in their thinking. A different *breed* of people come and work in Singapore [as FDWs]. That's fine with us. But these people leave their countries, many of them, invariably from rural areas. Some of them have never even seen a high-rise block and here, they are working in a high-rise apartment and you have people falling down when they hang clothes, when they clean windows, and then we have a maid problem."[30]

Excluded from the system of means and ends that the state wishes to enhance through the integration of professional and educated migrant workers, FDWs are viewed in terms of sheer technical utility: as mere means to the ends of others, without any ends of their own that need to be taken into account in the state's calculations. Hence, what we have is a form of governmental regulation without the welfare of the population. Instead of being the objects of productive regulatory techniques, FDWs need to be policed to mitigate what the state euphemistically refers to as "social costs": the negative consequences that their presence inflicts on Singaporean society, problems ranging from congestion of public space to strained bilateral relations with labor-exporting countries over their abuse by the local population.[31] The two main legal mechanisms of regulation are the foreign worker's levy and the bond. The levy is a pricing mechanism used to regulate the demand for foreign workers. It is a monthly cost borne by employers of foreign workers in addition to the worker's salary. The figures are reviewed and adjusted regularly according to changing market circumstances. It is a two-tier scheme designed to discriminate between skilled and unskilled foreign workers, encouraging retention and recruitment of the former and dampening demand for the latter.[32] Raising the levy is therefore part of the state's policy of encouraging the inflow of talented foreigners who could help Singapore maintain its economic competitiveness and its attempt to curb over-reliance on low-cost unskilled workers whose increasing numbers would prevent the upgrading of the local construction industry and the development of professional domestic and childcare services, and cause a whole array of "social problems." As an official of the Ministry of Manpower stated in an interview:

> We have 900,000 to one million households. If every one of them were to have a domestic worker, we would have one million FDWs. I mean, can you imagine the social implications? We are talking about one million FDWs alone, what about foreign

> construction workers and other foreign workers? The situation is not tenable. That will also have an impact on the way our children are raised, dependency problems of FDWs, bilateral problems that will invariably arise from time to time with the exporting countries. So there are social and management issues we have to grapple with, so we can't allow the population of FDWs just to rise. We can't allow the situation where every household who wants a FDW can have one.

The levy is a constant issue of contention in the national media and a major source of tension between the domestic worker and her employer. It is widely perceived by Singaporean women to be a means of lining state coffers at the expense of "the working class."[33] In fact, the costs are largely borne by the FDW in the form of a lack of wage increases or salary deductions. The rising costs of employing an FDW also lead employers to expect "to get more out of their maids."[34]

Whereas the levy reduces the number of FDWs, the security bond—$5,000 that employers are required to pay to the state—is an instrument for ensuring that the behavior and movement of FDWs is strictly policed and restricted by their employers during the term of their employment. An FDW is granted a work permit subject to various conditions.[35] The most repressive of these conditions are the prohibition of marriage to a Singapore citizen or permanent resident during her stay and the prohibition of pregnancy. The FDW is also required to submit to a medical examination for pregnancy and sexually transmitted diseases once every six months, and will be repatriated immediately if the test results are positive. Since the bond is forfeited if any of these conditions are violated, the mechanism transfers the monitoring of workers to the site of the household, where it can be performed most effectively and zealously by employers to prevent the possibility of any "illegitimate" activities even before the FDW enters into public space.

These legal technologies contribute to the systematic dehumanization of the FDW by articulating two principles or maxims of conduct. First, FDWs are a necessary but undesirable presence. Second, the employer has a responsibility to mitigate the social problems they cause. Indeed, it is almost a public duty of the employer to control the behavior and movement of her foreign maid. From the start, therefore, the FDW is viewed as a minor or delinquent, someone without a full moral personality who needs to be trained, corrected, and policed so that she will not err. The FDW's lesser status as a being to be excluded from the Singaporean population is repeatedly reinforced through state-education of the public via the print media about the gravity of the social problems FDWs cause. FDWs, on the other hand, are placed in the debased position of nonpersonhood. Employers who want to maximize their economic usefulness and are fearful of losing the bond engage in constant surveillance of maids, their working and eating habits, their social activities, and their use of the phone. Children are often the chief watchers. They are encouraged by their parents to tell tales about their maids, even rewarded for doing so.[36] As a caregiver who may not command the respect of her wards, the FDW's work is not reciprocated by the emotional rewards and recognition that constitute the subjectivating and human-redemptive dimension of mothering.

The nebulous sociolegal status and ambiguous site of paid housework renders maids especially vulnerable to poor treatment. Domestic workers are not governed by the Employment Act. The Singaporean government has repeatedly insisted that the employment of domestic labor involves a private contract between the worker and employer and that the conditions of service and wages should be determined by the free market rather than by labor legislation. The government has therefore staunchly rejected proposals for a standard employment contract for maids and employers, emphasizing instead the importance of bilateral contracts that spell out the terms and conditions of employment.[37] By refusing to regard the FDW as a genuine employee with clearly defined basic working conditions, the Singapore state exacerbates her vulnerability. This environment also fosters a culture of fear and self-suppression in FDWs similar to battered women's syndrome. A newspaper article reported that Filipina domestic workers who were aware of the standard contract set by their embassy said that they would not use it as a basis to seek redress if their employers did not observe its terms because they feared losing their job.[38] Similarly, although the Ministry of Manpower guidebook for FDWs clearly states that the abusive employer is punishable by law, an FDW may be unwilling to report abuses because they need the income and are afraid of being blacklisted by employment agencies and barred from returning to Singapore.

The plight of the FDW in Singapore exemplifies the tension between the law's inclusion and exclusion of the stranger in the exploitative trade in female migrant labor. The restricted hospitality offered by the law is here a direct consequence of territorial sovereignty. The cost-benefit calculations for the development of human capital actively prevent a fuller accommodation of these migrant workers even as they must be included because their labor is needed. From this perspective, we might view human rights instruments for the protection of migrant workers as constituting a higher law of hospitality that overcomes the limited hospitality of labor-receiving states insofar as such instruments transcend any economic calculations. The problem, however, is that these instruments are also caught in the web of economic instrumentality at various levels. Let us track this contamination of the higher law of hospitality in greater detail.

Today, there are an increasing number of international resolutions concerning migrant workers' rights, such as the 1990 UN International Convention on the Protection of the Rights of All Migrant Workers and Members of Their Families and the two main ILO conventions on migrant workers.[39] But their usefulness in protecting migrant female domestic workers is circumscribed by their scope and implementation. For present purposes, what is significant is that any attempt to establish minimum standards for the treatment of migrant workers based on the principles and provisions of existing UN and ILO conventions and recommendations faces the more profound obstacle of implementation. In a world of sovereign states, the execution of standards articulated in international documents depends on the action of individual states. These standards are binding only on states that have ratified the documents, something that is likely to occur only if a given state already has equitable labor policies for its own nationals. Thus far, these instruments have been ineffective because they have not been ratified by major labor-receiving states.[40] Until these instruments receive wider ratification, migrant workers' rights are not recognized and not concretely activated as universal human rights by labor-receiving states. Hence, although international law recognizes migrant workers' rights as universal rights that can be claimed by every individual, in the current conjuncture, the most feasible avenue for protecting them in cases of abuse lies with the individual worker's nation of origin.

Nor can the FDW be afforded greater hospitality by international feminist solidarity exemplified by the Platform for Action of the Fourth World Conference on Women, Beijing 1995.[41] The platform presupposes and relies on the same biopolitical technologies that have led to the dehumanization of FDWs. The entry of Singaporean women into white-collar work is precisely the upward mobility narrative of woman-in-the-developed or hyperdeveloping nation that the platform celebrates. Generally speaking, the platform incorporates some of the language of the Covenant on Economic, Social and Cultural Rights and includes provisions regarding the right to work, right to earn a living, right to protection, and right to fair treatment in a workplace. There are also sections explicitly concerned with the elimination of violence against women migrants and the right to sustainable development. However, like other progressive projects of transnational sorority, the platform's basic vision is to rectify inequality vis-à-vis men within the implicit framework of national advancement and development.

The platform necessarily presupposes but disavows the competitive nature of development. In place of an acknowledgment of the harsh realities of global exploitation, it gestures toward a benign internationalism forged out of the enlightened, benevolent, and, it is hoped, soon-to-be feminized mutual self-interest of nation-states each striving to maximize its own well-being without encroaching on other nation-states in post–Cold War globality. Despite its note of caution about the power of transnational corporations, Par. 11 offers an optimistic view of post–Cold War globality: "The end of the cold war has resulted in international changes and diminished competition between the super-Powers." Consequently, "international relations have improved and prospects for peace among nations have increased." The characterization of women's equality and right to development as a valuable human resource and target of biopolitical cultivation in the interests of the felicitous development of the *nation-state* is most obvious in Par. 159: "In countries that are undergoing fundamental political, economic and social transformation, the skills of women, if better utilized, could constitute a major contribution to the economic life of their respective countries. Their input should continue to be developed and supported and their potential further realized." Par. 41 expresses the platform's benign internationalism: "The advancement of women and the achievement of equality between women and men are a matter of human rights and a condition for social justice and should not be seen in isolation as a women's issue. They are the only way to build a sustainable, just and developed society. Empowerment of women and equality between women and men are prerequisites for achieving political, social, economic, cultural and environmental security among all peoples."

It has been suggested that the platform promotes "a slightly expanded identity for women that mandates the embracing of free market ideology in addition to maternity."[42] In uneven development, it is the transitory migrant worker, especially the migrant domestic worker, who sustains the advancement and entrepreneurial spirit of her more privileged fellow–Southeast Asian sister. As Par. 118 implies, the platform can understand violence against women only as something perpetrated by men. It cannot explain the fact that in Singapore, abused FDWs are mostly oppressed by female employers. The same fracture of the collectivity "women" compromises transnational sisterhood. Even though Par. 154 recognizes the contribution of women migrant workers such as domestic workers to the economies of both sending and receiving countries, global sorority was not strong enough to secure more support for the call of the Philippines for the ratification of the 1990 Convention on migrant workers' rights. Of the 132 countries participating in the Beijing Conference, only five countries (Bangladesh, India, Pakistan, Sri Lanka, and Thailand) responded positively, and they were all labor-exporting countries. As Carmela Torres notes: "[D]espite the liberalized trade among countries and moves to liberalize trade in services and movement of personnel, many of the richer countries which are expected to host migrant workers and their families tend to be protectionist in their attitude towards migrant workers."[43]

3. Unrightful Hospitalities: The Trade in Women from Mainland China to Hong Kong in Fruit Chan's *Durian Durian*

My account of the plight of FDWs in Singapore indicates that the nature of the hospitality offered by labor-receiving states is determined and limited by cost-benefit calculations in the service of the biopolitical cultivation of human capital. I have also argued that although international law instruments dealing with the human rights of migrant workers attempt to articulate a higher law of hospitality that transcends economic calculations, the implementation of this more open hospitality is complicated by the fact that the global stage of interstate relations and international civil society is necessarily caught within the web of economic instrumentality. In this final section, I consider alternative forms of hospitality to the stranger that do not issue from the laws of host countries by examining a filmic representation of the experiences of Mainland Chinese sex-workers in Hong Kong.

Like the FDW, the migrant sex-worker is also a necessary stranger in global capitalism. The important role of the sex-industry to economic development through global tourism in postcolonial Asia, especially in Thailand and the Philippines, has been well documented in social scientific studies.[44] Here, as in the case of domestic workers, there has been a gradual transnationalization of migration. What initially began as a circuit of rural-urban migration, where girls from impoverished rural areas moved to the capital city to engage in sex-work, has expanded into a genuinely global network. The situation is comparable to the need to import FDWs after the local supply of such labor has been depleted. The movement of sex-workers from a given Asian country to more lucrative destinations in and beyond Asia has given rise to the need to import sex-workers from poorer neighboring countries either through criminal trafficking or through consensual migration. Because of the nature of the work involved, the hospitality, if there is any, afforded to this type of migrant worker by the laws of host countries is inevitably much slimmer than that offered to FDWs.

The economic modernization of the People's Republic of China through its integration into the global capitalist system has led to the rise of transnational circuits for the migration of Mainland Chinese sex-workers. The global city of Hong Kong is a crucial terminal in such circuits. It was always the gateway to China for Chinese diasporic business networks and the corporate headquarters and eventual place of residence for many diasporic Chinese tycoons. From the standpoint of political sovereignty, HK may have been handed over to the PRC in 1997. But as a synecdoche of the permeability of the mainland's borders to the Chinese diaspora and its enlargement into Greater China, the handover also symbolically marked the irreversible integration of the PRC into the global capitalist system. It is effectively the handover of China to capitalism, its gradual weaning from communist principles. Thus, Hong Kong, and its broader economic hinterland in Southern China (especially the Guangdong area and the cities of Guangzhou and Shenzhen) is also a frontier, the source of change and innovation for the mainland. The PRC's integration into the global capitalist system has created channels for various types of labor migrants from the mainland into Hong Kong. The main focus of mainland development is directed at coastal cities and special economic zones. Such uneven development leads to rural poverty and mass migration of labor to the cities.

The hospitality shown by Hong Kong law to these necessary strangers is very limited. Under British colonial rule, people born in Hong Kong were second-class citizens of the United Kingdom. They had British passports of a restricted kind that did not give them the right of abode in Britain. Under the Basic Law that governs Hong Kong as a Special Administrative Region of China, however, Hong Kong-ers have special privileges in comparison to other PRC citizens because they (as well as Hong Kong residents who are not new immigrants—that is, those who have been there for more than seven years—and their children) have the right of abode in Hong Kong. Hong Kong identity therefore shifts from being excluded to being excluding, since it is defined after the handover in terms of desirable privileges that new immigrants from the mainland do not have. This distinction is part of a larger discursive construction of migrants from the mainland as economically and culturally backward "others" who threaten to overwhelm Hong Kong either as competitive labor for locals or as a drain on the welfare system.[45] The home of the host, the integrity of the site from which hospitality is offered, is therefore determined by various calculations. In the Hong Kong situation, the legal calculations that determine the limits of hospitality to the stranger and the rights a stranger has also presuppose cultural-discursive calculations about who belongs to a given community or group. As we will see, these calculations can divide an ethnicity or race (here, Chinese) into insiders and strangers. The splitting of Chinese-ness by these deep-seated prejudicial stereotypes is something that the mainland migrant confronts and brings back with her to the mainland despite the rhetoric of ethnic fraternity that figures all Chinese as descendants of the dragon.

A significant component of the out-migration of mainlanders is the movement and traffic of women for the purpose of sex-work from various parts of the mainland to Southern China onward to Macau, Hong Kong, and the rest of the world. Women constitute 80 percent of migrant workers to coastal cities, and this migration is a source of labor for the sex industry, which develops as a necessary offshoot of the flow of capital into the mainland. The permeability of borders that follows from the handover of Hong Kong extends these circuits of migration into Hong Kong, where the provision of sexual services to the local population is more lucrative than on the mainland.[46] Fruit Chan's *Durian Durian* (2000) takes as its central theme the completely inhospitable nature of Hong Kong law to these necessary strangers.[47]

The film is the first installment of an unfinished mainland prostitute trilogy that explores the implications of the transnational movement of sex-workers for the PRC as well as the position of China within the circuits of global capitalism. The film portrays the experiences of Xiao Yan, a mainland prostitute, and Ah Fen, a small girl from Shenzhen who overstays in Hong Kong and becomes an illegal immigrant. The film's opening sequence depicts the melding of Hong Kong and the mainland even as it keeps them apart. It begins with a shot of the Hong Kong harbor and the Star Ferry between Tsimshatsui and Hong Kong island, and this shot shades into a scene of Mudanjiang in the Northeast where the river is frozen in winter. The Mandarin voice-over, which is that of Xiao Yan, the mainland sex-worker, begins by describing the river in her hometown although the shot is of Hong Kong, and then proceeds to compare the two locations and marks their difference. In the next scene, a Cantonese voice-over by Ah Fen makes a similar contrast between their living conditions in the Hong Kong neighborhood of Mongkok and their house in Shenzhen. In both cases, therefore, the mainland is yoked to Hong Kong, indicating the porosity of the border between the two, even as a difference is repeatedly marked.

The identity in question here is not that of Hong Kong but of China. At the level of character or the aesthetic representation of personal experience (subjectivity), this difference between Hong Kong and China that is the mechanism for the interrogation of Mainland Chinese identity is registered in the two main characters' consciousness of their alien status in Hong Kong. In a scene that occurs roughly in the middle of the film, when both Xiao Yan and An Fen try to hide from the Hong Kong police, there is a poignant moment of recognition and solidarity where Xiao Yan looks at Ah Fen and intuitively recognizes herself and identifies her own social position. It is only later that this moment of recognition of herself in solidarity with the other is explicitly thematized. Xiao Yan's Mandarin voice-over in a later scene says that their friendship began in that alley, but it is only much later that she realized that she and Ah Fen are the same. They are both on a three-month visitor's pass. They have both come from the same place, Shenzhen, Ah Fen's hometown, and the location of a brothel where Xiao Yan has been working before moving on to Hong Kong. And they can both stay for only the same limited time. The only difference, Xiao Yan notes, is that Ah Fen wants to stay in Hong Kong permanently so that she can be with her father, a legal immigrant, even if it means being an illegal immigrant herself.

These two illegal immigrants are necessary strangers in two senses. Their paths have been scripted for them by processes of global capitalism that are beyond their control, and they perform tasks and services that are needed for the reproduction of social life in Hong Kong. Yet, as illegal immigrants, they are not offered any hospitality by the law. In Xiao Yan's case, although prostitution is not illegal in Hong Kong, Hong Kong laws criminalize the activities that are related to sex-work, such as solicitation. Xiao Yan is also violating the conditions of her visitor's pass by working. Her temporary presence in Hong Kong is therefore tolerated at the discretion of the police. She can be arrested at any time and become subjected to human rights violations at the hands of Hong Kong authorities. The human rights violations that migrant sex-workers can encounter at the hands of the law are not my main concern here. There is much to be said about the approach of the Hong Kong authorities who focus on prosecuting the women instead of investigating whether or not they are victims of trafficking despite the fact that Hong Kong has signed the Bangkok Declaration on Irregular Migration (April 21–23, 1999), which is partly concerned with the trafficking of women in relation to irregular migration, and is also bound by the Convention on the Elimination of All Forms of Discrimination against Women (1979), which calls on states to suppress all forms of traffic in women and exploitation of women for the purposes of prostitution.[48]

Moreover, it is questionable whether the UN Protocol to Prevent, Suppress and Punish Trafficking in Persons, Especially Women and Children (2000) is generally effective in offering greater hospitality to migrant sex-workers. Although Art. 14 emphasizes that the protocol should not be interpreted and applied in a way that discriminates against victims of trafficking, Art. 11 provides for the greater policing and strengthening of border controls in order to prevent and detect trafficking. This can have the effect of a de facto criminalization of sex-workers like Xiao Yan who willingly migrate to engage in sex-work. Indeed, since the protocol is ambiguous about whether the consent of the transported subject is a relevant factor in situations that do not involve force, coercion, and deception, it can potentially be interpreted and implemented in a manner that allows the host state to criminalize women who are moved across borders for sex-work by denying them victim status, as well as in a manner that grants legitimacy to the trafficker by placing the onus of proof on the trafficked person to show lack of consent.[49] However, a strict protectionist interpretation of the protocol that makes consent completely irrelevant can also enforce the anti-immigration policies of many Western countries and remove legal opportunities for migration for sex-work. As Kara Abramson notes, "[U]nder this scheme of trafficking, advocates bent on the prevention of trafficking become strange bedfellows with states eager to step up border controls to keep migrants out, or with regimes eager to restrict freedom of movement.[50]

For present purposes, what interests me is the permanent estrangement of the mainland sex-worker from all forms of legitimate community or *nomos*, her experience of inhospitality not only from the host city but also from her place of origin because of the cultural norms that define mainland society. In their different ways, both central characters rearticulate their identity in the mainland through the ways in which they have been defined as "other" by the law during their time in Hong Kong. At the beginning of the film, before she goes to Hong Kong, Ah Fen presents an idealized version of Hong Kong as a place of leisure, consumption, and self-improvement. She speaks of going to the Peak to see the night views of the city, of watching movies, learning English in school and going to Ocean Park. But her reality is bleaker. She spends most of her time in an alley, washing dishes with her mother. After she is arrested for having overstayed and is deported back to Shenzhen, Ah Fen tells Xiao Yan in a letter that being sent back is better because she is happier in Shenzhen, which she feels is her real home. This rejection of Hong Kong and identification with the mainland stems from her awareness that she will always be an alien in Hong Kong, someone who will always be rejected for cultural and legal reasons even though Cantonese is her mother tongue.

But Ah Fen is at least fortunate enough to be able to achieve repatriation in the mainland in the fullest sense of the word, unlike Xiao Yan, whose time in Hong Kong leaves her permanently dislocated and estranged even after she returns to Mudanjiang. Ah Fen is saved from this fate of perpetual limbo and alienation for two reasons. First, her youthful innocence does not permit her to see the infiltration of the same imperatives of consumption and profit-making governing Hong Kong society to the mainland. Second, and more important, her experiences as an illegal immigrant still occur within the relatively safe confines of her family who are there with her and provide her with a support system. In stark contrast, Xiao Yan's experience as an illegal migrant in Hong Kong is more spiritually corrosive because she is a sex-worker who must bear the memory of her experience in Hong Kong in utter isolation, since it must be forever hidden and kept separate from her life with her family back in Mudanjiang. (The contrast between the innocence of one protagonist and the other's sexual commodification, a veritable pair of Blakean songs of innocence and experience, however, also ominously implies that Xiao Yan's present could be Ah Fen's future.) The critical edge that Xiao Yan's experience gives rise to is more biting. It exposes the superficiality of transnational Chinese ethnic fraternity as a form of transnational hospitality offered to all Chinese people. Throughout her time in Hong Kong, Xiao Yan is repeatedly subjected to insulting slurs. Even the illegal Indian immigrants in the alley repeatedly call her a "Pak Ku" (Northern woman). Hence, when a client of hers with a body covered with tattoos of a dragon tells her that all Chinese are descendants of the dragon, the statement rings with hollowness.

One can understand economic globalization as a form of generous hospitality to the stranger qua business entrepreneur and bearer of capital flows. In this regard, Xiao Yan personifies an incisive critique of the myth of the Chinese diasporic entrepreneur. For the migrant sex-worker is intimately linked to the opening up of the mainland to economic globalization. It is not only that economic development and the porosity of the border between the mainland and Hong Kong has increased the flow of migrant sex-workers because young Chinese women who are adversely affected by modern development resort to prostitution to improve their standard of living. More strikingly, the migrant sex-worker embodies many of the traits and characteristics of the savvy and flexible diasporic entrepreneur that are celebrated as virtues and ideals both in Hong Kong and in the PRC, at the level of the state and society. In her decision to become a migrant sex-worker, Xiao Yan displays courage and self-determination, a willingness to cross borders and to sell herself as a commodity in order to make money to secure a future for herself back in the mainland. These are precisely the qualities of the old diasporic business subject as well as the values of the new Chinese transnational entrepreneurial subject who seeks foreign capital investment for China.

Yet, Xiao Yan is unable to find hospitality in either Hong Kong or her original home. Unlike Ah Fen, Xiao Yan's return home does not involve her felicitous reintegration into the fabric of life in her hometown. We learn that she is in fact married to her old childhood sweetheart, but her absence has so estranged her that she is getting a divorce. The second half of the film broaches in the most concerted manner the problem of what it means to be Mainland Chinese for a migrant sex-worker. What the audience witnesses in the film's second half is the crisis of Mainland China as host for the returning sex-worker, the fact that no homecoming is possible for Xiao Yan because there is no home to return to in the robust sense of the word, no social or collective substrate in which she can subsist as a member. As a result of the inhospitality that follows from the calculations and capitalist norms that determine Hong Kong identity, Xiao Yan's life there is deeply marked by solitude and alienation. She is always performing a role, putting on a mask in front of her clients. She adopts multiple names and tells each client that she is from different parts of China depending on what she thinks they want to hear and what will earn her more tips. She is variously from Szechuan, Hunan, Shanghai, Xinjiang, and so forth. When she has a mainland client, she even pretends to be a local, despite her thickly accented Cantonese.

One might reasonably expect traditional kinship or familial structures to provide the panacea that can alleviate or soften the experience of alienation and solitude that results from her commodification and her alien status as an illegal sex-worker in Hong Kong. In fact, however, these familial structures are also deeply imbricated in market-commodity relations. On the one hand, these familial relations always involve money and profit, since this is associated with honor and face. This is precisely the nexus between *guanxi* (personalized networks of influence) and capitalism axiomatic to the East Asian capitalist model. Xiao Yan's mother insists that she pay for an elaborate banquet to celebrate her return, with a minimum cost of 200 yuan per table with Western spirits, especially red wine, because she has returned as a successful business woman, and it has to "look good" so that they will not "lose face." On the other hand, these familial structures are also marked by a deep societal hypocrisy. They can revel in her newfound wealth and gleefully spend it. But she can never reveal to them its true source, much less seek support or solace for the humiliations and emotional scars that sex-work generates because of its stigmatized nature. They can accept capitalism but not the fact that modern capitalism also implies the rationalized or organized commodification of female sexuality. For the migrant sex-worker is quite literally playing an economic role opened up for her globalization. She is pushed by global economic forces to take up a relatively lucrative form of labor that has emerged as an option for uneducated women in rapidly industrializing

China, a form of labor that offers both economic and geographic mobility. But since this labor is stigmatized, Xiao Yan has to continue play-acting. She remains deeply alienated and lonely even when she is back in her hometown and among her closest friends and family. Back in Mudanjiang, she may appear to be an integral member of the community—someone's daughter, niece, cousin, daughter-in-law, or close childhood friend. But the fact that she must keep the truth of her profession in the south a secret means that she can never be fully integrated into mainland society and re-embedded in a hospitable support-system, a *nomos* or a *Sittlichkeit*, to borrow a Hegelian word.

This sociological fact of being a living secret is repeatedly exploited by Fruit Chan for irony at Xiao Yan's painful expense. For instance, she is repeatedly asked to take her young cousin to the south with her and teach her how to do business. It is also a source of psychical and emotional torture. Xiao Yan repeatedly receives phone calls from the madam at a brothel in Shenzhen where she used to work urging her to go back because business is booming. She receives one such call during her divorce proceeding, and she turns off the phone and throws it to the floor in obvious distress. The migrant woman sex-worker is therefore someone who is permanently in exile, someone who can never be received with hospitality, not even in her homeland. She can never return to the homeland fully, never be fully repatriated, even if she has returned physically, not because her consciousness has been irreversibly changed and because she doesn't wish to belong, but because there is no abode available that can receive her fully for what she is. As one NGO report puts it, "[A]lthough sex work has become a widespread phenomenon in the Mainland Chinese society, it is still not accepted by people under the mainstream social values. People tend to disregard the experience of sex workers and put it into underground, so as to avoid facing the discrepancy between the social reality and moral values. As a result, sex workers have to face many difficulties in their work and lives . . . without receiving desirable concern. The only general discourse on sex workers is negative and in all ways accuses them of chasing for enjoyment but being unwilling to work, or violating the ethics. As sex workers have a stigma attached to them, most of them do not tell their families about their work and problems. Instead, they have to face many conflicts with their families as they try to keep their secrets. . . . It more or less limits their possible change and development. All these problems have been disregarded in society."[51]

The true meaning of the mainland migrant sex-worker's movement is permanent dislocation. We commonly associate migration with freedom of movement and passage. But for this particular type of migrant, their very movement leads them to an aporia—literally, a road that cannot be crossed, a blockage where there is no passage. There is always some experience of blockage and nonmovement because, as we see in the case of Xiao Yan, the place of origin no longer provides any hospitable repose on return. Hence, there is no longer any home from which to move and no home to be nostalgically remembered. She is permanently a stranger. But it is precisely from this marginal place that is a nonplace that the migrant sex-worker and other examples of this new type of Chinese migrant worker can enable the critic to see the fraying of Mainland Chinese society, its cultural identity, and the increasing untenability of existing cultural resources for communal support.

I would like to conclude by looking at the solutions that *Durian Durian* offers to the dilemma of being a permanent stranger and their limits. We have already seen the solution that Ah Fen personifies: saying "no" to Hong Kong and affirming the mainland. At the end of the film, Xiao Yan performs a similar repudiation. She changes her cell phone number so that she can no longer be reached by contacts from her former profession. But as we have also seen, it is not so easy for Xiao Yan to affirm the mainland because of the secret she cannot disclose. The film seems to offer two solutions to this dilemma. First, at the very end of the film, after she has failed to stop her cousin from going to Shenzhen, Xiao Yan reaches back into her past training and performs a traditional dance. She assumes the role of the Goddess of Mercy in a performance for the New Year festival. But this attempt to find refuge in nostalgia and tradition seems too sentimental and escapist, given the film's harsh social realism.

Indeed, it is strongly suggested that we cannot simply say "no" to capitalist consumption. This culture is everywhere: the cell-phone that connects Xiao Yan to the brothel-keeper in Shenzhen, the cable TV in the apartment that she seeks to rent out has CNN, and all the channels available in a hotel. In an ironic scene at the beauty parlor where Xiao Yan and her friend Li Shuang are having facial treatments, they both emphatically demand to use imported cosmetic products such as Christian Dior instead of inferior local products. Yet it is precisely this desire for the consumption of imports that leads Xiao Yan to seek work abroad as a prostitute, a job that she would never undertake in the mainland despite the irony of her friend's suggestion that she should do whatever business she did in the south at home. Indeed, the escapism of Xiao Yan's final operatic performance is underscored by the fact that by the end of the film, most of her friends, including her former husband, have taken the train out of Mudanjiang, leaving the past behind them in search of the new, whereas she chooses nostalgically to stay put.

The film, however, points to another mode of hospitality that is neither that of legality or right, nor that of belonging to a group culture. During her time in Hong Kong, the one person that Xiao Yan is able to be genuine with, the one person with whom she doesn't have to play a role, is Ah Fen. Ah Fen does not judge her for being a sex-worker. She tells Ah Fen her real name and gives her her address and asks her to write to her. In her moment of despondency in Mudanjiang, she receives a parcel from Ah Fen, which turns out to be the exotic durian of the title, which Ah Fen gives to her in an act of generosity as a New Year gift. This suggests that precious solidarities and subcultures of support and hospitality can be found in the space of transnational migrancy even though they are necessarily transient, felicitous, and chancy and cannot be institutionalized into spaces for the building of permanent communities. Other examples can be found in this film and Fruit Chan's other films: the comradeship between mainland sex-workers, the friendship between the Indian immigrants and Ah Fen, or the affective ties between the Filipina maid and Little Cheung in *Little Cheung* or the friendship in *Hollywood, Hong Kong* between Tong Tong and the younger Chu son.[52] But these transient modes of transnational solidarity can no longer be understood under the sign of hospitality as right or law, even law in the expanded sense of communal norms, precisely because no hospitality can be found in the sphere of law.

Envoi

This paper has examined the conditional hospitality of the law toward the stranger in an era of global migration by looking at the law's construction and discriminatory treatment of two different types of female migrant labor in globalizing Asia. In the case of the FDW, we have seen how the purportedly universal hospitality of international human rights remains trapped by the competitive divisions of uneven globalization. In the case of the migrant sex-worker, the problem is not only that no hospitality can be offered because she is an illegal migrant. More disturbingly, the path that has been charted for her by global capitalism makes her a permanent stranger who cannot even fully return home and seek solace from the communal hospitality offered there.

These scenarios of restricted hospitality or nonhospitality raise several important questions about law as hospitality. In Kant's canonical understanding of hospitality, the hospitality of right was by definition conditional in comparison with the unconditionality of the moral law. This is because the various levels of right govern relations between individuals and collective subjects that both attract and repel each other because they need to associate but cannot be so close as to annul the differences between one another. Kant, however, suggested that the alliance between cosmopolitan right and world commerce signaled at a more universal hospitality to all of humanity that could asymptotically approximate the unconditional openness of a moral realm of ends that would include all rational beings. I have argued that today's version of this alliance—that between transnational human rights regimes and economic globalization—can lead only to forms of hospitality that remain restricted and conditional for various forms of migrant labor that are necessary to the global capitalist system.

It may be the case that the conditionality of law's hospitality in these cases is not merely a historical limit that arises from the unevenness of global capitalism and that can be overcome with the overcoming of this unevenness. For is not the hospitality of the law always going to be compromised insofar as these forces of attraction and repulsion of the stranger are always at work within law? For any law, whether we understand it in the strict or narrow sense as legality or right, or the rules and norms that define and bind together a cultural community, or even the moral law that applies to all rational beings, always involves the measure and calculative determination of some kind of secure or integrated unity. It articulates criteria that define an inside and an outside, adjudicates on who and what belongs within and who and what lies without, and regulates the permissible and tolerable intercourse between a community and its outside. The criteria for these calculations can be economic, political, or cultural. Hence, the hospitality of law can never be unconditional. The power or sovereignty that law necessarily presupposes always reserves the right to withhold hospitality according to its criteria for calculation—for instance, which migrant workers can be given a right of residence for economic reasons and which cannot. Even the moral law applies only to all rational beings.

In contradistinction, the hospitality that provides some relief from the inhospitality of state law and the laws of cultural community that Fruit Chan's film points to does not arise from any determinate criteria of calculative reason. Since it arises from chance encounters that cannot be predicted in advance, this hospitality is an openness to an other that is not defined in advance as this or that proper identity. It is thus a form of hospitality that is unconditional, that cannot be thought of in terms of the figure of lawfulness and right. It is in this spirit that Jacques Derrida has rigorously distinguished the unconditional hospitality of justice and ethics from the conditional hospitality of the law, even as he insists on the necessity of their aporetic embrace:

> Pure hospitality consists in welcoming the new arrival before imposing conditions on them, before knowing and asking for anything at all, be it a name or an identity "paper."[53]

> It is as though hospitality were the impossible: as though the law of hospitality defined this very impossibility, as if it were only possible to transgress it, as though *the* law of absolute, unconditional, hyperbolical hospitality, as though the categorical imperative of hospitality commanded that we transgress all the laws (in the plural) of hospitality, namely, the conditions, the norms, the rights and the duties that are imposed on hosts and hostesses, on the men or women who give a welcome as well as the men or women who receive it. And vice versa, it is as though the laws (plural) of hospitality, in marking limits, powers, rights, and duties, consisted in challenging and transgressing *the* law of hospitality, the one that would command that the "new arrival" be offered an unconditional welcome.[54]

The decoupling of unconditional hospitality from the hospitality of calculative reason conceived in terms of right would enable us to think of alternative forms of community and solidarity that are outside the law and can supplement its deficiencies, even as we insist on the urgent need for the legal protection of the rights of the various necessary strangers that globalization conjures up.

Notes

Portions of this chapter were adapted from: Pheng Cheah, "Another Diaspora: Chineseness and the Traffic in Women in Fruit Chan's *Durian Durian*," in Andrea Riemenschnitter and Deborah L. Madsen eds., *Diasporic Histories: Cultural Archives of Chinese Trans-*

nationalism (Hong Kong University Press, 2009), 160–64, 167–69. Portions were also reprinted and adapted by permission of the publisher from "Bringing into the Home a Stranger Far More Foreign: Human Rights and the Global Trade in Domestic Labor," in *Inhuman Conditions: On Cosmopolitanism and Human Rights* by Phen Cheah, 178–229, Cambridge, Mass.: Harvard University Press, Copyright © 2006 by the President and Fellows of Harvard College.

1. Joel Kotkin, "Flight to Safety," *San Francisco Chronicle*, August 7, 2005, B1, B6. The quotation is from B6.

2. Ibid.

3. Ibid.

4. The OED notes that etymologically, "city" derives from the Latin "*civitas, -tatem* was n. of state or condition f. *civis* citizen: its primary sense was therefore 'citizenship'; thence concretely 'the body of citizens, the community'; only in later times was the word taken as = *urbs*, the town or place occupied by the community. The historical relation between the Roman *civitas* and *civis* was thus the reverse of that between our *city* and *citizen*."

5. See Hannah Arendt, *The Origins of Totalitarianism* (San Diego: Harcourt, 1968), ch. 9, 267–302.

6. See, for instance, Saskia Sassen, *Globalization and Its Discontents* (New York: New Press, 1998), *Cities in a World Economy*, 2nd ed. (Thousand Oaks: Pine Forge Press, 2000), "Spatialities and Temporalities of the Global: Elements for a Theorization," *Public Culture* 12, no. 1 (2000): 215–32; and Jürgen Habermas, *The Inclusion of the Other: Studies in Political Theory*, ed. Ciaran Cronin and Pablo De Greiff (Cambridge: MIT Press, 1998), translation of *Die Einbeziehung des Anderen. Studien zur politischen Theorie* (Frankfurt am Main, 1996), and *The Postnational Constellation: Political Essays*, trans. and ed. Max Pensky (Cambridge: MIT Press, 2001), translation of *Die postnationale Konstellation. Politische Essays* (Frankfurt am Main: Suhrkamp, 1998). I have discussed the work of Sassen and Habermas in chapters 1–2 of my *Inhuman Conditions: On Cosmopolitanism and Human Rights in the Current Conjuncture* (Cambridge: Harvard University Press, 2006).

7. Michael Hardt and Antonio Negri, *Empire* (Cambridge: Harvard University Press, 2000), 397.

8. Ibid., 400.

9. See Immanuel Kant, *The Metaphysics of Morals*, in *Practical Philosophy*, trans. and ed. Mary Gregor (Cambridge: Cambridge University Press, 1996), §62, 489–90; *Die Metaphysik der Sitten*, in *Werkausgabe* VIII, ed. W. Weischedel (Frankfurt am Main: Suhrkamp, 1968), 475–77. Subsequent references to this text will be indicated by *MM*, with the page numbers to the original following that of the translation.

10. Immanuel Kant, *Toward Perpetual Peace: A Philosophical Project*, in *Practical Philosophy*, 330–31; "Zum ewigen Frieden. Ein philosophischer Entwurf," in *Werkausgabe*

XI, ed. W. Weischedel (Frankfurt am Main: Suhrkamp, 1968), 216–17. Further references to this text will be indicated by *TPP*, with the page numbers to the original following that of the translation.

11. On the different meanings of *Gewalt*, see Étienne Balibar, "Violence, Ideality and Cruelty," in *Politics and the Other Scene* (London: Verso, 2002), esp. 134–36.

12. Immanuel Kant, *Critique of Practical Reason*, in *Practical Philosophy*, 154; *Kritik der praktischen Vernunft*, in *Werkausgabe* VII, ed. W. Weischedel (Frankfurt am Main: Suhrkamp, 1968), 126.

13. Immanuel Kant, "Idea for a Universal History with a Cosmopolitan Purpose," in *Political Writings*, ed. Hans Reiss, trans. H. B. Nisbet (Cambridge: Cambridge University Press, 1991), 44; "Idee zu einer allgemeinen Geschichte in weltbürgerlicher Absicht," in *Werkausgabe* XI, 37–38. I have modified the translation where appropriate.

14. Ibid., 45/38.

15. As Derrida has noted, this communal right to possess the earth applies only to its surface and not to anything that is erected or instituted on that surface through human production and settlement.

16. Adam Smith, *An Inquiry into the Nature and Causes of the Wealth of Nations*, Chapter 4, "Of the Origin and Use of Money," ed. Edwin Cannan (Chicago: University of Chicago Press, 1976), 26.

17. Sassen, *Globalization and Its Discontents*, 21–22.

18. Ibid., 200.

19. See F. Fröbel, J. Heinrichs, and O. Kreye, *The New International Division of Labour* (Cambridge: Cambridge University Press, 1980); Scott Lash and John Urry, *The End of Organised Capitalism* (Cambridge: Polity, 1987); and David Harvey, *The Condition of Postmodernity: An Enquiry into the Origins of Cultural Change* (Cambridge, MA.: Blackwell, 1990).

20. The secretary of labor declared: "We no longer apologize for the outflow of Filipino labor abroad under such labels as the brain drain. We have decided it in such a manner that it will redound to the national interest. We are scouting aggressively for job markets for excess Filipino skills in many countries of the world" (Blas Ople, "Trends and Principles in the Labor Code," address before the National Tripartite Conference on the Labor Code, Development Academy of the Philippines [October 23, 1975], cited in Dan Gatmaytan, "Death and the Maid: Work, Violence, and the Filipina in the International Labor Market," *Harvard Women's Law Journal* 20 [Spring 1997]: 237).

21. World Bank, *World Development Report, 1991* (Oxford: Oxford University Press, 1991), 93.

22. World Bank, *World Development Report, 1995* (Oxford: Oxford University Press, 1995), 64–66.

23. For a comprehensive discussion that slightly predates the push to become an

information- and high technology–based economy, see Pang Eng Fong, "Absorbing Temporary Foreign Workers: The Experience of Singapore," *Asian and Pacific Migration Journal* 1, no. 3–4 (1992): 495–509.

24. The website for Contact Singapore is http://www.contactsingapore.org.sg.

25. "Singapore of the Future" (an extract from Deputy Prime Minister Lee Hsien Loong's book, *Singapore: Re-Engineering Success*), *Straits Times*, November 8, 1998.

26. See Brenda S. A. Yeoh and T. C. Chang, "Globalising Singapore: Debating Transnational Flows in the City," *Urban Studies* 38, no. 7 (2001): 1025–44.

27. As the female labor force participation rate, especially that of married women, increased dramatically, the number of foreign maids also catapulted from 40,000 in 1988 to more than 140,000 in 2001, with a 19 percent increase between 1998 and 2001 alone. The figures for foreign maids are from "Maid-Sharing Creates Too Many Problems," letter from Ministry of Manpower, *Straits Times*, December 1, 2001. There are around 100,000 households (out of 900,000 to 1 million households) that employ a foreign maid (communication from Ministry of Manpower).

28. Noeleen Heyzer and Vivienne Wee, "Domestic Workers in Transient Overseas Employment: Who Benefits, Who Profits," in *The Trade in Domestic Workers: Causes, Mechanisms and Consequences of International Migration*, ed. Noeleen Heyzer, Geertje Lycklama à Nijeholt, and Nedra Weerakoon (London: Zed Books, 1994), 63.

29. Interview with Ministry of Manpower, January 9, 2002: "I think their contributions are economic and social. Economic, because these people—FDWs—have actually given our females the opportunity to go out and work and contribute to the economy. 'Social' because they help manage the households too. Some of them end up teaching the children. Some of our domestic workers are fairly well-educated, so they end up also playing tutor to the young kids. Quite a lot of them are also active in voluntary work, church activities."

30. Ibid., emphasis added.

31. "'Social Costs' of More Maids Explained" (response by Ministry of Manpower), *Straits Times*, September 15, 2000.

32. In November 1997, the levy for unskilled foreign construction workers was increased by S$30 to S$470, and that for FDWs was increased by S$15 to S$345, whereas that for skilled foreign workers in the construction, marine, manufacturing, and service sectors was cut by half (from S$200 to S$100). See "Govt Revises Levy for All Foreign Workers," *Straits Times*, November 5 1997. The FDW levy was first introduced in 1982 and was set at $120. It has increased steadily and is now reviewed annually.

33. One employer complained in a letter to the national newspaper that "the recent government proposal to raise the maid levy is another instance where we can see how detached the Government is from the struggles and issues that are dear to the heart of the working class" (*Straits Times*, November 21, 1997).

34. Tay Lin Siau, "Review Maid Levy to Lower Abuse," *Straits Times*, December 11, 2001.

35. Security Bond, Immigration Regulation 21, Immigration Act (ch. 133).

36. Letters to the *Straits Times* often discuss the lack of respect shown by children to maids. See, for instance, "Teach Kids to Respect Maids," July 31, 2002.

37. "'No' to Standard Maid Contract," *Straits Times*, May 18, 1998.

38. "Just a Piece of Paper?" *Straits Times*, May 3, 1998.

39. Art. 25(1) of the UN Convention stipulates that migrant workers have the right not to be treated less favorably than national workers in respect of conditions and terms of employment "according to national law and practice." The two ILO Conventions are no. 97 Migration for Employment (1949) and no. 143 Migrant Workers (1975). For a fuller discussion of the differences between the ILO and UN conventions and the processes that led up to the UN Convention, see Roger Bohning, "The ILO and the New UN Convention on Migrant Workers: The Past and Future," *International Migration Review* 25, no. 4 (Winter 1991): 698–709; and Juhani Lonnroth, "The International Convention on the Rights of All Migrant Workers and Members of Their Families in the Context of International Migration Policies: An Analysis of Ten Years of Negotiation," *International Migration Review* 25, no. 4 (Winter 1991): 710–36.

40. Although it was adopted by the General Assembly on December 18, 1990, the UN Convention came into force only on July 1, 2003. As of June 10, 2003, the convention had been ratified by twenty-two states—namely, Azerbaijan, Belize, Bolivia, Bosnia and Herzegovina, Cape Verde, Colombia, Ecuador, Egypt, El Salvador, Ghana, Guatemala, Guinea, Mali, Mexico, Morocco, the Philippines, Senegal, Seychelles, Sri Lanka, Tajikistan, Uganda, and Uruguay. Eleven states— Bangladesh, Burkina Faso, Chile, Comoros, Guinea-Bissau, Paraguay, Sao Tome and Principe, Sierra Leone, the Sudan, Togo, and Turkey—have signed the convention. Note that none of the major labor-receiving countries have signed or ratified the convention. India and Indonesia are major labor-sending states from the South and Southeast Asian region that have not ratified it. ILO conventions no. 97 and no. 143 have been ratified by forty-two and eighteen countries, respectively. With the exception of Sabah, a component substate of Malaysia, none of the major Asian labor-sending countries or the major labor-receiving countries in the Middle East and Asia have ratified the ILO conventions.

41. *Report of the Fourth World Conference on Women* (Beijing, September 4–15, 1995), A/CONF.177/20, October 17, 1995.

42. Dianne Otto, "Holding up Half the Sky, But for Whose Benefit? A Critical Analysis of the Fourth World Conference on Women," *Australian Feminist Law Journal* 6 (March 1996): 27. Otto notes that "the emphasis of other strategic objectives is on equipping women to be able to better compete, equally with men, in the global capitalist

economy by such measures as making credit more available, directing finance to intermediary institutions that target women's economic activities and encouraging women's entrepreneurial ventures. But is the solution really for every poor woman to become a freelance entrepreneur?" (21).

43. Carmela Torres, "Asian Women in Migration in the Light of the Beijing Conference," in *Asian Women in Migration*, ed. Graziano Battistella and Anthony Paganoni (Quezon City: Scalabrini Migration Center, 1996), 188.

44. See, for instance, Pasuk Phongpaichit, *From Peasant Girls to Bangkok Masseuses* (Geneva: International Labour Organisation, 1982); Ryan Bishop and Lillian S. Robinson, *Night Market: Sexual Cultures and the Thai Economic Miracle* (New York: Routledge, 1998); and Ara Wilson, *The Intimate Economies of Bangkok* (Berkeley: University of California Press, 2004), ch. 2. All these studies deal with Thailand.

45. For a fuller discussion, see esp. Helen Siu's work on the construction of the mainland immigrant in her "Immigrants and Social Ethos: Hong Kong in the Nineteen-Eighties," *Journal of the Hong Kong Branch of the Royal Asiatic Society* 26 (1986): 1–16; and Agnes Ku, "Hegemonic Construction, Negotiation and Displacement: The Struggle over Right of Abode in Hong Kong," *International Journal of Cultural Studies* 4, no. 3 (2001): 259–78.

46. See the report by Zi Teng, the Hong Kong–based NGO, "Research Report on Mainland Chinese Sex Workers: Hong Kong, Macau, and Town B in Pearl River Delta," February 2000.

47. Fruit Chan (dir.), *Durian Durian* (Hong Kong: Nicetop, 2000).

48. On these issues, see Robyn Emerton, "Trafficking of Women into Hong Kong for the Purpose of Prostitution: Preliminary Research Findings," Centre for Comparative and Public Law, Faculty of Law, University of Hong Kong, Occasional Paper No. 3, February 2001. On the violation of sex-workers' rights, see Carolina Ng, "Policemen Humiliate and Hurt Us, Prostitutes Claim," *Sunday Morning Post*, July 24, 2005, 5.

49. The ambiguity with regard to consent is found in Art. 3(b), which states that "the consent of a victim of trafficking in persons . . . shall be irrelevant where any of the means set forth in subparagraph (a) have been used." This implies that consent could be relevant if the means set forth—the threat or use of force or other forms of coercion, abduction, fraud, deception, the abuse of power or of a position of vulnerability or the giving or receiving of payments or benefits to achieve the consent of a person having control over another person—are not employed. For a fuller discussion of this issue, see Kara Abramson, "Beyond Consent, toward Safeguarding Human Rights: Implementing the United Nations Trafficking Protocol," *Harvard International Law Journal* 44, no. 2 (Summer 2003): 473–502.

50. Ibid., 494.

51. Zi Teng, "Research Report on Mainland Chinese Sex Workers," 4–5.

52. Fruit Chan (dir.), *Hollywood, Hong Kong* (Hong Kong: Nicetop, 2001), and *Little Cheung* (Hong Kong: Nicetop, 1999).

53. Jacques Derrida, "The Principle of Hospitality," in *Paper Machine*, trans. Rachel Bowlby (Stanford, CA: Stanford University Press, 2005), 67.

54. Jacques Derrida, *Of Hospitality*, trans. Rachel Bowlby (Stanford, CA: Stanford University Press, 2000), 75, 77.

The Strangers in Ourselves: The Rights of Suspect Citizens in the Age of Terrorism

ROGERS M. SMITH

Like the jurisprudence of modern Western nations generally, American law has always drawn distinctions between "citizens" and "aliens." And as in perhaps all human societies, many Americans have often associated "aliens" with qualities they feared, from savagery to deceit to licentious sexuality to thirst for blood and conquest. But ever since the Declaration of Independence proclaimed that all men are endowed with certain inalienable rights, the United States has always also had strong traditions recognizing all persons as entitled to many rights, whether or not those persons were citizens. One of the twentieth century's seminal constitutional scholars, Alexander Bickel, eloquently argued that "the original Constitution presented the edifying picture of a government that bestowed rights on people and persons, and held itself out as bound by certain standards of conduct in its relations with people and persons, not with some legal construct called citizen."[1] Although I think Bickel overstated his case, it is nonetheless true that, with the important exception of the Alien and Sedition Acts, much in U.S. law, particularly at the federal level, did not sharply distinguish between citizens and aliens in terms of basic rights until the late nineteenth century, when mounting opposition to Chinese and then Southern and Eastern European immigrants led to new state restrictions on alien rights accompanied by federal bans on immigration.[2] In the nation's formative years, Americans' eagerness to grow and expand meant that they often extended to European aliens, at least, most if not all the rights they provided themselves.[3] To be sure, some gaps have always existed between the sets of rights that citizens and aliens possessed, and in different eras political and legal forces have sometimes widened, sometimes narrowed those gaps. Even so, American political leaders have not generally sought to gain support by expanding the rights of all citizens at the expense of all aliens. More commonly, they have cultivated some racial, ethnic, and cultural groups at the expense of others, regardless of citizenship—favoring whites over blacks, "Nordic" descended Americans against "Mediterranean" ones, Anglos versus Chinese, Japanese, and Mexican Americans.[4] The 14th Amendment, which formally guaranteed equal citizenship regardless of race, did mean that sometimes efforts to build racial, ethnic, and class alliances used the strategy of denials of rights to aliens. But just as often, that guarantee worked only to ensure that racially motivated reductions in rights formally applied to all citizens, though in practice, they most affected targeted minorities.

As a result, U.S. political struggles have more often worked either to expand citizenship and alien rights simultaneously or to reduce them in tandem than to differentiate sharply between them. In the late nineteenth and early twentieth centuries, American policy-makers and courts justified denials of rights to aliens on grounds of their racial and cultural unfitness to be Americans—and they used similar arguments to deny full rights to nonwhite U.S. citizens, consigned to "separate but equal" institutions.[5] And when the U.S. government "relocated" West Coast Japanese residents to internment camps en masse during World War II, they did not distinguish between Japanese aliens and Japanese American citizens. They reduced the rights of both groups.[6] When the Supreme Court minimized the due process rights of alien Nazi saboteurs in 1942, it also restricted the rights of any U.S. citizens who might be their allies.[7] In the civil rights era of the 1950s and 1960s and its immediate aftermath, similar linkages appeared, though in inclusive directions. Efforts to eradicate racially defined second-class citizenship eventually also won for aliens of all races and ethnicities rights more comparable to those of citizens.[8]

Toward the end of the twentieth century, the linkages remained, but a reverse dynamic began to emerge. Renewed anxieties about the dangers of immigrant aliens—seen as strangers in our midst who might at best be inclined to leech off American prosperity and at worse to engage in criminal activity and terrorist violence—increasingly were joined with fears that many Americans (often again nonwhite) presented like dangers. Concerns about alien threats have thus been used to win support for laws and judicial rulings that have sharply reduced the legal rights to social welfare, privacy, and due process of all who reside on U.S. soil, citizens and aliens alike, even if in practice, citizens with certain racial, ethnic, religious, class, and ideological identities remain far more affected. In crafting recent legislation, judicial rulings, and especially executive orders, Americans have raised alarms about the dangers of the strangers at our gates to justify efforts also to purge the strangers in ourselves. The events of September 11, 2001, greatly accelerated this trend, but it predated them, for its roots are deeper. They are long-standing traditions of treating those who do not fit dominant ethnocultural and ideological molds as too strange, too "un-American" to enjoy equal rights, whether or not the Constitution says they are citizens. How far those old roots will sprout new limits on the rights of aliens and citizens is one of the central political and legal questions facing the United States in the early twenty-first century.

Historic Distinctions between Alien and Citizen Rights. Even though American political battles have rarely turned on distinctions between citizen and alien rights, the history of how U.S. national, state, and local governments have defined the bundles of rights that could be claimed by each group is far too complex for full rehearsal here. I wish to highlight only a few broad patterns. In doing so, let me note that I stand firmly with the critics of policies and rulings that deny any meaningful role for the Constitution in constraining the U.S. government overseas and that grant only the most minimal role for its provisions in regulating treatment of aliens within the United States. These stances place me in opposition to much of what the courts have held historically as well as developments today, though I believe that they represent better readings of U.S. constitutional traditions.[9] Courts have frequently defined the gap between the constitutional protections afforded citizens and aliens as larger than I believe it should be.

I nonetheless think some distinctions between citizens and aliens make sense. For example, though they are not constitutionally compelled to do so, U.S. governments have generally confined voting rights to those who either already are members of the civic community or who have declared their intent to become so.[10] There are strong cases to be made for resident aliens voting in various sorts of specialized elections and for permitting dual citizenship, with voting rights in two countries.[11] Still, it is consistent with traditions of republican self-governance to restrict the franchise to those who accept the identity and responsibilities of citizenship, particularly when naturalization is reasonably easy to obtain. But it seems equally appropriate that the Bill of Rights, which consists extensively of protections against unfair criminal justice procedures, confers all its guarantees on persons, not citizens. Neither the United States nor any other government should hold that there are groups upon whom it is entitled to wield its coercive power arbitrarily.

Though practices surely varied, through the first part of U.S. history, few formal distinctions in the criminal justice rights of citizens and aliens existed. The federal government engaged in relatively little law enforcement, and the states and localities that primarily exercised police powers did so without any great regard for personal rights, but without any strong citizen/alien distinctions. In the antebellum years, casting a mold that has yet to be fully broken, it was nonwhites, and especially poorer nonwhites—African Americans, Native Americans, sometimes Mexican and Chinese residents—who were often denied basic procedural protections, whether or not they were citizens.

The Civil War produced the Fourteenth Amendment and a number of federal civil rights statutes that promised to change those racially inegalitarian patterns. But the political reaction against Reconstruction soon proved too great to hold back, and lawmakers zealously adopted new ways to deny rights to nonwhites and also to others they viewed as politically threatening, without explicitly violating constitutional and statutory standards of equal protection. Western legislators and, eventually, Northeastern blue-bloods feared immigrants from Asia and Southern and Eastern Europe on economic, racial, and ideological grounds, and Southern whites were happy to support restrictive policies toward immigrants in return for acquiescence in their construction of the Jim Crow South. In the Southwest and California, Anglo Americans also sought to gain and sustain ascendancy over Mexican Americans. In part these goals were pursued via laws at the state and national level that increasingly limited or eliminated the rights of aliens to own property, to hold jobs, to enter the country, and to receive basic procedural protections when detained by the government or deported. But they were joined by measures to segregate, disfranchise, and exclude from jury boxes and polling booths most African Americans, and sometimes Chinese and Mexican Americans as well. All these linked developments won endorsement from the U.S. Supreme Court.[12]

The seminal source of judicial denials of basic rights to aliens is the 1889 *Chinese Exclusion Case*, where the U.S. Supreme Court upheld the U.S. government's claim that it could prevent the return to the United States of formerly resident Chinese aliens to whom the government had given certificates guaranteeing their right to re-entry. Federal legislators had defended these exclusions on both economic and racist premises: the Chinese had evolved into "machines" of flesh and blood with which white workers could not compete, but who also had evolution-engrained "hideous immoralities."[13] They could be kept out regardless of any governmentally bestowed guarantees or even human rights, despite the absence of any explicit constitutional authority for doing so on these grounds. For the Court, Justice Stephen Field, a Californian, wrote that the Chinese "remained strangers in the land, residing apart by themselves, and adhering to the customs and usages of their own country," refusing to "assimilate with our people, or to make any change in their habits or modes of living." Exclusion of these "strangers" seemed necessary to keep the country from being "overrun."[14] The Court went on to hold that, because aliens were only in the country at the discretion of the U.S. government, it was not punishment to incarcerate or deport them when the government so desired, merely an administrative action to restore the civil status quo ante.[15] As Peter H. Schuck has written: "In view of what is inevitably and personally at stake . . . it is undeniable that deportation punishes the alien and punishes her severely. . . . without the safeguards that government must ordinarily afford before it can impose grave punishment."[16]

Citizens, in contrast, rarely faced threats of involuntary expatriation and deportation; but nonwhite citizens, in particular, faced parallel reductions in their rights during these years. The counterparts to the *Chinese Exclusion Case* and similar cases involving alien rights include *Virginia v. Rives* in 1879, permitting nonwhite Americans to be excluded from juries so long as the state did not officially espouse that goal; the *Civil Rights Cases* of 1883, limiting federal power to combat racial discrimination in places of public accommodation; *Plessy v. Ferguson* in 1896, upholding imposing "separate but equal" segregation on businesses; and *Giles v. Harris* in 1903, ruling that federal courts could do nothing about massive fraudulent, racially exclusionary voter registration systems. With limited access to many jobs, public transport, to jury service or the ballot, nonwhite Americans in practice possessed many fewer rights than whites.[17] But under the pressure of the 14th Amendment's equal protection clause, all these measures officially took the form of limits on the rights of all citizens, moving those sets of legal rights in the same direction as those of aliens, though in each case with severely disparate racial and class impacts.

After the Spanish-American War, the famous *Insular Cases* and their progeny underscored the notion that, even if they had some claim to membership in the American political community, those deemed ethnic and racial "strangers" really had only the most minimal legal rights, especially in regard to political rights and rights versus unfair criminal justice processes.[18] In those cases, the Supreme Court deemed the residents of the new U.S. colonies in Puerto Rico, the Philippines, Guam, and elsewhere to be ineligible for the full constitutional protections of the Bill of Rights. In response to arguments that the Constitution "follows the flag," extending its guarantees to wherever and whomever the U.S. governs, again legislators and courts held that these colonial inhabitants were too racially distinct and inferior to merit such rights. Those rulings remained in effect even after Puerto Ricans and residents of Guam gained U.S. citizenship. The fiction of equality was preserved because all U.S. citizens similarly lose protections should they move to those islands.[19] And again, in World War II, the U.S. government relied on assertions about the undesirable and unalterable "racial characteristics" of Japanese resident aliens *and* Japanese American citizens to defend its racially targeted curfews and internment camps, in which persons were placed without individualized examinations of whether they really represented security threats. The Supreme Court upheld these actions, most notoriously in *Korematsu v. United States*.[20] Although such racist justifications for denying aliens and citizens basic procedural rights have since been disavowed, most of the precedents for doing so still stand.

Then, just as the "rights revolution" of the Warren Court years restored long-denied rights to African Americans and other persons of color and expanded the rights of the accused (always disproportionately nonwhite and poor), the Supreme Court also limited the power of states to discriminate against aliens in several cases of the early 1970s. It even found a due process limit on federal power to deny some civil service positions to resident aliens.[21] But as conservative reactions to perceived "excesses" of the civil rights era gained power in U.S. politics and law, the Court began to stress instead that limits on state powers over aliens derived extensively from "federal preemption," the fact that primary authority to regulate the status of aliens lay with Congress, whose own powers over aliens had few limits. The Court also added that states could deny resident aliens access to a variety of "governmental functions" that the Court saw as integral to self-governance by the state's "political community."[22] Yet the Court did find that undocumented alien children could not constitutionally be denied public education in *Plyler v. Doe*, 457 U.S. 202 (1982), and in the ensuing two decades lawyers sometimes still succeeded in expanding due process rights of resident aliens and those seeking entry into the country in various contexts.

But the Supreme Court never overturned most of its harshest precedents denying aliens basic rights granted to citizens, and by the early 1990s, political forces were again pushing hard against any sort of generous treatment for aliens—or citizens—in social policy and in the criminal justice system. Conservatives sought to end redistributive forms of "big government," especially social assistance programs benefiting the poor, who were generally portrayed as even more extensively nonwhite than was the case.[23] Political leaders who sometimes portrayed inner city welfare beneficiaries as so alien as to be virtually another "species" sought to replace aid policies with more severe criminal justice policies.[24] Conservatives soon found immigrants, especially the burgeoning numbers of urban Latinos, an easy target who could be used to win support for putatively antialien laws that turned out ultimately to affect all Americans. Long-standing accounts of the "pathologies" of urban black cultures could be made to encompass Chicanos, Puerto Ricans, and other Latino immigrants. These groups often were Spanish-speaking, poor, and undocumented, and so they could be portrayed as incomprehensible, acquisitive, lawless "strangers in the land." This renewed linkage of fears of immigrants with fears of nonwhite "strangers" within the civic body is evident in a set of laws passed in 1996 that especially limited the rights of aliens, even as they also aimed to "end welfare as we know it" and most federal oversight of state criminal justice systems, in ways that reduced the social and due process rights of all Americans.

The 1996 Laws: AEDPA, PRWORA, and IIRIRA. The opportunity for these linkages arose because the early 1990s saw mounting anti-immigrant sentiments in the United States. Polls appeared to show some rise in the degree and salience of the long-standing public opposition to the prevailing levels of admissions. Governor Pete Wilson of California, who like many market-oriented conservatives had supported guest worker programs in the 1980s, now championed Proposition 187, a referendum proposal that sought to deny public benefits, including education, to undocumented aliens.[25] Probably the most widely read writer on immigration in those years was Peter Brimelow, who published various essays and then a book, *Alien Nation*, devoted to concerns about the "ethnic and racial transformation" that public policies were "inflicting" on the country. He insisted that "[r]ace is destiny" in American politics and life.[26] But though Brimelow sold books and Proposition 187 won at the polls, a U.S. district court declared it unconstitutional on "federal preemption" grounds, and the U.S. did not lower immigration levels. Thus many observers concluded that the nation had experienced one of its periodic spasms of anti-immigrant anxieties, but that its basically receptive policies and practices remained unaltered.

Congress did, however, pass three laws in 1996 that arguably represented significant victories putting "the government seal of approval" on the "wave of widespread anti-immigrant feeling," even though the laws also served employer interests.[27] Not coincidentally, they also included the triumph of a decades-long effort to end a landmark New Deal social welfare program that had come to be seen as breeding dependency and as rewarding undeserving, largely nonwhite Americans.

In June of 1996, Congress passed the Antiterrorism and Effective Death Penalty Act of 1996 (AEDPA). It greatly restricted federal habeas corpus review of state and federal prisoners and created a one-year statute of limitations for raising such claims. It also expedited the exclusion and arrest, punishment, and removal of those suspected of being alien terrorists or criminals by authorizing a special removal court, limiting judicial review of deportations, speeding up the timetable for deportation processes, limiting the discretion of the attorney general to admit or grant asylum to suspect aliens, and making many immigration law offenses subject to the expansive punitive measures authorized by RICO (the Racketeer Influenced and Corrupt Organizations Act).[28]

In August, President Clinton signed the Personal Responsibility and Work Opportunity Reconciliation Act (PRWORA). This historic measure ended the Aid to Families with Dependent Children (AFDC) program established in the original New Deal Social Security Act, replacing it with Temporary Assistance to Needy Families (TANF) block grants to the states. But it also made immigrants arriving after its enactment ineligible for all federally funded means-tested benefit programs like TANF and Medicaid for five years, with a state option to restore them thereafter; and it denied them Supplemental Security Income (SSI) and food stamps altogether. Immigrants could regain eligibility by naturalizing.[29]

In September, the Illegal Immigration Reform and Immigrant Responsibility Act (IIRIRA) increased resources for immigration law enforcement, including detentions; further streamlined procedures to expedite exclusions and deportations; further limited the attorney general's discretionary authority to grant entry to the needy via "parole"; banned Social Security benefits for undocumented aliens; authorized states to limit public assistance to aliens; mandated new data-collection on aliens, including requirements that educational institutions report on their foreign students; and authorized heightened worksite investigations, among other measures.[30]

Collectively, these laws meant that even though the United States did not restrict legal admissions during a decade when immigration was rising rapidly, it cut back sharply on the public benefits that immigrants as well as citizens could receive. Because the laws disadvantaged aliens even more than citizens, in some ways they deepened the gaps between the two sets of rights; but both were narrowed in the same direction. The main consequence of these policies for aliens was to make it more likely that they would take any sort of employment on any terms offered; and if they failed to find employment, the laws also made it easier to deport them. They also heightened pressures to naturalize, and naturalization rates rose. But most scholars agree that the laws succeeded in sharply reducing the number of immigrants who received various forms of public assistance, and many argue that problems of ill health, inadequate nutrition, and poverty rose in immigrant populations as a result.[31] They also prompted the states to undertake additional financial burdens of immigrant support that many have found difficult to sustain.[32] Even so, the laws seem to have placated some critics of high immigration levels while reducing welfare and criminal procedural protections for all residents, citizens and aliens alike—all without jeopardizing the availability of cheap immigrant labor favored by many employer interests and free market conservatives.

These laws may also have reinforced the Supreme Court's willingness to assert that old precedents limiting alien rights were still binding, even when it ruled in favor of aliens. For example, in *Zadvydas v. Davis*, a 2001 decision limiting the power of the attorney general to detain indefinitely immigrants who had been convicted of criminal offenses but who had served their time, both the majority and the dissent cited the *Chinese Exclusion Case* as a binding precedent. The majority also conceded that such indefinite detentions would be justified in the case of direct congressional authorization and if persons were suspected of terrorism.[33] That qualification would soon prove to be the pipeline for a powerful accelerant to efforts to reduce the gaps between citizen and alien rights by further limiting the rights of all.

The War on Terrorism and the Rights of Aliens and Citizens. The Supreme Court decided *Zadvydas v. Davis* on June 28, 2001. The following September brought the horrific terrorist attacks on the World Trade Center and the Pentagon that ushered in a new era in American foreign policy and in domestic law enforcement practices. The successful assaults showed that, despite the 1996 law and other measures, the United States had failed abysmally to prevent the entry and operations of foreign terrorists.

The federal government's political responses to these terrible events have created three important patterns that, together, combine to generate an even more significant one. For understandable reasons, the United States has severely eroded the Cold War distinction between foreign intelligence gathering and overt and covert security operations, on the one hand, and domestic criminal law enforcement, on the other. It has also breathed new life into the option of employing military instead of civilian criminal justice proceedings. And it has begun to undercut the long-standing practical separation of the enforcement of immigration control regulations from the enforcement of domestic criminal laws. In all these regards, the initiative for defining rights has shifted sharply toward the executive branch, traditionally regarded as having the crucial responsibilities and capacities in national security matters. Since taking office in January 2008, the Obama administration has been less assertive in these regards than the preceding Bush administration, but perhaps because of national security concerns, perhaps because of a sense of responsibility for executive prerogatives, there has been less change than many anticipated, as noted below. The continuing, now bipartisan support of executive branch officials for many of these measures makes them hard to challenge, politically and legally. Indeed, except in the case of threats to what they saw as their core institutional prerogatives, most members of the legislative and judicial branches of government have essentially followed the executive branch lead, even when doing so has meant acquiescing in sharp new limits on the rights of aliens and citizens alike. The exposure of numerous American abuses has reinforced insistent criticisms by international human rights organizations and foreign governments and courts of many of these American measures, particularly those unilaterally imposed by the executive branch.[34] It is reasonable to conjecture that in the modern global human rights environment, there are limits to how far the United States can detain and try persons in ways that appear to violate international treaties, such as the Geneva Conventions. Still, the U.S. government has in general been resistant to these pressures.

At present, the cumulative effect of chipping away at all these walls between traditional modes of governmental law enforcement, in the hopes of combating terrorism more effectively, has been to weaken severely most surviving legal barriers between the forms of coercion that American governments have used against aliens and the more restricted forms that are all they are officially allowed to employ against U.S. citizens. In modern antiterrorist America, all citizens are officially seen as potentially vulnerable to measures as invasive, extensive, and coercive as those imposed on the least protected group known to American law, "unlawful enemy combatants"—a group generally conceived as consisting of aliens, though it has in fact never been so restricted.

The first major steps taken to enhance the nation's ability to detect and deter terrorist threats included the September 18, 2001, Authorization to Use Military Force (AUMF) against terrorists;[35] passage of the U.S.A. Patriot Act on October 25, 2001;[36] the president's executive order issued November 13, 2001, authorizing detention and military trials for noncitizens suspected of terrorism;[37] and the opening on January 11, 2002, of a detention camp for unlawful enemy combatants at the U.S. naval base in Guantánamo, Cuba. Over 700 persons have been detained there, all initially declared by the U.S. to be not prisoners of war but "unlawful enemy combatants," without the individualized determinations of their status apparently required by the Third Geneva Convention of 1949.[38] Over innumerable objections from international lawyers and the courts and elected leaders of many Allied countries, the Bush administration contended that the convention did not apply because it does not recognize the category of "unlawful enemy combatants" into which, the administration insisted, all terrorist suspects fell.[39] President Barack Obama signed an order on January 22, 2009, to end the detentions at Guantánamo within a year, but critics noted that he did so without abandoning claims to unilateral executive power to impose detentions, and in fall 2009, efforts to place detainees elsewhere were still "sputtering."[40] In 2002, President Bush also secretly authorized the National Security Agency to monitor without warrants the international phone calls and e-mails of those suspected of links to Al Qaeda, aliens and citizens alike; and the NSA also reportedly secretly obtained millions of phone call records from several major telephone companies, analyzing calling patterns to identify suspected terrorists.[41]

These initial measures were soon followed by more sweeping institutional restructuring. The biggest step was the creation of a new Department of Homeland Security on November 25, 2002, which absorbed a large number of federal programs and agencies, including the Immigration and Naturalization Service and its antiterrorist "Special Registration Initiative," specifically targeted at keeping track of immigrants with Arabic and Muslim origins.[42] That initiative led to the questioning of roughly 130,000 male immigrants and alien visitors, the deportation of some 9,000 illegal aliens, the arrest of over 800 criminal suspects, and the detention of 11 suspected terrorists.[43] Though on April 30, 2003, the administration announced that the initiative was ending, in fact only requirements for annual reregistration were modified.[44]

Few believe, however, that any or all of these steps have overcome the nation's weaknesses in obtaining reliable data on terrorist activities, and they have been accompanied by acknowledged abuses in the treatment of prisoners in Iraq and Afghanistan and widespread accusations of similar offenses at Guantánamo and toward those subjected to "extraordinary rendition," removal from the United States to countries known to practice torture. In June 2003, an internal report also led the Department of Justice's inspector general to testify to Congress that some immigrant detainees in the U.S. had been treated abusively in ways that amounted to serious civil rights violations.[45] Many private groups and journalists also reported a wide range of discriminatory actions against aliens and Islamic and Arab citizens. In partial response, on December 17, 2004, President Bush signed the Intelligence Reform and Terrorism Prevention Act of 2004, extensively based on recommendations of the 9/11 Commission.[46] It created a new director of national intelligence with broad budgetary and personnel authority; a new National Counter Terrorism Center, which absorbed a Terrorist Threat Integration Center (TTIC) created in May 2003 but never made fully operational;[47] mandated more extensive information sharing among federal, state, and local agencies; and created a Privacy and Civil Liberties Board with investigatory and advisory powers to ensure that civil liberties are not violated by executive branch antiterrorist measures.

The U.S.A. Patriot Act, the Homeland Security Act, the Intelligence Reform and Terrorism Prevention Act, and arguably the secret wiretapping and phone records initiatives all involve self-conscious rejection of the venerable barrier between foreign intelligence operations and domestic criminal law enforcement that was a chief pillar of the structures the U.S. adopted to fight the Cold War in the late 1940s and early 1950s. Under those arrangements, the CIA and National Security Agency were expected to operate exclusively overseas, while the FBI, the Bureau of Alcohol, Tobacco and Firearms, and other federal criminal investigation bodies, along with state and local police, were to combat crime at home. Various federal laws and regulations specifically prohibited the foreign intelligence agencies from carrying on their activities within the United States. But in addition to the authorizations of more expansive surveillance procedures and searches in Titles II and IX of the U.S.A. Patriot Act, sections 203, 507, 508, 711, and 903 of the act also authorize extensive information sharing among all agencies, whether operating at home or abroad, whether federal, state, or local—including educational records, immigrant histories, and the fruits of surveillance methods that would ordinarily be deemed to violate constitutional rights if employed by federal, state, or local criminal law officers in more routine investigations. Section 502 also authorizes coordinated action among these heretofore generally distinct agencies.

The act authorizing the new Department of Homeland Security went further yet, by not only mandating information-sharing and coordination but also transferring various functions to the new agency, including immigration law enforcement and immigrant and naturalization services, now to be housed in separate Homeland Security bureaus (see, for example, secs. 221, 471, 891–99). And the Intelligence Reform and Terrorism Prevention Act mandated in section 1016 that the president appoint a "program manager" to work with a new Information Sharing Council to create policies and networks that would foster an "Information Sharing Environment" among "all appropriate Federal, State, local, and tribal entities, and the private sector." The information sharing mandates have been pursued through a bewildering variety of frequently changing mechanisms, including the presidentially appointed Information Sharing Council, made exempt from the requirements of the Federal Advisory Committee Act; a Joint Intelligence Community Council, consisting of the director of national intelligence and the secretaries of State, Treasury,

Defense, Energy, and Homeland Security, along with the attorney general; a Homeland Security Council including the secretary of defense, the director of homeland security, and the attorney general; and the creation of numerous "fusion centers" to promote intelligence sharing among various agencies.[48] The National Counterterrorism Center serves as the integrating institution in charge of analyzing threats and planning antiterrorist operations, even though information sharing and agency coordination remain problems. The director of national intelligence has a broad mandate to make it all work and has recently offered a vision statement for doing so, but critics contend that the position lacks sufficient budgetary, personnel, and operational authority to enable its occupant to succeed.[49]

But though many administrative problems clearly persist, under these new arrangements, classified information is now being made available to national, state, and local criminal law enforcement officials more extensively than ever before. Data on immigrants, including resident aliens, are being entered into the National Criminal Information Center (NCIC), even if the information has not been checked to see if it is current and accurate. Instead, on March 24, 2003, the attorney general issued an order exempting the NCIC's Central Record System from national Privacy Act standards requiring those records to be "accurate, timely, and reliable."[50] Using a provision of the Illegal Immigration Reform and Immigration Responsibility Act of 1996, the Justice Department also launched its "287(g)" initiative, seeking to involve state and local officials in enforcement of federal immigration laws for the first time.[51] The Obama administration has modified these efforts, seeking to focus on illegal immigrants who have committed serious crimes; but it is also seeking to expand them.[52]

It is understandable that the threat of terrorist groups organizing in distant lands to strike within the United States has prompted these concerns to make sure that all pertinent information is rapidly available to as wide a cross-section of U.S. law enforcement agencies as possible. The broader argument that the institutions that made sense for fighting the Cold War are not appropriate to current dangers is also hardly unreasonable on its face. For all officials, there can be no greater nightmare than the possibility that successful terrorist attacks will occur on their watch, at a time when the government as a whole has the information and enforcement capacity to stop the attacks, but is too administratively uncoordinated and inefficient to do so.

Yet it is also true that traditional American structures of law enforcement have reflected certain enduring values that are being put at risk by these momentous transformations in security institutions. Whether well founded or not, many judicial rulings hold that the U.S. government can take actions overseas, in regard to aliens, that would be unconstitutional if done to U.S. citizens, certainly if done within the jurisdiction of the United States. The United States has regularly taken such actions abroad, conducting warrantless wiretaps, coercing witnesses, seizing evidence, and detaining suspects without the procedural protections that are supposed to be provided citizens at home. When agencies long accustomed to acting without regard to constitutional restrictions overseas become entitled to join much more fully in domestic law enforcement efforts, there is clearly a danger that constitutional safeguards may be more often ignored at home as well. Even if intelligence-gathering agencies can merely make available information that could not be legally seized by a domestic criminal justice agency, the result may be that domestic law enforcement is less practically bound by constitutional restrictions.

The increased intermingling of immigration law enforcement and criminal law policing raises similar as well as distinctive concerns. Some state and local police are particularly concerned that when they get involved in immigration law enforcement, they receive less cooperation from immigrant communities, who fear that any contact with any sort of law enforcement agency might end in their deportation. Those fears are sustained, moreover, by the wealth of legal precedents that hold that immigration officials can constitutionally take peremptory actions against aliens that other law enforcement officers cannot. Because, ever since the *Chinese Exclusion Cases*, judges have viewed immigration law as something categorically different than criminal law, immigration hearings and decisions need not conform to the constitutional standards to which criminal justice proceedings are held. As noted, courts also have long ruled that in any case aliens have much less in the way of procedural protections against governmental coercion than citizens at least putatively have, even if the differences have fluctuated over time, and nonwhite citizens, especially, have often been denied rights. The 1996 laws, moreover, reaffirmed emphatic congressional support for these restrictive views of immigrant rights, positions greatly reinforced by the U.S.A. Patriot Act and subsequent laws. So today, if state and local police are simultaneously enforcing criminal laws and the more procedurally lax immigration laws, it becomes easier for them to act as though only the latter standards are binding on them. Thus, when we break down the walls between foreign and domestic enforcement efforts, and between policing immigration laws and criminal laws, we risk increasing the ways in which all governmental efforts may veer into infringements on constitutional rights, for both citizens and aliens.

The Current Convergence and Decline in Alien Rights and Citizen Rights. The degree to which post–September 11 antiterrorist measures would affect citizens as well as aliens was initially not so obvious, because the November 13, 2001, executive order authorizing military trials applied on its face only to noncitizens, and because the INS Special Registration Initiative targeted only aliens. That is probably one reason why few citizens found these actions disturbing. It has become clear, however, that if the government believes that anyone, even a U.S. citizen, is connected with terrorist activities, that citizen can be treated in almost exactly the same ways as any alien suspect. It is for this reason that the Bush administration relied heavily on a heretofore obscure World War II case, *Ex Parte Quirin*, as a legal basis for its most controversial measures, including indefinite detention without criminal charges or access to attorneys for those it suspected of being involved with terrorism.

It was this case that created the category of "unlawful combatant" or "unlawful enemy combatant" that became central to the government's claims to be exempt from the Geneva Conventions, to be able to detain persons on suspicion alone, and to conduct closed military trials of all terrorism suspects.[53] In *Quirin,* decided during World War II when national security concerns were at an unprecedented peak and concerns for rights of persons suspected of allying with the enemy were at a nadir (witness *Korematsu v. U.S.*), the U.S. Supreme Court upheld secret military trials for Nazi saboteurs captured in Florida and on Long Island. Justice Department officials repeatedly cited *Quirin* as authority for President Bush's order authorizing detentions and trials by military commissions of aliens that the executive branch designates as terrorism suspects, whether captured as part of foreign overt or covert operations, domestic criminal policing, or enforcement of immigration regulations.

Under that order, anyone so suspected could be arrested without showing of probable cause to a neutral magistrate and denied any opportunity to communicate with an attorney; detained indefinitely, or tried in secret military trials, on the basis of any evidence that military officials deemed to have "probative value," even if it was hearsay or illegally obtained; convicted on a vote of two-thirds of a panel of military judges, without trial by jury; and sentenced to death without appeal to the civilian courts. The Defense Department then added some further procedural protections, such as the requirement that guilt be found "beyond a reasonable doubt"; but even if persons were acquitted in such trials, the government claimed the power to continue to incarcerate them indefinitely if they were still thought to be national security risks. Collectively, all these measures represented major transformations in American law enforcement that imposed new pressures on the rights effectively enjoyed by U.S. citizens as well as aliens, and all were defended by the reasoning and authority of *Quirin*.

Though both government officials and critics of these policies have often referred to the case as validating severe measures aimed at "enemy combatants" or "enemy aliens," those terms are both too broad and too narrow to be accurate. *Quirin* did not focus on the powers of the U.S. government in relation to uniformed enemy combatants participating in a legal international war, nor did it focus on aliens alone. It defined power over "unlawful" enemy combatants of any nationality. That is the category the Bush administration stressed in defending its actions, because that description can reasonably be held to include participants in an undeclared war (though the *Quirin* opinion did not so specify). It is also a category into which suspects can be placed whether they are aliens or citizens.

To be sure, the military trial upheld by the Supreme Court in *Quirin* did in fact take place in the context of a declared war. But Chief Justice Stone's opinion suggested that secret military trials were appropriate for anyone accused of violating internationally recognized laws of war, whether in a declared war or other forms of combat. "Lawful combatants," he wrote, "are subject to capture and detention as prisoners of war by opposing military forces" according to international law. "Unlawful combatants are likewise subject to capture and detention, but in addition they are subject to trial and punishment by military tribunals for acts which render their belligerency unlawful." Such tribunals can, he made clear, be constitutionally conducted without the sorts of procedural safeguards, including Fifth and Sixth Amendment guarantees, ordinarily afforded to criminals and even to lawful enemy combatants. And though most of the saboteurs tried in *Quirin* were enemy aliens, Stone affirmed that, if the U.S. government deems a person to be an unlawful combatant, it did not matter whether the person was a U.S. citizen. National security required that citizens, too, be subjected to arrest, detention, and secret military trials if the executive branch deemed such measures appropriate.[54]

The reason this ruling has been so significant is that, even though it did not explicitly address combat outside the context of a conventionally declared war, it is in fact entirely plausible for the government to designate all those involved in terrorism as new kinds of "unlawful enemy combatants" or "belligerents." They clearly act in violation of international laws of war as well as domestic and international criminal laws. They are not conventional criminals, either in our eyes or their own, but they are also not lawful combatants. So what else can they be?

And if suspected terrorists can credibly be viewed as "unlawful" enemy combatants, then the *Quirin* precedent also makes it plausible to argue that they can indeed be arrested, detained, and secretly tried by military commissions without normal constitutional procedural protections, just as the Bush Justice Department asserted, whether the suspects are aliens, dual nationals, naturalized citizens, birthright citizens, or anything else. Yet plausible as those positions are, they are fraught with broad-ranging implications. Since *everyone* even suspected of being involved in terrorism is by this definition an "unlawful enemy combatant" or "belligerent," then every investigation of all possible terrorist activities can result in arrests, indefinite detentions, and secret trials on the basis of any sort of evidence that may give minimal credibility to allegations of such involvement.

Now consider what these legal powers mean in light of the heretofore largely unregulated new pooling of terrorist-related information among foreign and domestic security agencies, national, state, and local law enforcement bodies, and immigration officials that the U.S. is undertaking. The results of diverse forms of electronic surveillance, with and without warrant; so-called "sneak and peek" searches for which warrants need not be shown in advance; questioning that occurs during indefinite detentions, which may in practice involve torture; and the mappings of the social networks of suspects, all produce data on the activities of citizens with whom aliens communicate, as well as on their non-American connections. When international and domestic security agencies, national, state, and local police forces, and immigration officials are all entitled to share such information rapidly, even information that has not been checked for accuracy, on citizens and aliens alike, there is clearly enormous potential for citizens as well as aliens to be subjected to coercive measures that would ordinarily be deemed unconstitutional, on the basis of evidence that could not survive customary procedural safeguards. In sum, *Ex parte Quirin* provides the legal basis for treating all persons, citizens and aliens alike, as entitled only to rights of unlawful enemy combatants, the class of persons with the least rights when confronted by an accusing U.S. government; and the restructuring of American law enforcement institutions to conduct the war on terrorism more efficiently has greatly increased the capacities of American governments to designate persons as targets for such treatment.

The Supreme Court has repeatedly responded to this potential by asserting that the courts are entitled to preserve their role in ensuring that minimally fair procedural protections are provided to all those detained by the U.S. government, at least on U.S. soil. In *Sharif Rasul v. Bush* (2004), Justice John Paul Stevens ruled for a six-justice majority that the Guantánamo detainees had a statutory right to present habeas corpus petitions to U.S. courts, whether or not they were U.S. citizens. (Sharif Rasul was a British citizen who had actually been released by the time the case reached the Supreme Court. The remaining petitioners were Australian and Kuwaiti citizens.) In the Court's view, all the detainees were persons who were not nationals of countries at war with the United States and who were being detained indefinitely in a location that, the Court ruled, was under U.S. jurisdiction. None had received any formal process to determine if they were indeed unlawful enemy combatants. Because the Constitution and federal statutes promised due process rights and habeas corpus review for all persons detained by the United States within its jurisdiction, or at least all those who were not technically enemy aliens, the propriety of those detentions had to be reviewable by federal courts.

Justice Antonin Scalia's dissent argued that Stevens had failed to distinguish *Johnson v. Eisentrager* (1950), where the Court had denied that civilian courts had any right to review cases of enemy alien combatants in a declared war who had been captured and tried by military forces outside of U.S. jurisdiction. Scalia thought ruling otherwise extended "the habeas statute to the four corners of the earth," and he insisted there was a sharp line between citizen and alien rights. Only U.S. citizens were entitled to habeas corpus review if detained by U.S. agents outside the United States. The majority, however, refused to find such a chasm between citizen and alien rights, and in this case the Court insisted that aliens also receive the larger share of rights Scalia would have confined to citizens.[55]

In response, military officials established new boards, termed Combatant Status Review Tribunals, to provide individual determinations of whether each detainee was indeed an unlawful enemy combatant. After releasing some detainees, they then proceeded with military trials for others. Lower courts ruled in conflicting ways on the propriety of these procedures, and over the question of whether the right to petition for habeas corpus review upheld in *Rasul v. Bush* carries with it a right to have habeas review actually granted and a civilian trial held.[56] Pertinently, the same term that the Court decided *Rasul v. Bush*, it also considered whether U.S. citizens suspected of terrorism could claim greater procedural protections than aliens, especially if arrested and incarcerated in the U.S. itself. The president's November 13, 2001, order authorizing trials by military commissions explicitly applied only to "Certain Non-Citizens," but executive efforts to apply the same sorts of draconian measures to U.S. citizens were well established by 2004—even if the citizens selected for "enemy combatant" treatment were exclusively Islamic and, in many eyes, nonwhite, notably Yaser Esam Hamdi and José Padilla. (John Walker Lindh, a blond and blue-eyed U.S. citizen caught, like Hamdi, among Taliban forces in Afghanistan, instead received a regular civilian trial in the United States.)[57]

In the *Hamdi* and *Padilla* cases, the administration sought to justify its actions by claiming congressional authority via the 2001 AUMF and constitutional authority as recognized in *Quirin*.[58] Hamdi was a Saudi in his twenties who was born in the United States and therefore also possessed U.S. citizenship, and who was allegedly fighting in behalf of the Taliban and Al Qaeda when captured on a battlefield in Afghanistan. He always claimed to have been a noncombatant, out driving as part of his employment. Hamdi was held without formal charges in military prisons in Virginia and South Carolina for over two and a half years and was not permitted access to lawyers seeking to act in his case until the Supreme Court agreed to examine his detention.

In *Hamdi v. Rumsfeld*, the Court agreed that the AUMF authorized the use of force, and by implication detention, against terrorists, and it also affirmed the *Quirin* precedent that the United States could seize and detain enemy combatants. It held, however, that Hamdi had a due process right to a hearing by an "impartial adjudicator" to determine if he could reasonably be deemed an "enemy combatant," and that this right was enforceable via a writ of habeas corpus, until and unless Congress suspended the writ.[59] He was also entitled to "receive notice of the factual basis for his classification" as an enemy combatant and "a fair opportunity to rebut the Government's factual assertions before a neutral decisionmaker," though that hearing did not have to be accompanied by all the procedural protections afforded in criminal trials. Ironically, here Stevens and Scalia joined in dissent, both insisting that Hamdi was entitled not just to a military hearing but also to a full trial in the civilian courts. For Scalia, though not Stevens, it was the fact that Hamdi was a citizen that was decisive: he insisted that barring a specific congressional suspension of the writ of habeas corpus, citizens, and citizens alone, were always entitled to full civilian trials triggered by the writ.

The majority again refused to draw such a broad division between citizen and alien rights, but it defined the rights that Hamdi could claim less robustly than Scalia would have accorded to citizens and less robustly than Stevens would have accorded to all persons. Even so, rather than proceed with a military hearing concerning Hamdi's enemy combatant status as the Court required, the U.S. government concluded that he was no longer a threat to the United States. It permitted him to return to Saudi Arabia, on the (arguably unconstitutional) condition that he relinquish his U.S. citizenship.[60]

Similarly, for well over a year the courts refused to offer any but the most limited judicial review of the conditions of confinement imposed on José Padilla, also known as Abdullah al Muhajir, a U.S. citizen and long-term resident arrested at O'Hare airport. He was detained incommunicado for some months as a "material witness" to terrorist activities, and though officials then accused Padilla of having been sufficiently involved in a "dirty bomb" plot to qualify as an unlawful enemy combatant, he continued to be incarcerated in a military facility in South Carolina without formal charges. On December 18, 2003, two judges of the Second Circuit Court of Appeals ruled that the *Quirin* decision did not authorize the U.S. government to detain a U.S. citizen in this matter.[61] Without addressing the merits of the case, the Supreme Court subsequently ruled 5–4 that Padilla's petition had been filed in the wrong federal court.[62]

On September 9, 2005, a three-judge panel of the U.S. 4th Circuit Court of Appeals ruled that Padilla's continuing detention without charges was constitutional.[63] But when Padilla's lawyers sought to appeal to the U.S. Supreme Court, the president ordered that he be released from military custody and transferred to the control of the attorney general, to be tried in a Florida federal district court on lesser criminal charges of associating with terrorists, without any mention of his alleged involvement in a "dirty bomb" plot. Outraged, Judge Luttig of the Fourth Circuit sought to prevent the transfer as an apparent effort to evade Supreme Court review of his court's ruling.[64] But the Supreme Court declared the case moot, at least until such time as Padilla again faced the threat of a military trial.[65]

Though these cases collectively indicated that all the detainees under U.S. jurisdiction, whether citizens or aliens, were entitled to some sort of hearing to determine if they were indeed enemy combatants, they did not settle the question of whether detainees could be tried by military commissions or tribunals constructed with the truncated procedural protections laid out in the president's November 13, 2001, executive order. In *Hamdan v. Rumsfeld*, 2004, the Supreme Court ruled that any tribunals so constituted violated federal statutes. The case was brought by lawyers for a Yemeni, Salim Ahmed Hamdan, who had at that point been detained for five years, four at Guantánamo. His attorneys contended that trial by the proposed military commission would violate the Uniform Code of Military Justice, the Third Geneva Convention of 1949, and the U.S. Constitution as construed in *Rasul v. Bush*, so that he was entitled to habeas corpus relief and could not be subjected to trial by such a commission.[66] Newly appointed Chief Justice John Roberts, who ruled against Hamdan at the lower court level, recused himself from further consideration.

In taking the case, the Court appeared to reject continuing administration contentions that such military detentions and trials are simply unreviewable. But Congress then passed the Detainee Treatment Act of 2005, which denied the federal courts all habeas corpus review of the detention of aliens at Guantánamo. It did permit the decisions of Combatant Status Review Tribunals to be appealed to the U.S. Court of Appeals for the District of Columbia, which was authorized to consider the compliance of those tribunals with the standards and procedures established for them by the secretary of defense.[67] The legislation was in part an effort to override *Rasul v. Bush* and render *Hamdan v. Rumsfeld* moot. Because it denied habeas review to anyone designated an "enemy combatant," it too could be applied to U.S. citizens as well as to aliens.

Writing for a 5–4 majority in the *Hamdan* decision, Justice John Paul Stevens ruled that Congress had deliberately chosen to apply only part of the provisions of the Detainee Treatment Act to cases pending at the time of its passage, so that it did not take away the Court's jurisdiction in the case at hand.[68] Stevens next distinguished three types of military commissions: those that operate where martial law has been declared because civilian courts cannot function; those that operate as part of temporary military governments over occupied territories; and those that try enemies during wartime to determine if they have violated internationally accepted laws of war. The tribunals authorized by the president fell in the third category.[69] But Stevens contended that the "conspiracy" charge Hamdan faced was not part of the law of war (though he had only four votes on this point), and that in any case the Uniform Code of Military Justice required that these tribunals be as similar as possible to regular courts-martial in which military personnel are tried. Hamdan's inability to see the evidence against him represented an unnecessary violation of that procedural mandate. Finally, Stevens found at least some of the Geneva Conventions to be parts of the law of war, including the requirements that sentences be passed by "regularly constituted" courts, which forbade the sort of special tribunal prescribed in the president's order.[70] Justice Breyer's concurrence underlined, however, that though existing statutes denied the president the authority to create these kinds of military tribunals, "Nothing prevents the President from returning to Congress to seek the authority he believes necessary."[71]

The president responded in September 2006 by proposing that Congress provide authorization for military tribunals constructed much like those in his original executive order, including the denial to defendants of access to the evidence against them that the Supreme Court had criticized in the *Hamdan* decision.[72] On October 17, 2006, Congress complied by passing the Military Commissions Act of 2006 (MCA), which reinstated the major provisions of Bush's order, now as a duly enacted statute.[73] MCA tribunals were still entitled to use hearsay evidence and evidence obtained in violation of 4th and 5th Amendment guarantees, and defendants could be found guilty by two-thirds of the present military judges. As in the Detainee Treatment Act, ordinary habeas corpus review in civilian courts was prohibited, and the MCA specifically denied defendants rights to invoke the Geneva Conventions in court. Sentences could be appealed only to the Court of Military Commission Review, the U.S. Court of Appeals for the District of Columbia, and ultimately the Supreme Court.

On June 4, 2007, military judges in two separate cases dismissed charges against detainees brought before the new military commissions on the grounds that the preceding "combatant status review tribunals" had only declared the defendants to be "enemy combatants," not "unlawful enemy combatants," as required if they were not to receive trials via ordinary processes.[74] On September 25, 2007, the Court of Military Commission Review ruled that the military commissions could themselves decide if a defendant was an "unlawful enemy combatant," and the dismissed cases were resumed.[75]

In April 2007, the Supreme Court refused to hear two cases challenging the Military Commission Act's constitutionality; but on June 29, 2007, the Court unexpectedly reversed itself and agreed to hear them, consolidated into one case, *Boumediene v. Bush*, argued before the Court on December 5, 2007.[76] On June 12, 2008, a 5–4 majority of the Court ruled that the MCA could not constitutionally channel appeals through the special Court of Military Commission Review, for that restriction amounted to suspension of the writ of habeas corpus.[77] The dissenters insisted that this narrow appeal avenue was adequate. Many detainees immediately sought habeas review of their cases in a number of lower federal courts, and a federal district court soon ordered that Lakhtar Boumediene himself be released. But the story has not ended: though as a candidate Barack Obama opposed the MCA and when he entered the White House he suspended the commission system, in October 2009 he signed a revised Military Commission Act. It preserved the basic structure of the 2006 law and the original Bush executive order, while excluding statements obtained through torture and expanding the rights of defendants to attend their trials, examine the evidence against them, and call witnesses and cross-examine witnesses. Appeals were now to go through the U.S. Court of Appeals for the Armed Forces. Critics contended these changes did not resolve the constitutional problems of the military commissions system or bring it in alignment with the Geneva Conventions.[78] These developments made clear that the controversies concerning expansive executive powers over both aliens and citizens had not ended with the change in administrations.

Conclusion. Still, most Americans are likely to believe that they have little to fear from the developments reviewed here. They do not expect to be seen by any part of their government as terrorist suspects or as having information pertinent to terrorism. Rather, they see themselves as needing protection from terrorists. They also do not see themselves as suffering from the partial renunciation of modern federal responsibilities to provide social assistance to the poor. Rather, they see themselves as relieved of the burden of funding forms of aid that have only made worse the condition and character of their beneficiaries. For most Americans who are not Islamic, not Arab, not poor blacks or Latinos, and who do not appear as if they might be, these judgments are not unreasonable. The dangers of international terrorism do require heightened security measures of various sorts. It also is hard to say that AFDC as it was operating by the 1990s was a highly successful social policy.

Yet the broader political patterns of the last decade and half do provide grounds for concern. As I have briefly sketched, along with its many great achievements, the United States has a long history of treating whole classes of persons, usually those who seemed ethnocultural "strangers" to native white Americans, as undeserving of basic rights at various times, including due process, social, and political rights, whether or not those persons were officially U.S. citizens. Most of those policies are now widely seen as pernicious, including race-based immigration restrictions and denials of naturalization; the segregation, disfranchisement, and economic exploitation and exclusion of millions of nonwhite Americans; and horrendously biased criminal justice and immigrant deportation systems through much of American history. In light of that past, it is disturbing to see anti-immigrant fears, sometimes explicitly expressed in racial terms, used in the early 1990s to gain support for policies that ended legislated social rights for citizens and immigrants, without providing clear alternatives. It is also disturbing to see the judicial precedents spawned by some of the most repressive and racially intolerant measures in U.S. history revived as a basis for indefinite detentions that concededly can be based on rumor, suspicion, and certain ethnic and religious identities; for deportations without procedural safeguards; for potentially arbitrary military trials; and for limited or absent review by the civil courts. Since 1996 and especially since 2001, the American landscape of social rights and due process rights has been dramatically reshaped, with many guarantees cut back, by tools forged from some of the nation's worst expressions of hatred for strangers outside us and "strangers" among us.

With the exception of fear of deportation, citizens and aliens are positioned remarkably alike on this landscape, and that positioning must be seen as deliberate. Given the extraordinary size and heterogeneity of the United States population, many in government clearly expect that at least some citizens are in fact going to sympathize with terrorists, whether out of religious or ethnic loyalties, opposition to American policies, or (as the Bush administration stressed) involvement with the drug trade that has been exploited to fund terrorist operations in several parts of the world.[79] The linkage of drug trading to terrorism also helps connect in public discourse the criminal, culturally alien strangers abroad with what many perceive as the criminal, culturally alien inhabitants of American inner cities. And so it can seem not simply reasonable but also absolutely necessary to deny rights to those who seem threatening, at home and abroad, citizens and aliens, and instead to claim broad powers to incarcerate these groups indefinitely, in the Guantánamo detention camp, in military brigs, in the ever-growing modern system of federal and state prisons. Yet surely a government with expansive powers to incarcerate all on the basis of unproven suspicions and fears is not the same as a government with expansive capacities and commitments to provide liberty and justice for all.

Perhaps that is rhetorical excess; the dangers Americans confront are real, and so perhaps these added powers, many now endorsed by two successive administrations of different parties, are necessary. But they mean, quite literally, that the U.S. government is now viewing more of its citizens as if they were at least culturally "strangers," and more legal aliens and citizens as if they were enemy "strangers" of the worst sort. It is easy to say that courts and particularly Congress must in response engage in more vigilant oversight of these national security measures than they have, if constitutional rights are to be safeguarded. But judges and legislators have already shown that they are likely to do so only to protect their own prerogatives—or when pressured to do so by the public, within the United States and beyond its borders, but particularly at home. It is therefore incumbent on U.S. citizens themselves to take on the admittedly heavy burdens of being attentive to the new measures their government is undertaking—acting like those judges who believe that they should apply stricter scrutiny to claims of "public necessity" when basic freedoms are infringed. Now, more than ever, eternal vigilance is indeed the price of liberty, for citizens and noncitizens alike.

Notes

1. Alexander M. Bickel, *The Morality of Consent* (New Haven: Yale University Press, 1975), 36.

2. Peter H. Schuck, *Citizens, Strangers, and In-Betweens: Essays on Immigration and Citizenship* (Boulder, CO: Westview Press, 1998), 25–27.

3. Aristide R. Zolberg, *A Nation by Design: Immigration Policy in the Fashioning of America* (Cambridge: Harvard University Press, 2006), 62–66.

4. See, generally, Rogers M. Smith, *Civic Ideals: Conflicting Visions of Citizenship in U.S. History* (New Haven: Yale University Press, 1997).

5. Ibid., 429–53.

6. Philip A. Klinkner with Smith, *The Unsteady March: The Rise and Decline of Racial Equality in America* (Chicago: University of Chicago Press, 1999), 194–95.

7. *Ex Parte Quirin*, 317 U.S. 1 (1942), discussed more fully below.

8. Daniel J. Tichenor, *Dividing Lines: The Politics of Immigration Control in America* (Princeton: Princeton University Press, 2002), 207–24.

9. For my views on how Americans should see their citizenship today, including an argument that the pursuit of American democratic ideals requires allowing persons to be members of multiple political societies and supporting multilateral approaches to many national security issues, see Smith, *Stories of Peoplehood: The Politics and Morals of Political Membership* (Cambridge: Cambridge University Press, 2003), ch. 4.

10. Alexander Keyssar, *The Right to Vote: The Contested History of Democracy in the United States* (New York: Basic Books, 2000), 32–33, 104–5, 136–39.

11. See, for example, Peter J. Spiro. "Dual Nationality and the Meaning of Citizenship," *Emory Law Journal* 46, nos. 1412–85 (1997); Lisa Garcia-Bedolla, "Rethinking Citizenship: Noncitizen Voting and Immigrant Political Engagement in the United States," in *Transforming Politics, Transforming America: The Political and Civic Incorporation of Immigrants in the United States,* ed. Taeku Lee, Karthick Ramakrishnan, and Ricardo Ramírez (Charlottesville: University of Virginia Press, 2006).

12. Tichenor, *Dividing Lines*, 87–128; Smith, *Civic Ideals*, 371–85.

13. Smith, ibid., 358–69.

14. *The Chinese Exclusion Case, Chae Chan Ping v. U.S.* 130 U.S. 581, 595 (1889).

15. *Fong Yue Ting v. United States; Wong Quan v. United States; Lee Joe v. United States*, 149 U.S. 698 (1893), discussed in Smith, *Civic Ideals*, 368–69.

16. Schuck, *Citizens, Strangers, and In-Betweens*, 35.

17. *Virginia v. Rives*, 100 U.S. 313 (1879); *Civil Rights Cases*, 109 U.S. 3 (1883); *Plessy v. Ferguson*, 163 U.S. 537 (1896); *Giles v. Harris*, 189 U.S. 475 (1903).

18. *De Lima v. Bidwell*, 182 U.S. 1 (1901); *Goetze v. U.S. (Crossman v. U.S.)*, 182 U.S. 221 (1901); *Dooley v. U.S.*, 182 U.S. 222 (1901); *Armstrong v. U.S.*, 182 U.S. 243 (1901); *Downes*

v. Bidwell, 182 U.S. 244 (1901); *Huus v. New York & Porto Rico Steamship Co.*, 182 U.S. 392 (1901); see also *Balzac v. People of Porto Rico*, 258 U.S. 298 (1922).

19. See, generally, Smith, *Civic Ideals*, 429–39.

20. Peter Irons, *Justice at War: The Story of the Japanese American Internment Cases* (New York: Oxford University Press, 1983), 206–18; *Korematsu v. United States*, 323 U.S. 214 (1943).

21. See, for example, *Graham v. Richardson*, 403 U.S. 365 (1971); *In re Griffiths*, 413 U.S. 717 (1973); *Sugarman v. Dougall*, 413 U.S. 634 (1973); *Hampton v. Mow Sun Wong*, 426 U.S. 88 (1976).

22. See, for example, *Foley v. Connellie*, 435 U.S. 291 (1978); *Ambach v. Norwick*, 441 U.S. 68 (1979).

23. Martin Gilens, "'Race Coding' and White Opposition to Welfare," *American Political Science Review* 90 (1996): 593–604.

24. Klinkner with Smith, *The Unsteady March*, 333–35.

25. Tichenor, *Dividing Lines*, 275–78; American Bar Association Commission on Immigration, "American Justice Through Immigrants' Eyes." Online at http://www.abanet.org/publicserv/immigration/Due_Process.html, accessed June 27, 2005, 2.

26. Peter Brimelow, *Alien Nation: Common Sense about America's Immigration Disaster* (New York: Random House, 1995), 9–10, 264.

27. Audrey Singer, "Welfare Reform and Immigrants: A Policy Review," 2004, at 26. Online at http://www.brook.edu/dybdocroot/urban/pubs/200405_singer.pdf, accessed June 27, 2005.

28. See bill at http://www.fas.org/irp/crs/96-499.htm, accessed June 27, 2005.

29. In fact, PRWORA originally made even many immigrants present at the time of its enactment ineligible for SSI and food stamps, but Congress restored eligibility to most pre-enactment immigrants via the 1997 Balanced Budget Act, the 1998 Agricultural Research Extension and Education Act, and the Farm Security and Rural Investment Act of 2002. The states have chosen to provide TANF and Medicaid benefits to most pre-enactment immigrants (Singer "Welfare Reform and Immigrants," 23, 27–28).

30. See summary at http://uscis.gov/graphics/shared/aboutus/statistics/LegisHist/act142.htm, accessed June 27, 2005.

31. Michael Fix and Ron Haskins, "Welfare Benefits for Non-Citizens." Online at http:// www.brookings.edu/dybdocroot/es/wrb/publications/pb/pb15.htm, 2002, accessed June 27, 2005; Shawn Fremstad, "Recent Welfare Reform Research Findings: Implications for TANF Reauthorization and State TANF Policies," 2004. Online at http://www.cbpp.org/1-30-04wel.htm, accessed June 27, 2005.

32. Singer, "Welfare Reform and Immigrants," 29–30.

33. *Zadvydas v. Davis*, 533 U.S. 678 (2001) at III-A, III-B of J. Breyer's majority opinion and also J. Scalia's dissent.

34. Louis Fisher, *Military Tribunals & Presidential Power: American Revolution to the War on Terrorism* (Lawrence: University of Kansas Press, 2005), 177, 189–91, 198–201.

35. Public Law 197–40, Joint Resolution of the 107th Congress, September 18, 2001.

36. At http://www.eff.org/Privacy/Surveillance/Terrorism_militias/20022025_hr3162_usa-patriot. Congress renewed the act with minor changes in March 2006 (Sheryl Gay Stolberg, "Patriot Act Revisions Pass House, Sending Measure to the President," *New York Times,* March 8, 2006, A-20).

37. Available online at http://www.whitehouse.gov/news/releases/2001/11/print/20011113–27.html.

38. Human Rights Watch, "United States: Guantanamo Two Years On," January 9, 2004, hrw.org/english/docs/2004/01/09/usdom6917.htm.

39. This contention emerged as a result of a series of legal memoranda conveniently collected in Karen J. Greenberg and Joshua L. Dratel, eds., *The Torture Papers: The Road to Abu Ghraib* (New York: Cambridge University Press, 2005). See, esp., George W. Bush, "Memorandum on Humane Treatment of al Qaeda and Taliban Detainees," February 7, 2002, in ibid., 134–35.

40. Benjamin Wittes, "President Obama's Decision on Closing Guantánamo," at http://www.brookings.edu/opinions/2009/0929_guantanamo_wittes.aspx, accessed November 1, 2009.

41. James Risen and Eric Lichtbau, "Bush Lets U.S. Spy on Callers without Courts," *New York Times,* December 16, 2005, A1; Leslie Cauley, "NSA Has Massive Database of Americans' Phone Calls," *USA Today*, May 11, 2006, online at http://www.usatoday.com/news/washington/2006-05-10-nsa_x.htm.

42. Homeland Security Act of 2002, www.pfir.org/2002-hr5005 (accessed February 9, 2005). The Special Registration program, with targeted nations and groups, is described at www.ice.gov/graphics/specialregistration/index.htm (accessed February 9, 2005).

43. Rachel L. Swarns with Christopher Drew, "Fearful, Angry or Confused, Muslim Immigrants Register," *New York Times*, April 25, 2004, www. nytimes.com/2003/04/25/international/worldspecial/25REGI.html.

44. American Immigration Network, "Special Registration has NOT Ended—Many Requirements Continue," December 4, 2003, www.usavisanow.com/12-4-03.html.

45. Din Suleman, "Terror City." ColorLines v. 7, #3, 2004; online at http://www.arc.org/C_Lines/CLArchive/story7_2_02.html, accessed June 27, 2005.

46. Intelligence Reform and Terrorism Prevention Act of 2004, December 7, 2004, www.house.gov/rules/s2845crfulltext.htm.

47. Information on the Terrorist Threat Integration Center can be found at www.cia.gov/cia/public_affairs/press_release/2003/pr05012003.html (accessed February 9, 2005). Authorization to transfer the TTIC to the new National Counterterrorism Center occurs in sec. 1092 of the Intelligence Reform and Terrorism Prevention Act.

48. U.S. Department of Justice, "Fusion Centers and Intelligence Sharing," at http://it.ojp.gov/default.aspx?area+nationalinitiatives&page=1181, accessed November 1, 2009.

49. Intelligence Reform and Terrorism Prevention Act, sec. 1021; Markle Foundation Task Force, *Creating a Trusted Information Network for Homeland Security* (New York: Markle Foundation, December 2003), 2n2, 4n7; Shannon McCaffrey, "FBI and CIA Unite for Antiterror Fight," *Philadelphia Inquirer*, May 1, 2003; Richard A. Posner, "Important Job, Impossible Position," *New York Times*, February 9, 2005; John M. McConnell, "Vision 2014: A Globally Networked and Integrated Intelligence Enterprise," at http://terrorism.info.m.pt.org/pdf/vision-2015-globally-networked-integrated=intelligence-enterprise.pdf, accessed November 1, 2009.

50. *Federal Register*, March 24, 2003, v. 68, No. 56, 14140–41.

51. David Cole, "Driving While Immigrant," *Nation* 276, no. 18 (May 12, 2003): 6, 30.

52. Randal C. Archibald, "U.S. Alters Disputed Immigration Rules for Police," October 16, 2009, at http://www.nytimes.com/2009/10/17/us017.immig.html, accessed November 1, 2009.

53. Louis Fisher notes that though legal authorities at the time saw the Court in *Quirin* as building on earlier precedents holding that "war criminals" were not entitled to jury trials, those precedents did not authorize the kind of trial by secret military commission with minimal procedural protections that *Quirin* upheld. That is why executive officials claiming near-boundless authority over "enemy belligerents," "enemy combatants," or "unlawful enemy combatants," terms now often used interchangeably, virtually always rely ultimately on *Quirin* (Fisher, *Military Tribunals*, 117–24, 170, 221–22). Many administration memos have also stressed the somewhat more recent precedent of *Johnson v. Eisentrager*, 339 U.S. 763 (1950), but as discussed below, it upholds only the power of the president to prescribe military trials free from review by civilian courts in the case of alien combatants captured and held abroad in a declared war. It therefore cannot serve as a precedent for detentions and military trials on U.S. soil or territories subject to U.S. jurisdiction, as the Supreme Court has since held the Guantánamo Naval Base to be (*Rasul v. Bush* 542 U.S. 466 [2004]).

54. The full opinion can be found online at www. constitution.org/ussc/317-001a.htm (accessed February 9, 2005).

55. *Rasul v. Bush* 542 U.S. 466 (2004).

56. Neil A. Lewis, "U.S. Judge Halts War-Crime Trial at Guantánamo," *New York Times*, November 9, 2004, A-1; "Federal Judge Deals Setback to Guantánamo Bay Detainees," *New York Times*, January 20, 2005, A-20; "Judge Extends Legal Rights for Guantánamo Detainees," *New York Times*, February 1, 2005, A-12.

57. *United States v. Lindh*, 227 F. Supp. 2d 565 (E>D. Va. 2002).

58. See, for example, *Hamdi v. Rumsfeld*, 316 F. 3d. 450 (4th Cir. 2003), 19; *Padilla v. Rumsfeld*, U.S.C.C.A., 2d Cir. 02-7338, December 18, 2003, 40.

59. *Hamdi v. Rumsfeld*, 542 U.S. 507 (2004).

60. Joel Brinkley, "The Saturday Profile: From Afghanistan to Saudi Arabia, via Guantánamo," *New York Times*, October 16, 2004.

61. *Padilla v. Rumsfeld*, U.S.C.C.A., 2d Cir. 02-7338, December 18, 2003.

62. *Rumsfeld v. Padilla*, 543 U.S. 426 (2004).

63. *Jose Padilla v. C. T. Hanft*, U.S. Court of Appeals for the Fourth Circuit, No. 05-6396, September 9, 2005.

64. Ibid., filed December 21, 2005.

65. *Jose Padilla v. C. T. Hanft*, 126 S. Ct. 1649(2006).

66. Linda Greenhouse, "Justices to Rule on a Challenge to U.S. Tribunals," *New York Times*, November 8, 2005; Detainee Treatment Act of 2005, online at http://jurist.law.pitt.edu/gazette/2005/12/detainee-treatment-act-of-2005-white.php, accessed June 5, 2006.

67. Eric Schmitt, "Senate Approves Limiting Rights of U.S. Detainees," *New York Times*, November 11, 2005.

68. *Hamdan v. Rumsfeld*, "Opinion of the Court" at 14.

69. Ibid. at 31–32.

70. Ibid. at 38–39.

71. *Hamdan v. Rumsfeld*, "Justice Breyer, with whom Justice Kennedy, Justice Souter, and Justice Ginsburg join, concurring," at 1.

72. Stolberg, "President Moves 14," *New York Times*, September 7, 2006.

73. Public Law No. 109–366, 120 Stat. 2600, at http://frwebgate.access.gpo.gov/cgi-bin/getdoc.cgi?dbname=109_cong_bills&docid=f:s3930enr.txt.pdf.

74. William Glaberson, "Military Judges Dismiss Charges for 2 Detainees," *New York Times*, June 5, 2007, A1.

75. Glaberson, "Court Advances Military Trials for Detainees," *New York Times*, September 25, 2007, A1.

76. Glaberson, "In Shift, Justices Agree to Review Detainees' Case," *New York Times*, June 30, 2007, A1.

77. *Boumediene v. Bush*, 128 S. Ct. 2229 (2008).

78. Warren Richey, "Obama Endorses Military Commissions for Guantánamo Detainees," *Christian Science Monitor*, October 28, 2009, at http://www.csmonitor.com/2009/1029/p02s01-usju.html, accessed November 1, 2009.

79. See, for example, "Bush: Warn On Drugs Aids War on Terror," CBS News, December 14, 2001, online at http://www.cbs.news.com/stories/2001/12/14/politics/printable321433.shtml.

Strangers Within: The Barghouti and the Bishara Criminal Trials

LEORA BILSKY

How does domestic criminal law contend with those who are conceived by the state as strangers, as the enemy, falling under the rubric of "terror"? This question has recently gained urgency in light of growing efforts by democratic states to bring "terrorism" within the scope of criminal law. This development challenges the structure of criminal law in liberal democracies since it mandates addressing the lack of a fundamental condition that grants legitimacy to the court: a common legal basis shared by the two groups (represented by the prosecution and the accused) upon which to adjudicate the actions under consideration. The difficulty is compounded by the fact that modern criminal law has anchored its claim for legitimacy (or nonpoliticization) in the exclusion of political "motive" from the court's deliberation regarding the responsibility of the defendant.[1] This exclusion becomes problematic in "terror trials," since the very definition of terror is at the heart of the dispute. For one side it is a legitimate act of resistance against occupation and is based on the right of self-determination, while for the other side it is a violent action no different from ordinary murder. I call this condition "radical difference" and ask what changes should be introduced to criminal law to allow it to confront the problems it presents.

My claim, which I will seek to establish on the basis of the *Barghouti* and *Bishara* criminal trials, is that it is precisely in situations lacking shared community values and an inclusive democratic process that domestic courts are called to delineate the boundaries of political discourse, distinguishing legitimate criticism from illegal violence. The court can restrict the conditions for political deliberation that have been threatened by the growing violence, or it can enhance them. In other words, it becomes the court's decision whether and to what extant to ensure that the opposition is given space, that the defendant's narrative is heard, and to ensure the equal and inclusive enforcement of the law on members of both sides to the dispute.[2]

However, this role of the court is often obscured and it is particularly so in criminal trials. My question is what changes are needed in the criminal law if it is to contend with its new political role of judging the "terrorist" as an ordinary criminal. In order to understand the need for this reform we should first examine how the terror trial reverses the standard order of things: instead of working within the well-known boundaries of a political community from which it draws its legitimacy, the court itself participates in the act of drawing the boundaries of the political discourse community to which it belongs, while deciding questions of procedural and substantive criminal law. I claim that forcing the criminal court to decide such political cases engenders a crisis of legitimacy for the court, which cannot be addressed if we continue to ignore or deny the new political role of the criminal trial. This essay investigates the relation between criminal law and a political community and maintains that it is a dynamic and a constitutive one.[3] The court in the terror trial is an active participant in the redrawing of the boundaries of political community by taking certain arguments outside the scope of political discourse and defining them as criminal actions, or by resisting this attempt. When the democratic system functions in an inclusive way the groups that are threatened by such a move can oppose this process before the legislator. However, when there is a democratic deficit—for example, when one of the groups is denied access to the political process—this opposition is channeled to the criminal trial itself. However, under the ordinary criminal process there is no place to seriously consider such political challenges since they undermine the claim of the law for neutrality and the exclusion of politics from its domain. This position of traditional criminal law cannot be maintained in terror trials without undermining their legitimacy. Since I do not believe that terror trials are going to disappear anytime soon, we should address this problem. We need to develop a legal channel to discuss the political question raised by the terror trial, as a way to enhance its legitimacy. Instead of denying any place for politics in the trial, we should find ways to confront the political issue directly. The tools for this change can be adopted from constitutional jurisprudence that has long been struggling with similar issues.

My argument relies on the works of various liberal thinkers who have suggested ways to allow liberal theory to contend with the existence of political trials.[4] In this essay I concentrate on the level of criminal law doctrine. I suggest that constitutional law, and the doctrines it has developed over the years for addressing the problem of the political trial, can offer insights into ways of facing the new challenge of criminalizing the "terrorist." In particular, it is useful to consider how constitutional law attempts to walk the fine line between legitimacy and legality by granting various discretionary powers to the court. In this context I examine what jurist Alexander Bickel has termed "the passive virtues,"[5] and ask whether and to what extent it is desirable to allow criminal courts to develop similar mechanisms of judicial discretion. More specifically, I compare two ways to infuse the criminal court with political discretion—the defense of "abuse of process" (which has been adopted and developed by the Israeli court in recent years), and the practice of jury-nullification (which has been recognized in Anglo-American law)—both of which, I argue, can give the criminal court (judge or jury) much needed discretion for examining the broader constitutional ramifications of the case. As we shall see, under traditional liberal theory these doctrines have been given a narrow interpretation, and were therefore shorn of their full potential for confronting structural problems of group discrimination through the criminal law. I suggest reinterpreting the scope of these doctrines in light of the new challenges introduced by the jurisprudence of terror.

Radical Difference in the Court

Criminal law cases and constitutional law cases are usually regarded as separate fields, at both the substantive and institutional levels (in Israel the former is decided by the ordinary courts and the latter by the Supreme Court sitting as the High Court of Justice). The general view is that there are only narrow points of convergence between the two fields—with regard to the constitutional rights of the defendant and, recently, also with regard to the rights of the victim.[6] Instead of asking what are or should be the constitutional rights of the defendant or the victim, I suggest asking what is or should be the constitutional role of the criminal trial in a liberal democracy. In other words, I am more interested in the deeper layer of constitutionalism affected by criminal law. I call this the question of "boundary drawing": identifying how criminal law actually participates in delineating the boundaries of citizenship, of who belongs and who does not belong to a political community of discourse.

Boundary drawing is much more apparent in constitutional law cases. A recent decision of the Israeli Supreme Court [May 2006] regarding law of citizenship and denial of the right of family unification for Israeli citizens who are married to a Palestinian from the "territories" can demonstrate this role, and the choices made by the judges in this regard.[7] Thus, for example, Justice Cheshin, leading the majority position of court, focused on the Palestinian spouse, who was described as "foreigner" and as belonging to an enemy state, and therefore, not enjoying a constitutional right to become a member of the Israeli state. Justice Barak, the president of the court, leading the minority position, focused on the Arab Israeli spouse, and thus could see clearly how his or her constitutional rights to equality and family life in Israel were breached. In other words, the preliminary decision on whom to focus, and how to see the Palestinian—as foreigner or as belonging to the political community through family ties—determined to a large extent the legal outcome reached by the different justices.

The process of boundary drawing is not explicit in criminal law adjudication. Since modern criminal law is connected to the nation-state, it presupposes the existence of a political community over which it has authority (monopoly of violence). It assumes that the issue of effective sovereignty has been settled.[8] Challenges to the authority of the court are therefore relegated to a preliminary stage of the criminal trial involving questions of jurisdiction, which, it is assumed, can be properly answered with the tools supplied by domestic criminal law. This preliminary process is not seen as relevant to the constitutional matter of determining the boundaries of the political community.[9] I would like to look more closely at this process—namely, how criminal law actually participates in drawing the boundaries of a political community.[10]

Political trials often begin with what can be characterized as a situation of radical difference in which two groups with antithetical or irreconcilable ideas about law and society meet in court. The conflict is radical in the sense that the two sides cannot agree on the substantive law that governs the dispute or on the evidentiary and procedural rules that can be legitimately applied to resolve it. The controversy cannot be resolved solely by legal means, since it does not concern a legal question such as the interpretation of the law or a disagreement about facts, but raises the preliminary question of which legal system has the right to adjudicate the conflict and which tribunal has jurisdiction over the case. In effect each side calls for the recognition of a different normative system, anchored to a different historical narrative, which determines which court should adjudicate the case. In such cases, the triad structure of the trial collapses into a binary structure of two parties facing each other in a power struggle without an accepted overriding law that can function as arbiter. In an ordinary trial, the two disputing parties can bring their case before a third party, whose position as an outsider to the dispute can guarantee its impartiality and thus endow its ruling with legitimacy.[11] In cases of radical difference, there is no such third party, because the court itself is deemed by one of the parties (and the group he or she represents) as its adversary, and hence illegitimate. This crisis occurs, for example, after a war or a revolution when one regime judges its predecessor's crimes, or in cases of a national uprising against a colonial power, or in situations bordering on civil war, when the courts of the current regime are called upon to judge those who seek to change it. In all such situations, the judiciary is identified with one of the parties to the dispute. But this can also occur in criminal trials in nontransitional situtaions, especially when there is an unresolved conflict between ethnic, religious, or national groups over the basic values of the polity.

The problem of "radical difference" has been central to two "terror" cases that have been tried before the Israeli courts: *The State of Israel v. Azmi Bishara*,[12] and *The State of Israel v. Marwan Barghouti*.[13] These cases are of special interest since here the state chose to conduct ordinary criminal trials instead of resorting to the military courts' system.[14] This decision has been informed by political changes that have taken place since the outbreak of the second uprising (*Intifada*) in 2000. During that time and under the growing circles of violence between the groups, Palestinian political leaders have undergone a process of delegitimization in the Israeli media and in political discourse.[15] Criminal law carried a central role in this process, in particular when it was directed against public leaders whose criticism of Israeli policy in relation to Palestinians was formally considered a legitimate part of the political discourse in Israel. This transformation, when it takes place incrementally, is very hard to trace. But when we examine criminal trials of central Palestinian public figures, these subtle processes can be identified, and the role of the law in this transformation can be analyzed. The trials of Palestinian leader Marawan Barghouti, and Arab Israeli leader Azmi Bishara, provide us with such an occasion. Both trials, I maintain, partake in a process of boundary drawing of Israeli political community vis-à-vis the stranger within, the political leader whose familiarity has to be rejected, and who has to be redefined as falling squarely beyond the pale of legitimate political discourse.[16]

Both trials were directed against Palestinian political leaders, but one, Bishara, is an Israeli citizen while the other, Barghouti, is not a citizen of Israel. Both defendants were viewed by the Israeli political authorities as involved in "terrorist" activities to different degrees. In particular, both were charged for making speeches inciting to terrorist attacks against Israeli citizens. Since they were both political leaders the trials had the further potential of delegitimizing the groups they represented. For the purposes of this essay, the difference between the two cases is no less important than what they had in common. Legally, Bishara was indicted for speech related offenses while Barghouti was charged for complicity in murder. Politically, Bishara was an elected Arab member of the Israeli Knesset (parliament)—representing a group that is considered de jure an integral part of the Israeli polity, but de facto suffers from discrimination,[17] while Barghouti was an elected member of the Palestinian parliament, a political leader in the Fatah faction and the military Tanzim faction, representing a group that was engaged in a violent struggle for national liberation and self-determination.

How did the problem of "radical difference" manifest itself in the two trials? The trial of Bishara dealt with two speeches he delivered, in Umm el-Fahem, Israel, and in Syria, in favor of the Palestinian right to "resist" Israeli occupation. The trial of Barghouti revolved around speeches he made in support of the violent uprising against the Israeli occupation and his role in supplying weapons and financial support to members of his organization who had carried out terrorist acts. He was charged, among other things, with murder. In both cases, the path to the criminal trial passed through the category of "terror," which was translated into specific criminal offenses,[18] and in both cases the defendants advanced oppositional narratives competing with the hegemonic narrative about the basic values of the state of Israel. Bishara was the leader of a political party that advocates turning Israel into "a state of all its citizens" as opposed to a

"Jewish and democratic state" as the basic (constitutional) laws of Israel define it.[19] Barghouti advocated military resistance to the Israeli military occupation, but, in contrast to some more radical Palestinian leaders, he favored limiting the violent resistance to the Occupied Territories (that is, against soldiers and settlers), claiming that this restriction makes the resistance actions legitimate under international law.[20] This argument collided with Israel's claim that these distinctions do not stand and that all acts of violent resistance are terror.

In both cases, the underlying theme of the two competing narratives is the ongoing conflict between Jews and Palestinians in the region. The one important difference between the trials is that Bishara, as an Israeli citizen and an elected MK (member of Knesset), was able to compete with the dominant Israeli narrative at the political level and to work to incorporate his views (and his political motive) into the law.[21] His demand that the Israeli polity become more inclusive of its Palestinian citizens can explain his decision not to question the competence of Israeli courts. to rule on the legality of his speeches. Instead, he claimed that, under existing law, he was answerable only to the Knesset, since political speeches by MKs enjoy parliamentary immunity under the law.[22] Bishara argued that if the court ruled against him on this preliminary question of immunity, and asserted its authority to adjudicate the case, it would be redrawing the lines of legitimate political speech in Israel, thus de facto criminalizing Arab opposition to the Zionist ethos of the state.[23] He further claimed that such a decision could change the balance between the legislative and the judicial branches, thus undermining two cornerstones of Israeli democracy—the separation of powers and freedom of speech. The state prosecution denied the validity of this claim, maintaining that Arab citizens of Israel and Arab MKs most certainly do enjoy freedom of speech, but that Bishara had crossed the line between legal and illegal activity when he had advocated violent actions of resistance by Palestinians to the Israeli occupation.

The problem of "radical difference" was even more pronounced in the trial of Barghouti where the two parties not only disagreed about the legitimate jurisdiction of the court but were also divided over which law should govern the dispute (the international law of war or domestic criminal law). This latter disagreement had to do with the place of "political motive" in the criminal trial, since international law still recognizes the legitimacy of resorting to armed conflict in certain situations, while criminal law is premised on the idea that violence is never a legitimate response to conflict, and that its use is the exclusive prerogative of the state. The only justified resort of individuals to violence is in cases falling under certain defenses (such as "self-defense"), but there is no recognition of a right to "collective self-defense."[24] These opposing legal categorizations of the case relied in turn on two contrasting historical narratives of the Second Palestinian *Intifada* (uprising). While Israel characterizes the *Intifada* as acts of terror that pose a severe threat to the state, Palestinians, relying on a historical narrative of occupation and oppression, see it as a collective struggle over their right to self-determination. These differences were pronounced in the trial. Barghouti tried to distinguish between legitimate violent resistance (aimed against Israeli soldiers and settlers) and terror acts (against civilians within pre-1967 Israel). The prosecution argued that no such distinction is legally recognizable and that they should all be viewed as terrorist attacks that amount to ordinary crimes of murder and assault.

The Law of Jurisdiction

The issue of legitimacy is central to the political trial. As explained by jurist and political philosopher Otto Kirchheimer,[25] a political trial can be crudely characterized as an attempt by political authorities to eliminate a political opponent by legal means. They resort to the court because it provides legitimacy, placing their actions within the "rule of law," giving them a legal rather than a political coloring. The role of legitimization played by the criminal trial is therefore a key to understanding the choices of the prosecution. This problem of legitimization is also the main reason for the defendant to search for ways to raise his political concerns to the court without endowing it with legitimacy.

The jurisdiction stage of the trial is the only stage in which such division between participation and legitimation can be made. At this stage the parties do not have to engage the substantive claims about the guilt or innocence of the defendant but, rather, to debate what the proper tribunal is for addressing these questions. Interestingly, unlike liberal theory's general insistence on maintaining the ideal of the "rule of law" by preserving a distance between the tribunal and the parties to the dispute,[26] at this preliminary stage the opposite is required. Before the parties can present their substantive arguments, the court requires that its jurisdiction over the dispute be established, that the parties show a meaningful link between the case of controversy and the court. In a criminal trial, the most important connection is based on a territorial link—that the acts causing the dispute occurred on the territory over which the court has jurisdiction (the territoriality principle). Another link is a personal one, in cases where one of the parties to the dispute is considered a member of the political community over which the court is authorized to judge (the nationality principle). In addition, a temporal connection has to be proven—that there is no statute of limitations applicable to the act under consideration. These three links establishing the court's jurisdiction are also the three basic relations that constitute a political community—space, time, and people.[27] In other words, in order to establish its jurisdiction, the parties have to establish the court's proximity to the dispute, that there is a meaningful link to the court. The community basis of criminal law is thus exposed.[28] The principle of territorial jurisdiction represents the modern understanding of criminal law as one of the most important expressions of state sovereignty, which is usually delimited in terms of territory and geography (promising to apply the criminal code in an equal manner to all the inhabitants of a certain territory).[29] The law of jurisdiction can thus give us a first hint about the connection between criminal law and political community, a connection that might be too easily overlooked in an age of "universal jurisdiction."[30]

Given the problems of "radical difference," "legitimacy," and "divided community" in the Barghouti and Bishara trials, it is not surprising that the two defendants concentrated their arguments regarding the broader constitutional aspects of the trials at the jurisdiction stage—the only stage in a criminal trial in which engaging in legal arguments does not endow the court with legitimacy on part of the defendant. In the Bishara trial the "external" quality of this stage acquired an institutional character. The question whether an Israeli MK enjoys parliamentary immunity from criminal charges is first decided by the Knesset Committee. Only after immunity is removed by the Knesset can the court acquire jurisdiction over the case. In the Bishara case the trial court decided to postpone its decision regarding the issue of immunity to the end of the trial, after the substantive issues of criminal responsibility were decided.[31] The defendant petitioned the Supreme Court sitting as High Court of Justice on this decision, and on February 1, 2006, the Supreme Court ruled in his favor. In the Barghouti case the jurisdiction stage did not bear an institutional character, since the same tribunal decided both the question of jurisdiction and the substantive question of criminal liability (the decision can be appealed only as a whole). However, Barghouti, as a political defendant, attributed considerable weight to this qualitative difference and acted accordingly. Thus, regarding the issue of jurisdiction he was legally represented and submitted a legal answer, while he refused to have legal representation or to cooperate with the Israeli court or the Public Defense Office on any other issue so as to avoid the effect of legitimization.

In the Bishara case, the main claim against the court's jurisdiction concerned the issue of parliamentary immunity: since his political speeches had been made as a MK and a political party leader, in order to fulfill his political mandate, he claimed that they were protected by his parliamentary immunity. Thus, the Knesset Committee had erred in removing his immunity, and any criminal proceedings advanced against him were therefore void. In other words, the argument about the court's lack of jurisdiction was presented as an internal one, pertaining to the separation of powers between the legislative and judicial bodies within Israel as a democratic state. Barghouti's claim against jurisdiction was far more radical: since the Palestinian people base their right of violent resistance on their collective right to self-determination, and since Israeli law does not acknowledge such a right, Israeli courts cannot serve as legitimate arbiters. He translated this claim into five main arguments against the jurisdiction of the Israeli court.[32] Barghouti relied on the Oslo accords, which he claimed had effectively ended Israel's jurisdiction over Palestinians who injure Israelis, and on international law, which he claimed does not recognize Israel's right to bring him to trial since he was a "freedom fighter" resisting military occupation. Further, he argued that he had been illegally kidnapped by the Israeli army (IDF) and should enjoy "prisoner of war" status. Barghouti also claimed that he enjoyed immunity from criminal prosecution as a member of the Palestinian parliament, and that the indictment was purely political, amounting to an indictment against the Palestinian people as a whole, and therefore should be withdrawn. The court rejected all these claims,[33] insisting that Barghouti's actions were not political but criminal, and therefore "it is the duty of the state of Israel to bring the likes of Barghouti to trial."

It is clear from both cases that issues relating to the political nature of the trial underlay the defendants' argument regarding the jurisdiction of the court.

Both defendants sought to expose the political underpinning of the trial by showing the unequal treatment that they received—Bishara stating that his trial constituted a first precedent for prosecuting an Israeli MK for political speeches, and Barghouti maintaining that Israel was deviating from the norms of the international law of war by treating him as criminal defendant instead of a "war prisoner" and conducting a political trial against him. Both defendants thus questioned the legitimacy of resorting to domestic criminal law. For this reason both also stressed the collective nature of the prosecutions—that in each case, the real defendant was the group represented by the legal defendant.

The doctrines of jurisdiction point to the basic problematic of modern criminal law. Barghouti, who bases his claims against Israeli jurisdiction on the general right of resistance, is more radically opposed to the jurisdiction of Israeli courts, maintaining that criminal law allows no distinction between legitimate and illegitimate acts of resistance (exclusion of political motive). As I pointed out, the exclusion of "political motive" from modern criminal law depends on the guarantee of equal citizenship (and the ability to contest the terms of criminal law before the legislator). However, since this condition is not satisfied in the case of military occupation, and an ongoing national conflict, a domestic criminal court can no longer be justified in ignoring the political motive of the defendant.

The jurisdiction stage of the trial was thus haunted by the political motive excluded by criminal law. The question is whether dividing the criminal trial into two stages, and delegating the "political" question to the preliminary stage of jurisdiction, can allow the court adequate discretionary powers to contend with the political basis of the trial and its constitutional ramifications. I believe the answer is negative. This is so because jurisdiction in criminal law is binary (it either exists or not),[34] and is therefore not adequate to addressing cases that require a more subtle balancing of legal and political issues. For example, in the Barghouti case, even according to the principle of territorial jurisdiction, the Israeli court clearly enjoys jurisdiction since the violent attacks were directed against Israeli citizens and were not confined to the West Bank but also within the June 4, 1967, borders, and not only against soldiers but also against civilians. Although Barghouti claimed that these "transgressions" were carried out by members of his organization against his explicit orders, this fact could not bear on the jurisdiction issue, since it concerns matters of substantive law

(law of participation in a criminal enterprise). The jurisdiction of Israeli courts stems from the basic understanding of sovereignty. If the court cannot establish its jurisdiction in a case where the life of Israelis within Israel is taken, then the very basis of state sovereignty (monopoly of violence) is placed in question. Nevertheless, the defendant's need to shape his constitutional concerns in terms of jurisdiction seems to miss an important component of the problem. Even if Israeli courts can claim valid jurisdiction over the case, the political aspects of the trial remain to be addressed. The neutrality and impartiality of the court are undermined when the defendant belongs to a collective engaged in a violent struggle with the state to which the court belongs. In our case, while one side to the conflict enjoys de facto immunity from criminal prosecution for what Israel defines as collective acts of "self-defense,"[35] the other side to the conflict is exposed to criminal prosecution for what it defines as justified acts of "resistance." But does such bias that is endemic to situations of radical difference mean that Israeli courts should be exempted in principle from judging such cases? I would like to suggest that we abandon the binary understanding of the law of jurisdiction and develop more refined tools that could enable the defendant to raise his concerns about the neutrality of the prosecution and the court. In other words, I suggest that Israel can assert legitimate jurisdiction over such cases only if its legal system develop legal tools that enable the courts to address concerns about unequal enforcement of the domestic criminal law on both sides to the violent conflict.

The jurisdiction stage seems to better serve the Bishara case since his actions were doubly distanced from violent acts. First, he was not charged with participating in the violent acts of "resistance" but only with speaking in their favor. And second, since Bishara was an elected MK, he did not challenge the constitutionality of the substantive criminal law proscribing such speeches, but only insisted on an MK's immunity from prosecution under such laws. He also enjoyed the institutional advantage of bringing his claims before the Supreme Court sitting as High Court of Justice, once the trial court rejected his claims (an option closed to Barghouti, whose appeal on jurisdiction could take place only after the conclusion of the trial). However, also in the Bishara case, the law of jurisdiction was ill suited to illuminating one important aspect of Bishara's claim, the unequal treatment he was receiving by the political bodies.[36]

"Terror" trials present us with the risk of selective prosecution, of criminalizing only one side to the conflict in domestic national courts. It might be argued that domestic courts are so "tainted" that the only solution is to transfer such cases to international tribunals. I believe that this solution is problematic. First, it is unlikely that national courts will relinquish such cases, which are often viewed as the very symbol of the state's sovereignty (the right to adjudicate those who claim unrestricted "war" against the state and its citizens). This may lead to direct conflict between domestic courts and international tribunals. Second, if domestic courts are prevented from adjudicating such cases, the political authorities are likely to resort to the alternative—the use of brute force (which is of great concern to liberal thinkers dealing with problems of state authorized assassinations, administrative detentions, or military committees in the war on terror.)[37] The solution of recognizing universal jurisdiction to third-party courts, which is proposed in order to enhance the "rule of law," may in fact create its own problems of politicization. In any case, the controversy over universal jurisdiction deserves a separate article. In this essay I restrict myself to contemplating an alternative solution, one that invests domestic courts with legal tools to address the issue of selective prosecutions in trials of terror.

Midway Conclusion

The law of jurisdiction can teach us that the key to solving the problem of political trials in national courts does not necessarily lie in trying to maintain the strict separation of politics and law. "Blind justice" does not always result in a just trial. We are used to thinking about the rule of law in terms of maintaining a distance between the court and the parties to the dispute, but at the same time, as noted above, the rule of law requires that a meaningful link be established between the court and the community injured by the deed. The problem of a political trial can arise when there is too much distance between the tribunal and the disputing parties, just as it arises when there is too much proximity. It is therefore necessary to devise more creative ways to balance the political bias of national courts by endowing the courts with more subtle tools of discretion for handling the political issues that such cases inevitably raise—in particular, the problem of equal treatment before the law in situations where the national "community" is divided (such as in the Bishara case), or where two communities are engaged in an ongoing violent conflict against a military occupation (such as in the Barghouti case). My contention is that the legitimacy of applying criminal law to such cases should not be conditional on the (fictional) existence of one community of shared values, but rather that we should try to develop constitutional tools that can enable the criminal trial to address these concerns about equal treatment by national courts under conditions of radical difference.

The Constitutional Analogy

During the years in which the constitutional balance of powers between courts and the other political branches has been shaped, jurists have given much thought to the problem of how to strike the proper balance between legality and legitimacy when faced with the political question. Two main approaches to this problem can be broadly identified: implicit and explicit. The former can be called the "passive virtues" approach, the other the "substantive discretion" approach.

In his book *The Least Dangerous Branch*,[38] American jurist Alexander Bickel suggested that it is crucial for a court adopting an active stance of judicial review on constitutional matters to insist on developing what he terms the "passive virtues"—that is, various legal doctrines such as "standing," "ripeness," "non-justiciable questions," and so forth, all of which enable the court to choose to confront the political branch at the time and with a case that seems most suited to maintaining both the rule of law and the legitimacy of the court. These tools allow the court to avoid deciding cases on merit when they are too explosive politically, without taking a principled position in favor of the executive decision. These are therefore "silent" tools of avoidance that permit the court to balance prudence and principle.

The opposite approach to the danger of politicization has been to endow the court with explicit discretionary powers. Instead of a "yes-no" approach to judicial review (valid and void decisions), it is proposed that the court should develop doctrines of degrees such as "reasonableness," "proportionality," "partial voidance" and so forth,[39] which admit the existence of gray areas in which the executive and the court should resort to discretion. These doctrines, while allowing the court the needed leeway (between principle and prudence), stipulate that such balancing will be carried out explicitly, in the reasoning of the court.[40] These tools are no longer "silent"; rather, they require elaborate justification. Although constitutional law jurists in Israel and elsewhere have long debated the advantages and disadvantages of each of these approaches,[41] here I propose to extract from this complicated controversy those elements that may be useful for dealing with the political question in criminal law.

I have argued that when "terror" enters the realm of criminal law, it can create a crisis of political legitimization, since the very act of judging the terrorist as a common criminal carries a huge symbolic message. Historically, courts in democratic societies have resorted to the law of procedure to handle such difficulties. For example, in the United States, giving a constitutional basis (4th and 14th amendment) to doctrines for excluding tainted evidence ("the fruit of the poisonous tree") was designed to discourage the police from overzealousness in prosecuting suspects and it could be used to temper unequal enforcement of the law on different groups.[42] In general such doctrines invoke the equity idea of "estoppel"—that is, that the authorities are barred from proceeding with the case if they violate the accused's procedural guarantees of due process. Such doctrines allow the court to dismiss cases suspected of abuse of power without ruling on the merits.[43] In the area of criminal law, resorting to tools of avoidance may lead to public criticism of the courts for allowing criminals to go free because of a seeming "technicality," or for preserving the constitutional rights of defendants at too high a cost to society. Indeed, in Israel the court decided against resorting to this rigid sanction in criminal law cases and instead opted for a more discretionary approach to the problem.[44] Another, more explicit way to mitigate the political tendencies of the prosecution, can be found in the interpretation of substantive criminal law in light of constitutional concerns. Of special concern for liberal courts are crimes that undermine the principle of individual fault (such as crimes of criminal conspiracy),[45] crimes undermining freedom of political speech (libel, incitement), and crimes directed against the polity (treason, espionage).[46] Courts that were willing to restrain the political authorities' tendency to misuse these crimes against political adversaries relied on strict construction of the criminal law.[47] As Kirchheimer indicated, notwithstanding the natural tendency of national courts to identify with the position of the authorities in times of "security emergency," they often find ways to resist such pressures.[48]

These traditional tools of criminal law, important as they are, are not sufficient to deal with the dangers of the political trial. Therefore, I would like to suggest applying the constitutional framework of the "passive virtues" and "substantive discretion" approaches to examine discretionary tools available to courts in the field of criminal law. Particularly, I will be looking at two ways to address issues of selective prosecution. One way, that of jury nullification in Anglo-American law, can be characterized as a "silent" tool, opening up the binary structure of jurisdiction by allow a "third way" for the court: a means for acquitting defendants that suffer from discrimination or abuse of process without involving the judges themselves in a direct collision with the political authorities. The second way, the defense of abuse of process (developed by Anglo-American courts and recently adopted by Israeli courts), is a discretionary tool that demands explicit reasoning. It allows the court to delay or dismiss a case based on broad constitutional consideration of factors such as selective prosecution and discrimination. In the following sections I discuss the possible contribution of these tools to contending with the problems presented by trials of terror.

The Defense of "Abuse of Process"

We have seen how the very question of whether the defendant has to answer to the court in a political criminal trial carries with it constitutional ramifications. The problem stems from the situation of radical difference, as well as from the court's apparent proximity to one party to the conflict. The very willingness of a national court to adjudicate the case is viewed by the defendant as undermining the court's authority, making it a party to the dispute. The alternative possibility, of making the court answerable to the defendants for the constitutional basis of the trial, has not been seriously considered by jurists.[49] In this section I argue that finding ways to address this problem can enhance the legitimacy of the trial by creating a deliberative space that has previously been closed to the defendant by the political authorities.

We have seen that arguments about jurisdiction in criminal law are not tailored to tackling the problem of political bias. I therefore suggest that we should not consider the jurisdiction phase as exhausting the constitutional arguments against the trial. Rather, we can explore an intermediate approach—that the jurisdiction of the court might be valid, yet, because of various concerns about selective prosecution the court has to further establish its authority by meeting the condition of answerability to the defendant. This can be done, for example, by changing legal presumptions. In cases of alleged radical difference we could consider adopting a presumption of the "partiality" of national courts because of their structural closeness to one of the parties. The court will then have to overcome such presumption before it can adjudicate the case.[50] But short of such radical solutions we can consider a more moderate tool for reviewing the constitutional basis of the case through the introduction of the "abuse of process" defense.

In recent years, Israeli courts and legal scholars have been deliberating the introduction of the defense of "abuse of process." Scholars argued that this defense has the potential of bridging the gap between criminal law and constitutional law, since it directs the court's examination to the larger political framework of the trial.[51] The need for such a defense is especially acute in legal systems like the Israeli one, in which the prosecution enjoys broad discretion whether to press criminal charges.[52] Since broad prosecutorial discretion creates the potential for abuse of power, the Israeli Supreme Court, sitting as High Court of Justice, has gradually recognized its power of judicial review over decisions of the public prosecutor and attorney general, but applied it in very rare occasions in which the decision not to prosecute seemed highly unreasonable.[53] A similar power of review, however, was not exercised by criminal trial courts. For many years Israeli courts have not recognized their power of acquitting a defendant on the basis of a preliminary argument of "bar to trial" such as "I was illegally brought to trial" (Eichmann, Barghouti), or "I was discriminated against—the state charges me for a crime while letting others commit similar crimes." The need for reform was first acknowledged by the courts that developed the defense of "abuse of power" relying on their discretionary powers to interpret the law, and in 2007 the Israeli legislature amended the criminal procedure act and recognized this defense.[54]

The defense was first recognized in the Yefet case [1996], which dealt with the conviction of bankers and banks for the manipulation of their shares. The defense claimed that the state was barred from prosecuting the defendants because of its own involvement in the matter. The court recognized the defense of "abuse of process" in principle but limited its application to very rare cases of "unbearable and scandalous conduct of the authorities that amounts to persecution and oppression of defendants . . . cases that shock the conscience and affront the universal sense of justice."[55] Thus, the court restricted the defense to cases of "gross misconduct" and "bad intent" on the part of the prosecution (subjective criteria).[56] One reason for limiting the defense to cases of "subjective" discrimination might be to protect the court from having to decide political issues that it lacks the expertise to decide. However, this narrow scope of review left the problem of structural bias and group discrimination unaddressed. Under this interpretation the defense could not be used to address the difficulty raised in cases of "radical difference" when the law is applied against people belonging to only one side to the conflict.[57]

In the Borowitz case (Borowitz, 2005),[58] the Israeli Supreme Court adopted a broader test for examining "abuse of process," and it therefore opened the door to raise the defense in cases such as *Bishara* and *Barghouti*. In the Borowitz case, the court allowed itself more discretion to bar or limit criminal prosecutions when there is "substantial harm to the sense of fairness and justice," and was willing, in principle, to recognize discrimination also in cases in which the authorities acted in "good faith." Legal scholars called the court to adopt the broader criteria to encompass arguments that refer to the intersection between criminal law and constitutional law.[59] The legislature followed suit and article 149(10) of the amended criminal procedure law adopted the broader test for review according to which the court should examine whether the indictment by the prosecution or the conduct of the trial "stand in substantial contradiction to principles of justice and legal fairness."[60]

Adopting the broader test for review under the "abuse of process" defense has the potential of creating a better system of checks and balances on the executive by making the issue of equal treatment in criminal prosecution subject to judicial review.[61] It allows the court to refrain from judging the case on its merits, and instead, to stay, limit, or annul the charges until the concerns about equal protection of the laws are addressed. Thus, the defense of "abuse of process" in its broader interpretation can create a new incentive for the prosecution to eradicate unjustified immunities enjoyed by certain classes of defendants. It can thus work to enhance the legitimacy of domestic courts in adjudicating cases of "radical difference." In principle it can discourage the prosecution from targeting only one side to the conflict and hence also reduces the need to send the case to a "third-party" court or to an international tribunal (an option that creates new kinds of problems of selective prosecution, as I elaborated elsewhere).[62]

How could the defense of "abuse of process" have changed the dynamic of the Barghouti and Bishara cases?[63] As we saw, Bishara as an Israeli citizen and a parliament member chose not to raise this defense and relied instead on the substantive immunity enjoyed by MKs. This choice reflects the current state of law in which constitutional claims against the criminal proceedings are often channeled to the jurisdiction phase. Given the difficulty of establishing the defense of "abuse of process," and given the uncertainty about the proper criteria for its application (subjective or objective), Bishara's lawyers opted to rely solely on the Law of Parliamentary Immunities. But if, for the sake of argument, Bishara had raised claims of discrimination under the abuse of process defense, and if the court had opted for the broader test adopted by the Borowitz case, how could the defense have been applied to Bishara? The court could have examined Bishara's criminal prosecution in relation to the Israeli attorney general's policy of refraining from prosecuting, for instance, leaders of Israeli settlers in the Occupied Territories for speeches advocating violent resistance to the August 2005 withdrawal from the Gaza Strip.[64] However, we should bear in mind that there are substantial legal barriers to the success of such "abuse of process" claims: 1. Selective prosecutions as such are not prohibited. 2. The courts have a choice between a "subjective" or an "objective" criterion for review. 3. The proper criterion for comparing classes of defendants is not clear and subject to political contestation (should Jewish rabbis be compared with Arab political leaders?). All these difficulties might well have convinced Bishara to stick with the parliamentary immunity argument that constitutes a general block for prosecution and does not require a substantive review by the court of the prosecution policy of the attorney general. Obviously, this constitutional channel available to an elected MK is not an option for other Arab citizens of Israel who might find themselves accused of incitement to violence.[65] The Supreme Court's decision to uphold Bishara's immunity without deciding on the merit of his speeches only underlines the need to create a more general doctrine that would allow the court to review the constitutional ramifications of the criminal prosecution in ordinary criminal cases.

A similar case for the defense of "abuse of process" can be made with regard to the Barghouti trial. Under this defense Barghouti could have claimed that he was facing criminal charges for the killing of innocent civilians, while leaders of the Israeli army enjoy de facto immunity for killing civilians during acts of "targeted killing."[66] One answer to such criticism can be that there is a principled way to differentiate between the two cases (intentional killing of civilians is nothing like killing civilians unintentionally, as "collateral damage"). However, this answer presupposes the existence of a legal channel through which such claims can be raised and examined by the courts. As long as the legality of the policy of "targeted killing" is left outside the jurisdiction of Israeli courts in principle, and the petitions to the Supreme Court about their legality are not accepted, the preliminary claim about unequal treatment (and hence the abuse of process defense) remains the only channel in which to raise the constitutional concern. This can be done through the "abuse of process" defense. Applying the defense to the Barghouti case raises difficult problems for an Israeli court, since it would have to compare the nonprosecution of Israeli soldiers for 'targeted killing' with the prosecution of Barghouti for terrorist attacks. Moreover, since the defense amounts to a "bar to trial," the more horrendous the crime, the less likely it is that the court will stay the proceedings (balance between fairness to defendant versus public security).[67] These difficulties seem to make the "abuse of power" defense in the Barghouti case into a theoretical possibility at best.

The hypothetical attempt to apply the "abuse of process" defense to our cases clearly shows its limitations, which can be attributed to its explicit character. Although this defense allows the claim of discrimination to be directly addressed, and the court's decision to acquit or to stay the process on the basis of discrimination has the potential of creating incentives to the prosecution to apply the criminal law in a more equal and universal manner, the obstacles nevertheless seem to outweigh the benefits. The very fact that domestic courts tend to apply the "abuse of process" defense only on rare occasions and under stringent conditions reveals their difficulty in intervening in such cases, especially with regard to serious crimes. Moreover, since cases of radical difference implicate the court as well as the prosecution, asking the court to recognize the "abuse of process" defense requires it to make a statement about the structural bias of the legal system to which the court has contributed. Finally, the defense of abuse of process places the court in direct confrontation with the executive, and could undermine the legitimacy of the court in the eyes of large sectors of its domestic public.[68]

The "abuse of process" mechanism offers only a partial solution, as it raises another problem—that of the court's own legitimacy. Once the court begins to openly deliberate questions of group discrimination, for example having to compare between Palestinian leaders (who are indicted) and the settlers' political leaders (who aren't), or between Palestinian terror attacks on civilians and the policy of "target killing" by the Israeli Army (with civilians killed as "collateral damage"), the court is bound to lose its legitimate status in the eyes of the broad Israeli public. I therefore turn in the following section to consider an alternative to this explicit review, based on the Anglo American practice of jury nullification.

Jury Nullification

"Jury nullification" has been practiced in English and American courts for hundreds of years, but it has been on the decline since the nineteenth century.[69] Even though this solution is purely theoretical in Israel, which does not have a jury system,[70] it is an interesting option to consider, since it tackles the problem of the community basis of the criminal trial from the opposite direction. We saw that the "abuse of process" defense requires that the court explicitly engage the constitutional issue of equal enforcement of the law, and in cases of accepting the defense, provide an elaborate justification. Jury nullification, on the other hand, is recognized only implicitly, as it is not a recognized right. This practice has not been acknowledged or justified in the open court and therefore its scope remains ambiguous and uncertain. While "abuse of process" is practiced in the light of day and vigorously scrutinized and reviewed by the Supreme Court, jury nullification needs the dark of night and at most, is silently recognized. For this reason the two solutions offer a strong analogy to the constitutional framework that contrasts the "explicit discretion" approach and the "passive virtues" approach to the problem of the political question.

Jury nullification is a controversial doctrine that recognizes that jurors have the right (or enjoy the power) to refuse to enforce the law against defendants whom they believe in good conscience should be acquitted. They can acquit defendants for conduct that formally falls under a criminal prohibition and does not enjoy any recognized defense. This power was first recognized in 1670 in England, following the refusal of a jury to convict two religious leaders of the Quaker movement (William Penn and William Mead) for unlawful assembly and breach of the peace. After the court fined the jury, one of the jurors, Edward Bushel, refused to pay the fine, was imprisoned, and appealed. This appeal changed the course of jury history. In a landmark decision the appellate court ruled that jurors might never be fined or imprisoned for their verdicts.[71] This meant a de facto recognition of the power of jurors to acquit on grounds other than the existing law. However, the practice has not been recognized as a right of the jury, and its current power comes from the fact that under American law there can be no appeal on jury acquittals (on the basis of the constitutional guarantee against double jeopardy). Thus it has become a corrective device to the criminal system. Jury nullification bears special importance in cases that reflect an unresolved clash of values within society, when criminal defendants rely on their oppositional value system that collides with the one expressed by the law. Modern examples are the legality of abortions, the illegality of mercy killing, the illegality of drug use, and so forth.[72] Jury nullification in such cases can be viewed as an extension of civil disobedience, since it invites the jury not to punish what they believe to be justified acts of lawbreaking. But it can also be exercised as a protest against an unequal and discriminatory application of the laws over certain classes of people in society.[73] The danger in jury nullification results from its unaccountability. Juries might, and often did, resort to this practice not just to enhance noble causes but also out of various prejudices (racism, sexism and the like).[74]

Since jury nullification has not been recognized as a right (but only as a power), and since juries do not provide reasoning for their verdicts, the practice amounts to an implicit power of abstention from applying the law. Judges cannot instruct juries to exercise their power of nullification, since it is not a right. Indeed, much of the current debate about the practice revolves around the formal issue of whether to instruct or not.[75] This debate touches on the question that interests us here—what form constitutional deliberations should take in the criminal process: explicit or implicit.

Israeli scholar Amnon Lehavi argues that the power of jury nullification lies in its secrecy, which enables it to ameliorate injustices inherent to the criminal system without undermining the integrity of the court and without creating bad precedents.[76] The tool of jury nullification is regarded as "just" as long as it remains "silent"—that is, as long as the jurors' opinions are unanimous, as long as their discussion is held behind closed doors, and their considerations remain concealed. Practically, this means not knowing when exactly the jury has used the power of nullification and when it is actually convinced that the accusation is unfounded. In this manner, jury nullification upholds the formal commitment of criminal law to the exclusion of political motive from its deliberation, and simultaneously enables the court to reach a "just" result based on these considerations. In other words, the secretive nature of the practice enhances the legitimacy of the trial by preventing an unjust result without forcing the judge to distort the law for that purpose. According to this analysis jury nullification offers a way to protect the integrity of the system, while correcting local injustices to specific defendants. This solution is a manifestation of a broader structure of the criminal law that has been previously identified by Meir Dan Cohen as "acoustic separation." The idea is to allow both the affirmation of the rule of law and the needed deviation from the law in cases of gross injustice. Such devices help the court achieve conflicting goals of the criminal law.[77]

The question is whether this mechanism is suited only to correcting individual cases of injustice, or whether it should be used to correct "structural" problems stemming from racism, sexism, and other biases in the implementation of the criminal law such as in cases of "radical difference." For example, when criminal law definition of "self-defense" does not encompass the needs and life-experiences of battered women, should we put our hopes in jury nullification as a corrective mechanism? Or, when the criminal system is biased against one class of defendants who belong to a certain minority, should we resort to jury nullification as a corrective device? This question leads us back to an important role that jury nullification played in the past as a check against political trials. Indeed, several participants in the current debate argue that the jury should be informed of their historical role as "value" articulators of the community, a role that goes beyond and above their fact-finding role recognized today.[78] Lehavi takes a strong position against this approach. He argues that given its delicate mechanism of "secrecy and harmony," jury nullification can only work to ameliorate individual injustices. Any attempt to enlarge its scope to address structural bias against minority groups poses grave risks to the integrity of the criminal system, and is likely to produce more harm than good (as the case of O. J. Simpson demonstrates).[79]

I agree with the diagnosis (that the power of jury nullification lies in its secrecy) but do not agree with the prescription (against applying it as a check in political trials). My reasons can become clearer if we compare "jury nullification" to the "abuse of process" defense. Both doctrines offer opposite directions for tackling structural problems that are typical in cases of "radical difference." I suggested that the problem of legitimacy faced by the court in such cases is the result of a lacuna in criminal law adjudication—the lack of discretionary tools for addressing the political question. In other words, the problem does not lie in the substance of the accusations, but in the constitutional framework of the trial. Both approaches are meant to infuse the court with discretion to address the constitutional structure, either explicitly or implicitly. Here we can see the relative advantage of the "jury nullification" mechanism over the "abuse of process" defense. Since the latter requires that the court justifies its decision explicitly and therefore puts the court in direct conflict with the political authorities, the court is likely to narrow down its scope, thus avoiding dealing with the most difficult cases of radical difference. In contrast, jury nullification allows the court to reach the same result of avoiding ruling on the merit, without explicitly condemning the executive policy of unequal enforcement of the law. This said, I agree that jury nullification is unlikely to work in cases where it is most needed—namely, where the democratic system suffers from endemic problems of democratic participation.

The history of the jury shows that although its conception and roles have changed over time, the jury has consistently been perceived as being connected to a concept of participatory democracy (either active participation in the shaping of a community's laws, or more passive participation in restraining the power of nonelected judges). The jury represents a popular instinctive justice, the "conscience of the community," and can thus contribute to the legitimacy of the criminal trial by implementing the widely agreed values of the community.[80] Thus, the power of jury nullification to remedy the problem of legitimacy in political trials derives not from the jury's "expertise" in the law or from its special capacity to determine the facts, but from its perceived connection to a political community. As the notion of "community" has changed in modern times from homogeneity to heterogeneity, the belief in the jury as the articulator of common values of society has been abandoned. However, the jury can still help connect criminal law to a political community by serving as a negative check against abuse of power by prosecutors or judges. Although the practice of jury nullification can cause havoc to all attempts of systematization and harmonization of the laws, it is "tolerated" precisely because it preserves the connection between criminal law and a living community.[81] It thus fulfills the promise of "self-rule" vis-à-vis the most feared aspect of sovereignty—relinquishing the monopoly over violence to state officials. As a corrective device it reflects a democratic suspicion of "perfect laws" or "perfect judges" as sufficient in and of themselves to protect the liberties of the people in whose name the laws were legislated.

Having recognized this modern reason for acknowledging the power of jury nullification, it seems unjustified to limit it to instances of "individual injustice." Rather, we should see jury nullification as capable of ameliorating also structural biases that are endemic to a heterogeneous society. Juries from local communities can offer a check on discrimination and unequal enforcement of the law over minority groups. However, this also suggests the limits of such a corrective mechanism. It can work only when some kind of political representation and participation is given to a minority group. In situations of military occupation this condition cannot work and hence the practice loses its corrective function. Under such conditions, it is left to the court to exercise review over the constitutional foundation of the criminal law.

In this essay I cannot offer a definite answer to the question of which tool, jury nullification or abuse of process defense, is better suited to deal with situations of "radical difference," but I maintain that without some kind of check over the equal enforcement of the criminal law, terror trials in domestic courts will lose their legitimacy. Adopting a mechanism to address these problem into the process of criminal law is essential to address the problems of politicization created by such trials. [82]

How does this analysis bear on the Barghouti and Bishara cases? The practice of "jury nullification" points to an essential difference between the cases that is related to the factor of community. The Bishara case exposes the discord between two communities: within the Israeli polity, the majority community of Jews, and the minority community of Arabs. Although both communities are part of a larger civil community, Israel's Basic Laws endorse a specific conception of the state (Jewish and democratic) that is tilted toward the majority community, thus creating a tension that is exacerbated when it is translated into provisions of the criminal code.[83] An amendment from 1995 that proscribed incitement to violence or terror (art. 144d2) remained neutral between the two communities. However, Bishara argued that it was applied unequally to leaders of the two communities. The case was adjudicated by the Nazareth district court, the domicile of Bishara.[84] If Israel had a jury system, a jury constituted of the inhabitants of the district of Nazareth might have had a good chance of nullifying the verdict as an act of protest against state discrimination against Arab leaders by means of political prosecutions. This is all hypothetical, but given the history of African American discrimination by the criminal law system in the United States, analogies to cases of jury nullification there could be telling.[85] The need to enhance the legitimacy of courts in criminal cases bearing on internal Jewish conflicts has been also acknowledged by Israeli legal system by appointing "representative" judges in political trials that dealt with defendants from various Jewish minority groups.[86] Of course, this midway solution (between professional judges and jury system) is more cosmetic than real, given the centralized structure of the court system in Israel. But it points to a growing understanding of the problem in terms of equal representation. Adopting the jury system in Israel would bring some of the risks of the practice (judging according to local prejudices) as well as some of its advantages (infusing the legal system with local community values). In either case it could have introduced a check on political persecution of Arab Israeli leaders and to mitigated their political overtones.

The Barghouti case, by contrast, is unlikely to benefit from a hypothetical adoption of a jury system in Israel. Under the current political conditions of Israeli occupation over Palestinian land, and terror attacks of Palestinian organizations against Israeli citizens, it is hard to find a jury that can remain neutral. In an explosive political case such as the Barghouti case any Israeli jury would most likely be susceptible to the general public mood and conform to the conception of the political authorities. Moreover, a jury system embodies a conception of participatory democracy, while Palestinians under Israeli occupation are not citizens of Israel and thus do not enjoy even the elementary right to vote for the Knesset, let alone the right to participate in our hypothetical jury. Hence, the systemic bias of the trial can hardly be corrected by exposing it to a jury of Israeli citizens. Nevertheless, our hypothetical experiment shows that the problem lies not in the attempt to bring Barghouti to a criminal trial, but in the weak constitutional basis of the trial. The exclusion of the political motive as irrelevant to a criminal trial, combined with the exclusion of the group represented by the defendant from any participation in the democratic process in Israel, creates a structural bias against him. This problem is unlikely to be identified, let alone addressed, within the current structure of criminal law. The two legal mechanisms that I have explored as a way to address the problem also point to the source of the problem as lying in the larger political context of democratic participation. Thus, they expose the connection of criminal law to a conception of democratic participation as the main source of legitimacy for the court, a connection that a formalist understanding of jurisdiction tends to overlook.

From Hypothetical Trials to Real Trials

Given the very limited margins of maneuver enjoyed by the criminal court and the lack of direct doctrines to address the political bias of the trials, what were the solutions adopted by the Israeli court? In particular, how did it try to walk the fine line between legality and legitimacy? We can identify two distinct approaches. The Barghouti trial court rejected the claims against its jurisdiction and was thus left only with the interpretive tools of substantive criminal law to balance the political overtone of the case of the prosecution. The Bishara trial court proceeded in a similar manner until it was barred by the intervention of the High Court of Justice, which accepted Bishara's argument of parliamentary immunity and barred the trial against him. These two opposite approaches require some clarification because they do not accord with what we would expect in cases of "radical difference"—that the more radical the "difference," the less inclined the court will be to judge on the merit and will try to resort to the "passive virtues" of avoidance in order to protect its own legitimacy. My explanation is that lacking discretionary tools to confront the political question, the different results of the two cases reflect the different circumstances of the two cases. The Bishara court could rely on the constitutional tools provided by the law of parliamentary immunity and thus avoid direct confrontation with the political authorities, while the Barghouti court had no such tools at its disposal. It is interesting that the Barghouti court did attempt to "control" the damage with the only tools available to it—tools of legal interpretation—but these tools were ill fitted to addressing the problem of legitimacy. Having come to this point, let me summarize briefly the results of the two trials.

The Barghouti Trial

We have seen that the prosecution had the choice between conducting a criminal trial in the civil courts or relegating the case to military courts. In order to gain legitimacy in the eyes of the international community, and in order to strip Barghouti of his political pretensions in the eyes of segments of the Israeli public, it opted to conduct an ordinary criminal trial. However, in order to convict him of murder on the basis of speeches and the supply of finance and weapons, the law of criminal partnership had to be greatly expanded. Indeed, Barghouti was charged with thirty-seven counts of murder based on his general support of terror attacks through speeches and supply of weapons. The Israeli prosecution argued that since Barghouti advocated and supported the *Intifada*, any terror attack by his group could be attributed to him. The court decided to reject this grand conception of the trial promoted by the prosecution, which sought to build a case similar to the Eichmann trial in which the defendant is found guilty for all the acts committed by subordinate members of his organization. The political need to make Barghouti into an ordinary criminal threatened a cornerstone of Israeli criminal law—individual responsibility. In order to convict Barghouti the court would have had to erase the distinction between principal actor and accomplice, between political speeches and criminal actions. The judges therefore dismissed thirty-three of the thirty-seven counts of murder and found him guilty only in four instances where his direct involvement could be proven. The court explained that political speech encouraging military resistance, or the supply of finances or weapons to the terrorists, did not constitute participation in murder.[87] In terms of criminal law this was a legal victory for the prosecution, since Barghouti was convicted of four counts of murder. In terms of politics, however, the Israeli authorities failed to criminalize the political leadership of the Palestinian people for abandoning the Oslo agreements in favor of violent resistance. However, this did not help Barghouti to change Israeli public opinion. Lacking a legal channel to raise his concerns about the politicization of the trial, he was perceived by the Israeli public as a terrorist, a common criminal. The trial, however, carried the opposite effect on the Palestinian public, who saw Barghouti as a persecuted political leader.[88] Thus, the bifurcated perceptions of the trial manifest the condition of "radical difference" that was only enhanced by conducting a criminal trial.[89] As of 2010,

Barghouti is still arrested. The Palestinians often compare him to Nelson Mandela, and his popularity and influence has only increased since the trial in the eyes of his own people. In the elections that were conducted in August 2009, Barghouti was elected a member of the central committee of Fatah.

The Bishara Trial

To repeat the main facts of the criminal case against Bishara: On November 7, 2001, the Knesset voted to lift Bishara's parliamentary immunity, and on November 12, 2001, the attorney general filed two indictments against him. The first indictment charged Bishara with violating the Prevention of Terror Ordinance [1948] in two public speeches he had made, one in the city of Umm al-Fahem on June 5, 2000, and the other in Kardaha, Syria, on June 10, 2001, at a memorial service marking the first anniversary of President Hafez al-Assad's death, which had been attended by leaders of the Hizballah Party. The indictment claimed that Bishara's speeches were a call to commit terrorist acts against Israelis. He was indicted for supporting a terrorist organization.

We have seen that Bishara based his defense on the preliminary argument of parliamentary immunity. After the trial court decided to postpone the decision on this issue to the end of the trial, Bishara petitioned the Supreme Court, which, in its decision of February 1, 2006 (in a majority of 2:1) granted his petition and barred the criminal proceedings against him.[90] In deciding the case the justices considered the impact of their decision on the constitutional structure of Israeli democracy, in particular the relation between the criminal proscription against incitement to violence and support of terrorist attacks and the protection of political speech. The court relied heavily on its prior decision to annul the decision of the Election Committee to disqualify Bishara's party from participating in the elections because of its platform of transforming Israel into "a state of all its citizens." The Supreme Court did not see this policy as contradicting the Basic Law of the Knesset that declares Israel to be a "Jewish and democratic" state. In our case the Supreme Court decided to go a step further and to recognize the application of parliamentary immunity to speeches that seem to fall under the criminal proscription against incitement to violence and terror. In both these decisions the court struggled to uphold the distinction between protecting political speeches while not endorsing the content of the speech. The court expanded the protection granted to elected representatives of the Arab citizens in order to allow them to continue to criticize the fundamental values of the polity without fearing criminal prosecution. The constitutional value of equal opportunity for political representation seems to outweigh the value of the rule of law.[91]

The decision of the Supreme Court reflected the need to find a way to infuse the criminal process with tools of constitutional discretion. Since Bishara was an MK, the court could rely on the availability of such a tool. It offered a third way for the court between acquittal and conviction—one that addresses the constitutional problematic of the criminal prosecution without deciding on the merits of the case.[92] The "passive virtues" solution, which was available only to Bishara through the parliamentary immunity channel, highlights the urgent need to create such constitutional tools for the criminal court in its jurisprudence of terror.

On April 8, 2007, it became public that Bishara had left Israel. On May 2 it became known that another criminal investigation had been carried against him for allegedly contacting a Hizballah agent and supplying information that could risk Israeli security interests and receiving in return money. In a newspaper interview Bishara claimed that this investigation amounted to political persecution, as he was conducting friendly conversations discussing the common knowledge that Hizballah's missiles hit Arab villages in the north of Israel. Nevertheless, Bishara decided to leave the country instead of having to face the possibility of a criminal trial about charges of espionage.

The two Palestinian leaders, the Stranger within, had become a criminal prisoner and a fugitive from the law; Israeli society was far from facing the challenge of treating the "stranger within" as an equal. Using the criminal law had a direct effect on limiting the boundaries of political discourse in Israel.

Epilogue

Our journey has brought us a long way. We witnessed the crisis of legitimacy faced today by criminal law given its systemic failure to adjudicate on equal terms crimes such as "crimes against humanity" and "war crimes." Our cases focused on the danger of selective prosecution of one side to a violent political conflict via the criminalization of terror. We identified the double function of such trials—convicting the criminal, while depoliticizing his or her actions—which makes these trials vulnerable to the dangers of the political trial (advancing a political agenda under the guise of law). I argued that the sources of this problem lie in the situation of "radical difference" and the inability of the criminal law to remain reflective about its own inability to overcome such biases.

Our theoretical examination helped expose a lacuna in the heart of criminal law—the lack of formal ways to raise concerns about the universal application of the law in an unbiased manner toward different groups. This lacuna is made all the more problematic in the age of "terror trials" conducted by national criminal courts. In the absence of legal venues to address these concerns, the legitimacy of these trials is undermined in the eyes of the international community, and by groups identified with the defendant. Parallel to this development we witness the growth of third party courts exercising universal jurisdiction over "war crimes" and "crimes against humanity," thus piercing the shield of sovereignty and advancing a regime of accountability. One might say that the two developments should be understood together—as balancing each other, and correcting structural biases in the system of national criminal law. Elsewhere I have argued that universal jurisdiction cannot really fix the problems of politicization in international law, and in many cases it might increase these problems. In this essay I therefore turned to explore the road of "terror trials"—trying to see if there exist internal mechanisms that can control the inherent political bias of such trials. I looked at ways to supply domestic courts with improved legal tools to review the political question. The two "tools" I examined: the defense of "abuse of power" and "jury nullification" were found wanting precisely in cases where the community basis of the criminal law is undermined by the systematic exclusion of the defendant and his group from equal participation in the political process. However, as a heuristic exercise, our investigation can help us identify the crisis of legitimacy that criminal law is now facing and to find its source in the organizing principle of modern criminal law—the principle of territoriality. This organizing principle found its expression in the principle of territorial jurisdiction, which set a bright line limit to the reach of criminal law. This principle has been undermined from without (universal jurisdiction) and from within (terror trials), and a new balance has to be found that will help reconnect the criminal law to the community that is its subject.

Let me conclude by relating to an academic debate between Alan Norrie and Anthony Duff regarding the ability of criminal law to stand up to its liberal values. Norrie criticizes liberal criminal law for containing a fundamental contradiction that cannot be resolved. On the one hand, the law is committed to the establishment of individual guilt as a condition for criminal liability. On the other, criminal law removes the motive from the trial deliberation and thereby expresses its unwillingness to distinguish between categories of individual guilt. Particularly troubling is the exclusion of "political motive." Norrie claims that while the liberal legal system is committed to the principle of individual guilt, it nonetheless discounts completely subjective motives that have direct ramifications for the moral guilt of the accused. This inconsistency, he claims, is intrinsic to the liberal legal system, which is obliged to ignore political/ideological motives but cannot admit to this.[93]

Duff responds that Norrie does not succeed in showing such a fundamental contradiction in the liberal legal system, since he overlooks important distinctions in criminal law.[94] Criminal law does not ignore the subjective motive. Rather, it distinguishes between the role of the legislator and that of the judiciary: the legislator decides which among the possible motives is relevant, and the judge applies this determination. As long as the democratic system functions, all citizens in the community must accept these decisions. In grounding his thesis, Duff rejects outright the radical subjective approach to criminal law. The law's commitment is to arbitration according to the defendant's understanding of the facts, not according to his or her value system. In order to establish subjective guilt on the basis of a community's value system, it is sufficient under criminal law that the defendant could have understood the community's values even though he or she preferred his or her own values.

This response in fact rests on a theory of political legitimacy. It is the role of the legislator and not the (nonelected) court to determine the values according to which we assess the defendant's actions. Duff emphasizes that the criminal law is the law of the community—the values of the community are channeled to the law by way of the elected legislative body. The judiciary must implement these values, and as long as the democratic process functions—whereby the political opposition can present its alternative values—the criminal law (with its value system) legitimately applies to all members of the polity.

This short exchange can cast light on our two cases. I argued that it is precisely this kind of sensibility that directed the Supreme Court to grant Bishara's petition and bar his criminal prosecution. The exclusion of political motive from criminal law is premised on the working of the larger democratic structure—the legislature's ability to deliberate the distinction between different political motives. However, if the court had removed Bishara's immunity in the hard case of political speech in support of the Palestinian *Intifada* (the right of violent resistance to military occupation), it would have undermined the very legitimacy of applying the criminal law to cases of incitement to violence and support of terror. Another way to look at it is in terms of equal membership in a political community. The legitimacy of applying the criminal law to members of the territorial community is based on the premise of a working democracy. The decision of the Supreme Court in Bishara's case concerned the problem of how to draw the boundaries of the political community in a way that will legitimize the exercise of criminal law over a deeply divided society. The Barghouti court, on the other hand, could only restrict the political overtones of the trial, but it could not resist the very act of using the criminal law to redefine a political adversary as a criminal, a stranger to Israeli political community of discourse.

Notes

Assistant Professor, Tel Aviv Law Faculty. Thanks to Hanoch Dagan, Tali Fisher, Daphne Barak Erez, and Kenneth Mann for their comments on earlier drafts; and to Inbal Djalovski, Magi Ostri, Avi Lubin, Michal Saliternik and Rivka Brot for their help in research. I would like to thank the Minerva Center for Human Rights and the Cegla Center for Interdisciplinary Research of the Law in the Buchman Faculty of Law at Tel Aviv University for their generous financial support.

1. See exchange between Antony Duff and Alan Norrie. Alan Norrie, *Crime, Reason and History: A Critical Introduction to Criminal Law,* 2d ed. (London: Butterworths, 2001), 35; Anthony Duff, "Principle and Contradiction in the Criminal Law: Motives and Criminal Liability," in *Philosophy and the Criminal Law: Principle and Critique,* ed. Antony Duff (Cambridge: Cambridge University Press, 1998), 176, 179–84.

2. I developed a theoretical model for such a role in my book, Leora Bilsky, *Transformative Justice: Israeli Identity on Trial* (Ann Arbor: University of Michigan Press, 2004).

3. James Boyd White, *Justice as Translation: An Essay in Cultural and Legal Criticism* (Chicago: University of Chicago Press, 1990).

4. Otto Kirchheimer, *Political Justice: The Use of Legal Procedure for Political Ends*

(Princeton: Princeton University Press, 1961); Judith N. Shklar, *Legalism* (Cambridge: Harvard University Press, 1964); Lawrence Douglas, *The Memory of Judgment: Making Law and History in the Trials of the Holocaust* (New Haven: Yale University Press, 2001); Mark Osiel, *Mass Atrocity, Collective Memory, and the Law* (New Brunswick, NJ: Transaction Publishers, 1997), Ruti G. Teitel, *Transitional Justice* (Oxford: Oxford University Press, 2000).

5. Alexander M. Bickel, *The Least Dangerous Branch: The Supreme Court at the Bar of Politics* (Indianapolis: Bobbs-Merrill, 1962): 111–98.

6. Douglas E. Beloof, *Victims in Criminal Procedure* (Durham, NC: Carolina Academic Press, 1999).

7. HCJ 7052/03 Adalah—*The Legal Center for Arab Minority Rights in Israel v. The Minister of Interior,* PADOR [Hebrew data base] 217 (10) 06.(2006) [Hebrew]. The petitions demanded the annulment of the Nationality and Entry into Israel Law (Temporary Order) 2003. A 6–5 Majority of the Supreme Court approved the law.

8. Bruce Ackerman, *Before the Next Attack: Preserving Civil Liberties in an Age of Terrorism* (London: Yale University Press, 2007). Ackerman opposes the resort to criminal law in addressing the problem of terrorism because the terrorist threatens the effective sovereignty of the state while the criminal law presupposes it (pp. 43–44). I agree with Ackermann's diagnosis, but do not accept his prognosis of designing an "emergency constitution," since I do not think terror can be simply moved into a discrete category neatly separated from ordinary criminal law cases, as the Barghouti and Bishara cases demonstrate. Ackerman concedes that indeed the Palestinian uprising demonstrates this difficulty (p. 185 fn 28).

9. Although it is understood that the very issue of jurisdiction of the court is a constitutional matter, once decided by the legislative body, the role of the court is viewed as one of application. My view is that the community basis of criminal law cannot be reduced to questions of jurisdiction, and it is often this reduction that does not allow us to see the constitutional role of the judges conducting criminal trials against alleged terrorists. For debate in Israel regarding the scope of jurisdiction and its larger implications for the concept of sovereignty, see Yoram Schachar, "Against Extra-Territorial Application of Criminal Law on National Grounds," *Plilim: Israel Journal of Criminal Justice* 5, no. 1 (1996): 5–64; and Shneor Zalman Feller and Mordechai Kremnizer, "Reply to Yoram Schachar," in ibid.: 65–99 [Hebrew]; in the U.S., see Ronald Dworkin "What the Court Really Said," *New York Review of Books* 51, no. 13 (August 2004) (discussing recent terror trials in the United States: *Rumsfeld v. Padilla,* 542 U.S. 426 [2004]; *Rasul v. Bush,* 542 U.S. 466 [2004]; *Hamdi v. Rumsfeld,* 542 U.S. 507 [2004]). Dworkin recognizes the political aspects of jurisdiction issues and suggests that the jurisdictional rule that aims to discourage "forum shopping" should apply not only to defendants but also to the government.

10. Ackerman, *Before the Next Attack*, 24–38. Ackerman believes that the abandonment of criminal law in the cases of Hamdi and Padlila (U.S. citizens who were denied a trial by jury, since the American authorities saw them as falling under the rubric of "war on terror" and not "criminal law") demonstrates the real danger that "war against terror" poses to civil liberties in the United States, but he also argues that the traditionalist attempt to view these cases as falling easily into domestic criminal law is misguided. He therefore suggests that a constitutional change is due, but it should not be "judges made." In contrast, I call to recognize the court's constitutional role in such trials. One important aspect of how such awareness can shape the court's response is revealed in the decision of the British House of Lords in December 2005 to strike down antiterrorist legislation that authorized the government to detain aliens (and not citizens) for indefinite periods without trial (*A and Others v. Secretary of State for the Home Department*, UKHL 56 [2005] AC 68).

11. Martin M. Shapiro, *Courts: A Comparative and Political Analysis* (Chicago: University of Chicago Press, 1981).

12. Cr.C. (Nazareth) 1087/02 *The State of Israel v. Bishara* (unpublished, on file with author) [Hebrew]; H.C.J. 11225/03 *Mk Dr. Azmi Bishara v. The Attorney General*, PADOR 294 (3) 06 (2006) [Hebrew].

13. S.C.C. 1158/02 (Tel Aviv) *The State of Israel v. Marwan Barghouti*, PADOR 664 (4) 04 (2004) [Hebrew].

14. Although in the Bishara case the military court was not an option since he is a citizen of Israel, a security investigation by the security forces was feasible under certain conditions. The decision to bring a Knesset member to face criminal charges for political speeches marked the irregularity of this case. The decision to conduct a criminal trial to Barghouti in an Israeli civil court instead of a military court, stood out against a policy of turning away from the court system. Such was the assassination of Sheikh Yassin and the general policy of target killing, administrative detentions, and military trials against Palestinians suspected of involvement with terror. The decision to conduct an ordinary criminal trial against Barghouti can be explained as an attempt by the Israeli general prosecution to gain legitimacy in the international community. See Amos Harel and Avi Isacharoff, *The Seventh War* (Tel Aviv: Miskal, 2004): 163 fn 60 [Hebrew].

15. The outbreak of the second *Intifada* in October 2000 signified the eginning of the use of overt violence by and against Arab citizens of Israel on the grounds of their alleged support of the Palestinian struggle. During the first week of October 2000, thirteen Israeli Arabs who participated in violent demonstrations against the Israeli government were killed by the Israeli police forces, and many other demonstrators were injured and detained. According to an official report of the Israeli government, more than 200 Israeli Arabs were involved (most of them in cooperation with Palestinian organizations) in the execution of terrorist attacks during the first four years of the conflict (a

summary of the report can be found at http://www.intelligence.org.il/sp/pa_t/i_a.htm [Hebrew]).

16. Until their trials both Bishara and Barghouti were considered by the Israeli mainstream as political adversaries who are legitimate members of a larger discourse community of Israelis and Palestinians. The change in their image can be noticed when we follow the reports in the Israeli daily *Ha'aretz* about the two leaders. See, for example: Lili Galili, 23.04.96; Gideon Alon, 22.10.01; Shaul Seter, 22.3.06 (regarding Bishara); and Amira Hess, 23.1.02; Vered Levi-Barzilai, 3.5.02; Shamay Leibovich, 29.9.02 (regarding Barghouti).

17. See report of the Israeli Association for Civil Rights (ACRI) on discrimination of Arabs in the Israeli criminal system, from December 1999. Summary can be found at http://www.acri.org.il/hebrew-acri/engine/story.asp?id=306.

18. In the Bishara case the charges were based on article 4 of the Prevention of Terror Ordinance (1948): "4. A person who (a) publishes, in writing or orally, words of praise, sympathy or encouragement for acts of violence calculated to cause death or injury to a person . . . or (b) publishes, in writing or orally, words of praise or sympathy for or an appeal for aid or support of a terrorist organization; or (c) has propaganda material in his possession on behalf of a terrorist organization; . . . shall be guilty of an offence and shall be liable on conviction to imprisonment for a term not exceeding three years or to a fine not exceeding one thousand shekels or to both such penalties." Barghouti was charged with murder and with conspiracy to murder on the basis of article 300(a)(2) (combined with articles 30–31) and article 499 of Penal Law 5737-1977. He was also charged on the basis of article 2 and 3 of the Prevention of Terror Ordinance (1948).

19. Basic Law: Human Dignity and Freedom (1992), article 1a (1992) S.H. [Sefer Ha-hukim, Israel formal laws publishing, Hebrew] 1392 at 150; Basic Law: Freedom of Occupation (1994), article 2 (1994) S.H.454 at 90; Basic Law: The Knesset (1950), article 7a(a)(1) (1985) S.H. 1155 at 196. For elaboration on Bishara's political views regarding the state of Israel, see Amal Jamal, "The Vision of the Political Nation and the Challenge of a State of All Its Citizens, Reflections on Azmi Bihara's Writings," *Alpayim* 30 (2006): 71–113 [Hebrew]; for a different view of Bishara's vision of a "state of all its citizens," see Dan Shiftan, "The New Identity of Arab Knesset Members," *Azure* 13 (Fall 2003): 23 [Hebrew].

20. Barghouti was advancing an interpretation of international law that is contested as is explained by the court decision. International law has recognized the resort to force against a colonial power as not merely an internal matter. The Consensus Definition of Aggression (1974), which was adopted by the UN General Assembly, presented in article 7 the right of people entitled to but forcibly deprived of the right to self-determination, "to struggle to that end and to seek and receive support, in accordance with the prin-

ciples of the Charter and in conformity with the 197 Declaration." See Malcolm N. Shaw, *International Law,* 5th ed. (Cambridge: Cambridge University Press, 2003), 1036–39. UN General Assembly Resolution 3314 (XXIX). Definition of Aggression [http://jurist.law.pitt.edu/3314.htm].

21. However, see the decision of the Central Election Committee to ban Bishara's party, the NDA (National Democratic Assembly), from participating in the 2003 general elections because its policy of turning Israel into "a state of all its citizens" seemingly clashed with article 7a of Basic Law: The Knesset. This decision was overturned by the Supreme Court, Election Confirmation 11280/02 *The Central Elections Committee v. MK Tibi,* 57(4) P.D. 1 (2003). The court gave a narrow interpretation to article 7a of Basic Law: The Knesset that enables its elections committee to ban a party that denies the existence of the State of Israel as a Jewish and democratic state or supports terror activities from participating in elections. According to the court's interpretation there should be solid evidence that the party was taking actual, forceful steps to turn its ideas into reality.

22. Knesset Members Immunity, Rights and Duties Law, 5711-1951. Article 4(a) states that "a Knesset member shall not stand criminal charges for a crime committed while or before becoming a Knesset member, unless his immunity is first removed." The court ruled that the purpose of this procedural immunity is to ensure the proper working of the Knesset and to protect against the persecution of Knesset members by the government for political motives (H.C.J. 507/81, *Abu Hatzira et al. v. The Attorney General et al.,* 35(4) P.D. 561, 568).

23. See "H.C.J. 11225/03 *MK Dr. Azmi Bishara v. The Attorney General.*" A summary of the claims posed by the petitioner is available at http://www.adalah.org/eng/legaladvocacypolitical.php#11225.

24. George Fletcher, "Liberals and Romantics at War: The Problem of Collective Guilt," *Yale Law Journal* 111 (2002): 1499, 1518.

25. Kirchheimer, *Political Justice.*

26. For elaboration on the triangular structure of the trial as a basis for its legitimacy, see Shapiro, *Courts.*

27. In legal terms international law recognizes five bases for jurisdiction (the territorial principle, the nationality principle, the protective principle, the passive personality, and the universality principle). See Steven R. Ratner and Jason S. Abrams, *Accountability for Human Rights Atrocities in International Law: Beyond the Nuremberg Legacy* (Oxford: Clarendon Press, 1997): 140–41. For our purposes I generalized these doctrines according to their constitutive elements in order to distill the element of community that lies behind them.

28. It has other manifestations, such as the right to jury trial in criminal law cases. For elaboration of this aspect of the jury system and for its history in English law, see

Thomas Andrew Green, *Verdict according to Conscience: Perspectives on the English Criminal Trial Jury, 1200–1800* (Chicago: University of Chicago Press, 1985).

29. For a different conception during the Middle Ages that linked criminal law to a community of people rather than territory, see Marian Constable, *The Law of the Other: The Mixed Jury and the Changing Conceptions of Citizenship, Law and Knowledge* (Chicago: University of Chicago Press, 1994).

30. The question of how universal jurisdiction fundamentally changes the relations between law, tribunal, and community deserves a separate discussion. In my view the move of cases of "radical difference" to third party courts practicing universal jurisprudence does not necessarily solve the problems of politicization. See Bilsky, *The Eichmann Trial and the Legacy of Jurisdiction, in Politics in Dark Times: Encounters with Hannah Arendt,* ed. Seyla Benhabib, Cambridge University Press, forthcoming. Some writers have been raising the problem by pointing to the democratic deficit of universal jurisdiction trials. See Seyla Benhabib, "Reclaiming Universalism: Negotiating Republican Self-Determination and Cosmopolitan Norms," the Tanner Lectures on Human Values (delivered at the University of California at Berkley, March 2004), available at http://www.tannerlectures.utah.edu/lectures/documents/volume25/benhabib_2005.pdf; Benhabib, *The Rights of Others: Aliens, Residents, and Citizens* (Cambridge University Press, 2004); Diane F. Orentlicher, "Whose Justice? Reconciling Universal Jurisdiction with Democratic Principles," *Georgetown Law Journal* 92 (2004): 1057; John B. Jordan, "Universal Jurisdiction in a Dangerous World: A Weapon for All Nations against International Crime," *MSU-DCL Journal of International Law* 9, no. 1 (2000): 1. For criticism of some of the shortcomings of universal jurisdiction, see Fletcher, "Against Universal Jurisdiction," *Journal of International Criminal Justice* 1 (2003): 580–84; Anthony Sammons, "The 'Under-Theorization' of Universal Jurisdiction: Implications for Legitimacy on Trials of War Criminals by National Courts," *Berkeley Journal of International Law* 21 (2003): 111; Madeline H. Morris, "Universal Jurisdiction in a Divided World: Conference Remarks," *New England Law Review* 35 (2001): 337, 342; Henry A. Kissinger, "The Pitfalls of Universal Jurisdiction: Risking Judicial Tyranny," *Foreign Affairs* 80 (2001): 86.

31. C.C. (Nazareth) 1087/02 *The State of Israel v. Bishara* (decision of November 12, 2003), see fn. 13.

32. D.C. (Tel-Aviv) 92134/02 *The State of Israel v. Marwan Ben-Hatib Barghouti.* Takdin (Hebrew legal data base) 2002 (4) ,18443 (2002) [Hebrew].

33. The court explained that Israel had the authority to guarantee the safety of Israelis even in the occupied territories and that this authority is specifically expressed in the Oslo accords. The court added that since the Oslo agreements had been systematically broken by the Palestinians, "by any standard of human logic" the claim that the agreement should be enforced should not be accepted. The court ruled that Barghouti was not entitled to "prisoner of war" status since he did not fulfill the requirements of

the Geneva Convention (such as bearing a recognizable sign of being a soldier, openly carrying weapons, and not attacking civilians), and should therefore be seen as an "illegal combatant" who should stand trial for his crimes. According to the court, there was no breach of international law, which allows arrests of those who may be of risk to Israel's security interests. Moreover, the legality of the way in which Barghouti was brought to trial was a separate issue and did not bear on the jurisdiction of the court (on this argument the court relied on the Eichmann trial precedent). The court also ruled that international law does not recognize the immunity of a member of parliament in state A who commits crimes in state B.

34. It may be argued that the universal jurisdiction era we live in undermines the binary discourse (see discussion on Universal Jurisdiction, below). For elaborations on the concept of sovereignty in binary terms, see Thomas Hobbes, *Leviathan* (Cambridge: Cambridge University Press, 1991); and Carl Schmitt, *Political Theology*, trans. George Schwab (Chicago: University of Chicago Press, 2005). For a critical evaluation of the concept and an alternative history, see Michel Foucault, *Society Must Be Defended: Lectures at the Collège de France, 1975–76,* trans. David Macey (New York: Picador, 2003).

35. For decisions of the Israel High Court of Justice not to intervene in the policy of "target killing," see H.C.J 769/02, *The Public Committee against Torture v. The Government of Israel*, PADOR 578 (31) 06; and H.C.J. 8794/03, *Yoav Hess v. Dan Haluts,* PADOR 677 (40) 08 (2008) (available also at http://www.stoptorture.org.il/eng/images/uploaded/publications/76.pdf).

36. The issue of discrimination and political persecution was raised in the discussion of the Knesset Committee. See protocol of Knesset committee, September 25, 2001, and November 5–7, 2001, pp. 655–85 (esp., pp. 661, 668, 670–71, 674) (unpublished, file with author).

37. A striking example is the U.S. administration's position on Guantánamo. For a critical discussion and alternative to "war on terror" solutions, see Ackerman, *Before the Next Attack.*

38. Bickel, *The Least Dangerous Branch.*

39. On the use of "proportionality" and "reasonableness" in European administrative law, see Jurgen Schwarze, *European Administrative Law* (Luxembourg: Office for Official Publications of the European communities, Sweet and Maxwell, 1992): 677–867. On the use of these principles in Israeli law, see Aharon Barak, *The Judge in a Democracy* (Princeton: Princeton University Press, 2006): 248–60.

40. For a critical evaluation of the use of these doctrines in the jurisprudence of Justice Aharon Barak, see Ronen Shamir, "The Politics of Reasonableness," *Theory and Criticism* 5 (1994): 7 [Hebrew]; Menny Mautner, "The Reasonableness of Politics," *Theory and Criticism* 5 (1994): 25 [Hebrew].

41. See Ruth Gavison, Mordechai Kremnitzer, and Yoav Dotan, *Judicial Activism: For and Against the Role of the High Court of Justice in the Israeli Society* (Jerusalem: Hebrew University Press, 2000); Dotan, "Ripeness and Politics in the High Court Justice," *Tel Aviv University Law Review* 20 (1996): 93 [Hebrew]; Mautner, "The Decline of Formalism and the Rise of Values in Israeli Law," *Tel Aviv University Law Review* 17 (1993): 503 [Hebrew].

42. For historical interpretation of this move, see Potter Stewart, "The Road to Mapp v. Ohio and Beyond: The Origins, Development and Future of the Exclusionary Rule in Search-and-Seizure Cases," *Columbia Law Review* 83 (1983): 1365.

43. For discussion of estoppel doctrines, see R. A. Duff, "'I Might Be Guilty, But You Can't Try Me': Estoppel and Other Bars to Trial," *Ohio State Journal of Criminal Law* 1 (2003): 245; John W. Lundquist, "'They Knew What We Were Doing': The Evolution of the Criminal Estoppel Defense," *Wm. Mitchell Law Review* 23 (1997): 843; Anne Bowen Poulin, "Prosecutorial Inconsistency, Estoppel, and Due Process: Making the Prosecution Get Its Story Straight," *California Law Review* 89 (2001): 1423; Cynthia L. Randall, "Acquittals in Jeopardy: Criminal Collateral Estoppel and the Use of Acquitted Act Evidence," *University of Pennsylvania Law Review* 141 (1992): 283.

44. Eliahu Harnon, "Illegally Obtained Evidence: Has the Law Been Affected by the Basic Law on Human Dignity and Freedom?" *Bar Ilan Law Studies* 13 (1996): 139 [Hebrew].

45. Neal Kumar Katyal, "Conspiracy Theory," *Yale Law Journal* 112 (2003): 1307.

46. See Michal R. Belknap, ed., *American Political Trials* (Westport, CT: Greenwood Press, 1981). For discussion of various degrees of politicization of crimes, see Otto Kirchheimer, "Politics and Justice," *Social Research* 22 (1955): 408, 413–22.

47. See, for example in Israel, F.H. 8613/96 *Muhammad Yusef Jabareen v. The State of Israel*, 54(5) P.D. 193; C.A. 2831/95 *Alba v. The State of Israel*, 50(5) P.D 221; F.H. 1789/98 *Kahana v. The State of Israel*, 54(5) P.D. 145.

48. Different factors contribute to this possibility: the special institutional position of the courts, their concern with precedents and consistency, and their need to adhere to procedural safeguards.

49. Duff relates briefly to this matter with the following: "[If] the law is to be a rational enterprise that treats its citizens as responsible agents, such 'opposing political ideological reasons' must be heard: There must be a space for dissenters to try to persuade others of their opposing values, and thus to change the law . . . . [We] could imagine a legal system in which the courts provide part of this space: in which courts had not only to apply the law, but to justify it to the defendant, to attend to any opposing view he wanted to offer, and to acquit him if persuaded by this view." Duff, "Principle and Contradiction in the Criminal Law," 181.

50. For similar suggestions in the context of African American defendants suffering

from racism under the U.S. criminal law system, see Andrew D. Leipold, "Symposium on Race and Criminal Law: Objective Tests and Subjective Bias: Some Problems of Discriminatory Intent in Criminal Law," *Chicago-Kent. Law Review* 73 (1998): 559.

51. Zeev Segal and Avi Zamir, "Abuse of Process, Fairness and Judicial Stays: Constitutionalism of Criminal Proceedings," *Hapraklit* 47 (2003): 42 [Hebrew].

52. Gavison, *Discretion in Enforcement of the Criminal Law: The Power to Stay and Renew Criminal Proceedings* (Jerusalem: Hebrew University of Jerusalem, 1991); Daniel Fridman, "Judicial Discretion in Criminal Prosecution," *Hapraklit* 35 (1983): 155 [Hebrew].

53. It was recognized initially in regard to cases in which the prosecution decided *not* to press criminal charges. H.C.J. 935/89 *Ganor et al. v. Attorney General*, 44 (2) P.D. 485 (1990).

54. Criminal Law Procedure Act (Amendment No. 51) 5767—2007, Article 1) S.H. 2095 at 308, adding Article 149(10); Yisgav Nakdimon, Judicial Stays of Criminal Proceedings (2d ed. Nevo, 2009), 47–205.

55. CA. 2910/94 *Yefet v. State of Israel*, 50(2) P.D. 221, 370. The defense was recognized but was not applied here, nor in later cases. See, for example, H.C.J. 1563/96 *Katz v. Attorney General et. al.*, 55(1) P.D. 529; H.C.J. 6781/96 *Olmert v. Attorney General*, 50(4) P.D. 793; C.A. 10960/03 *Hason v. State of Israel*, PADOR 280 (14) 05 (2005).

56. This narrow formulation of the defense can be traced back to English law where it originated as an estoppel type of argument See *Connely v. D.P.P.*, [1964] 2 All E.R. 401 (H.L.); and also, for example, *R. v. Heston-Francois*, [1984] 1 All E.R. 785 (C.A.); *R. v. Brentford JJ*, ex parte Wong [1981] 1 All E.R. 884 (Q.B.). In U.S. as well as Canadian law, we can trace two sources for the defense, common law, and constitutional law. In both we can find instances in which the criterion that was adopted by the court was the objective one. See, for example, in U.S. law *Hampton v. U.S.*, 425 U.S. 484 (1976); *U.S. v. Russell*, 411 U.S. 423 (1973). In Canadian law, see *R. v. Keyowski*, [1988] 1S.C.R. 657 (adopting the objective test); *R. v. O'Connor*, [1995] 4 (explaining the relations between the common law defense, and the Canadian charter).

57. Such is the problem, for instance, both with the under-prosecution of "crimes against humanity" and "war crimes" by national courts (discretion not to prosecute) and with the selective prosecution against one side to a military conflict on the basis of "terror"-related crimes, while the other side enjoys de facto immunity (discretion to prosecute).

58. C.A. 4855/02 *State of Israel v. Borowitz*, 59 (6) P.D. 776 (2005).

59. For Israeli literature recommending the injection of constitutional considerations to the criminal process through the defense of abuse of process, see Boaz Okon and Oded Shahm, "Due Process and Judicial Delay of Proceedings," *Hamishpat* 3 (1996): 265 [Hebrew]; Zeev Segal and Avi Zamir, "Abuse of Process, Fairness and Judicial Stays:

Constitutionalism of Criminal Proceedings," *Hapraklit* 47 (2003) 47 (2003): 42 [Hebrew]; Mordehai Levi, "About the Essence of 'Abuse of Process' Defense and the Criteria for Accepting It," *Hamishpat* 19 (2005): 80 [Hebrew].

60. Criminal Law Procedure Act (Amendment No. 51) 5767—2007, Article 1, S.H. 2095 at 308, adding Article 149(10). For discussion of this test, see "Yisgav Nakdimon . . . ," 77–125.

61. For a similar call to adopt "objective" tests to discrimination of African American defendants, see Leipold, "Symposium on Race and Criminal Law," 559.

62. Bilsky, "Territory, Community and Political Trials: A New Challenge for International Law," *Tel Aviv University Law Review* 27 (2003): 655.

63. The abuse of process defense had been raised by Bishara in another criminal trial, C.C. (Nazareth) 5196/01 *State of Israel v. Bishara*, TAKDIN 9 (02) 2003, in which Bishara and his parliamentary assistants were indicted for assisting Arab Israelis to cross the border into Syria in order to meet their families. Assisting a person to cross the Israeli-Syrian border is a felony according to Regulation 18 (a) and (d) and Regulation 5 of the Emergency Regulations (Foreign Travel) Ordinance 5709-1948. Bishara raised the Abuse of Process defense, claiming that this was a humanitarian act, that the authorities were aware of the very public actions and did not prevent them, and that the authorities also behaved in a discriminatory and abusive manner toward the defendants. However, these claims were discussed only in regard to Bishara's assistants, since Bishara himself was acquitted by the court because of his parliamentary immunity.

64. Nadav Shragai, "Mazuz: There Shall Be No Investigation on Elitzur Comments Regarding the Eviction," *Ha'aretz*, September 28, 2004. Yoaz Yovel, "Another Link in the Chain of Weakness," ibid., December 21, 2005. Nana Editorial board, "Rabbi Eliyahu Commanded, and the Soldiers Refused to Follow Orders," *Nana News*, July 18, 2005 (available at http:// news.nana.co.il/Article/?ArticleID=194374&sid=16)%20" Rabbi).

65. Compare F.H. 8613/96 *Muhammad Yusef Jabareen v. State of Israel*, 54(5) P.D. 193, in which the court acquitted Muhammad Jabareen, who had published several articles in support of throwing stones at IDF soldiers, of the felony of supporting a terror organization, under the Prevention of Terrorism Ordinance. In this case, the court's protection of freedom of speech was achieved by strict construction of the ordinance due to the lack of other constitutional tools at its disposal.

66. For decisions of the Israel High Court of Justice not to intervene in the policy of "target killing," see "H.C.J 769/02 *The Public Committee against Torture v. The Government of Israel*"; and "H.C.J. 8794/03 *Yoav Hess v. Dan Haluts*." Note, however, that the High Court of Justice of Israel has intervened and completely banned the army practice of using Palestinian civilians as "human shields" against attacks during arrests of terror suspects, in H.C.J. 3799/02 *Adallah v. GOC Central Command*, IDF PADOR 586 (22) 05 (2005). (English version available at http://elyon1.court.gov.il/eng/verdict/framesetSrch.html.)

67. "C.A. 4855/02 *State of Israel v. Borowitz,*" at paragraph 21 ("[T]he more severe the crime, the more weight should be given to public interest in prosecution").

68. These difficulties may be reduced if the case is removed from the trial court to the Supreme Court sitting as High Court of Justice, which is indeed an option when dealing with the conduct of the prosecution [C.A. 4855/02*State of Israel v. Borowitz*, at paragraph 2]. It can be argued that these are constitutional matters that are not for the criminal trial court to decide and should be brought before the Supreme Court. Indeed, in a previous criminal case against Bishara (dealing with the assistance he gave Israeli citizens in order to visit their relatives in Syria), it was ruled that the proper forum for deciding discrimination contentions raised by the defendant under the "abuse of process" defense should have been the High Court of Justice [C.C. (Nazaret) 5196/01*The State of Israel v. Azmi Bishara*), paragraph 36]. The judge reasoned that since the issue was the reasonableness of the attorney general's decision to press charges against the defendant and not against others, it should be brought as a petition before the Supreme Court. Academic articles have left this question open. I believe that a distinction can be drawn between different types of contentions brought currently under the "abuse of process" defense. It might be preferable to leave arguments requiring a factual decision about the specific circumstances of the criminal charges to the trial court. However, in cases of structural discrimination that require a broad perspective on the attorney general's policy of criminal prosecution against different classes of defendants, the better forum is the Supreme Court acting as High Court of Justice. This could also create an institutional separation that is often needed in political trials.

69. The historical background on jury nullification cited here is based mainly on Jeffrey Abramson, *We the Jury: The Jury System and the Ideal of Democracy* (New York: Basic Books, 1994); Green, *Verdict according to Conscience.*

70. The historical reasons why the British refrained from creating a jury system in Palestine are not clear, although it is common knowledge that the political tensions between Arabs and Jews were the source of this reluctance. The practice of "jury nullification" may have been one reason to fear this system, since historically it was used most successfully against colonial power by local communities.

71. Bushell (1670) 1 Vaufhan 135, 124 Eng. Re. 1006 (C.P. 1670).

72. For elaborate discussion of such trials, see Abramson, *We the Jury,* 57–95.

73. Several famous acquittals of African American defendants in the United States can be attributed to this kind of jury protest—for example, the trial of African American mayor Marion Barry for use and possession of narcotics (1990); the trial of O. J. Simpson (1995).

74. Thus it was used in the United States both to acquit defendants who helped runaway slaves and to acquit Ku Klux Klan members who murdered African Americans. See Abramson, *We the Jury.*

75. A. Scheflin and J. M. Van Dyke, "Jury Nullification: The Contours of a Controversy," *Law & Contemporary Problems* 43 (Autumn 1980): 51; D. C. Brody, "Sparf and Dougherty Revisited: Why the Court Should Instruct the Jury of Its Nullification Right," *American Criminal Law Review* 33 (1995): 89.

76. Amnon Lehavi, "Discreet Actions, Happy Ends? On 'Harmony through Secrecy' in Criminal Law," *Plilim* 10 (2001): 9 [Hebrew]. Lehavi argues that although the formal reason to keep jury deliberation secretive is to protect free deliberation, it also reflects the goal of the criminal law to protect the superiority of the rule of law and harmony in society through the use of secrecy. It allows the court to diverge in certain cases from the letter of the law, as long as this decision remains secret.

77. Meir Dan Cohen, "Decision Rules and Conduct Rules: On Acoustic Separation in 97 Criminal Law," *Harvard Law Review* (1984): 625–77. The article demonstrates that by relying on acoustic separation between conduct rules (addressed to the public) and decision rules (addressed to the officials who apply conduct rules), society accommodates competing values at stake in criminal law.

78. For a history of jury nullification, see Green, *Verdict according to Conscience.*

79. Lehavi, "Discreet Actions, Happy Ends?" 31–38.

80. On the relation of the jury and the community, and specifically the tension between the notion of local jury that reflects the community's moral values, and the impartiality of the jury, see Abramson, *We the Jury,* 18.

81. Ibid., 88–90.

82. Cf. Robert F. Schopp, "Verdicts of Conscience: Nullification and Necessity as Jury Responses to Crimes of Conscience," *Southern California Law Review* 69 (1996): 2039. The author argues that the necessity defense is more consistent with the values of political liberalism. The explicit defense of necessity is better equipped to reflect the balancing of values in a rational way. This position, however, ignores problems of "radical difference"—situations in which criminal law cannot reflect the true values negotiated within a heterogeneous society, given some systemic problems of participation in the democratic process by minority groups. For such problems, I argue, both explicit defenses or implicit mechanism of jury nullification are needed in order to legitimize the application of criminal law over all sections of society.

83. For example, when it explicitly prohibits travel to "enemy" countries, thus placing an unequal burden on the Arab citizens of Israel who often have relatives in those countries (see the first Bishara case, C.C. (Nazareth) 1087/02 *The State of Israel v. Bishara*).

84. The original indictment was submitted to the court in Jerusalem. However, Bishara's request to transfer the case to the court in Nazareth where he resides (based on the Courts Law [consolidated version], 5744-1984, Section 78), was accepted by the Supreme Court, despite the prosecutor's objection.

85. Two famous examples from recent years are the Rodney King and O. J. Simpson trials. For a discussion of their relationship, see Shoshana Felman, *The Juridical Unconscious: Trials and Traumas in the Twentieth Century* (Cambridge: Harvard University Press, 2002), 54–105.

86. The appointment of a religious Mizrahi Jew (of North African and Middle Eastern origin) to preside over the trial of Aryeh Deri (leader of the ultraorthodox Mizrahi Party, Shas, who was accused of various corruption felonies, and also over the trial of Yigal Amir (the religious Mizrahi Jew accused of assassinating Prime Minister Yitzhak Rabin). For in depth discussion of the two cases, see Bilsky, "J'accuse: Deri, Political Trials and Collective Memory," in *Shas: The Challenge of Israeliness*, ed. Yoav Peled (Tel Aviv: Miskal, 2001), 279 [Hebrew]; Bilsky, *Transformative Justice*, 202–36.

87. It wrote that the defendant "cannot be attributed with the general and sweeping crime of premeditated aiding and abetting of murder for each and every terrorist attack only due to his general awareness that his people were executing attacks using weapons and funds that he secured for them" (paragraph 171).

88. Indeed, Barghouti participated from Israeli prison in the 2006 elections to the Palestinian Authority and was elected to the parliament. He also initiated and signed the "prisoners agreement" between the various Palestinian sections regarding the borders of '67 (*Haaretz*, May 11, 2006).

89. Interestingly, after the army capture of Ahmed Saadat for his alleged participation in the assassination of Israeli minister Rehavaam Zeevi, the Israeli prosecution decided not to conduct his trial in civilian courts, but in a military court. See *Haaretz*, April 27, 2006.

90. HCJ 11225/03 *Mk Dr. Azmi Bishara v. The Attorney General.*

91. Interestingly, even the dissenting judge, who thought that the immunity should not apply to these speeches, agreed that greater protection should be given to elected members of parliament even in cases where their speech seems to infringe criminal proscription.

92. This tool was not available in a previous case brought against an Arab journalist (the Jabareen case) in which the court opted for acquittal on the basis of a strict construction of the law. "F.H. 8613/96 *Muhammad Yusef Jabareen v. The State of Israel.*"

93. Norrie, "Crime, Reason and History," 35–58.

94. Duff, "Principle and Contradiction in the Criminal Law," 179–84.

Conflict of Laws and the Legal Negotiation of Difference

PAUL SCHIFF BERMAN

In a world of multiple normative communities, law constantly confronts the stranger. Indeed, if globalization means anything, it is that territorial borders are even less able to keep the unfamiliar at bay, forcing legal systems to consider how to adjudicate disputes involving the norms of multiple, perhaps far-flung, communities.[1] Accordingly, law must constantly negotiate the permeable and ever-shifting divide between the familiar and the strange.

Further, the very idea of the stranger fundamentally implicates concerns with law because law is a social discourse that helps to mediate disputes between Self and Other. Even in the most homogenous societies, it is precisely because selves are inevitably distanced from—and therefore strangers to—each other that law is necessary. Law provides fora for both dispute resolution and (ideally) some moments of communication across both literal and psychic distances.

In this essay, I begin by exploring ideas of strangerness and otherness, building on works of sociologists and political theorists analyzing interpersonal and societal communication. I contrast a vision whereby difference is overcome by assuming commonality with one in which "strangerness" is seen as an inevitable part of human interaction. And I argue that it is unwise to attempt to "overcome" difference by trying to forge sameness. Instead, we should aspire to a state of unassimilated otherness. In such a state, we seek communication across difference rather than annihilation of difference.

Then, I turn to law and suggest that the three legal doctrines grouped under the rubric of conflict of laws—jurisdiction, choice of law, and judgment recognition—provide a site for viewing this sort of negotiation among strangers. Jurisdiction involves the decision of a community to assert legal dominion over an act or actor. Choice-of-law analysis considers which community's legal norms should apply to a dispute involving members of multiple communities. And recognition of judgments asks communities to decide whether to enforce prior judgments of other communities, even when those judgments would not (or could not) have been issued by the enforcing community as an original matter. Each of these doctrines, therefore, is crucial to analyzing how law confronts "strangerness" and conceptualizes ideas of space, place, distance, territory, sovereignty, and pluralism. Yet, neither sociolegal scholars studying the interaction of legally defined communities nor scholars interested in the multiplicity of legal and quasi-legal norms under conditions of globalization have focused sufficiently on these conflicts doctrines. This is unfortunate, and so one aim of this essay is merely to stake a claim to conflict of laws as a crucial area of interdisciplinary inquiry. Indeed, it is largely on the terrain of conflict of laws that communities delineate Self and Other and consider the alternative normative communities that are all around.

But beyond simply identifying conflict of laws as a fruitful subject of further study, I also want to argue that conflict of laws provides a potentially *useful* framework for viewing disputes among multiple normative orders. If taken seriously, a conflicts analysis could offer a forum for creative engagement with questions of community affiliation, extraterritorial effects, and the development of hybrid norms. Moreover, following the insights of legal pluralists, who have long argued that the state does not hold a monopoly on "law," we can use conflicts analysis to consider interactions with nonstate normative communities as well. Accordingly, conflicts analysis can become a form of cultural anthropology, permitting an inquiry that acknowledges that we are all members of multiple overlapping normative communities, that some of those communities are state-based and some are not, and that all of these communities may assert norms that have real impact on the world stage of law. This vision of conflicts of law, because it is both *cosmopolitan* (recognizing multiple, possibly nonterritorial, community affiliations) and *pluralist* (recognizing nonstate community affiliations) may help to better negotiate the inevitable divide between Self and Other by requiring communities both to acknowledge competing community norms and to wrestle explicitly with the question of how much to assimilate or give deference to those competing norms. Such an approach does not annihilate difference in the vain search for uniform rules; instead it fosters engagement among strangers and negotiation of unassimilated otherness.

Self, Other, and the Negotiation of Difference

Sociological studies of communication often start from the idea that interpersonal interaction requires both parties in an encounter to believe (or at least assume) that the other is not truly other at all.[2] According to this view, most associated with Alfred Schutz,[3] differences in individual perspective are overcome only if each party tacitly believes that he/she could effectively trade places with the other. As Schutz describes it, "I am able to understand other people's acts only if I can imagine that I myself would perform analogous acts if I were in the same situation."[4] Thus, differences in perspective are reduced to differences in situation. Any possibly more fundamental differences are suppressed in order to facilitate dialogue.

As a result, the deliberate "assuming away" of the unfamiliar is seen as a constant part of everyday life. The unfamiliar is relegated to the category of "strange," and "strangeness" necessarily is placed elsewhere, somewhere other than the interaction at hand.[5] Moreover, Harold Garfinkel and other ethnomethodologists have argued that individuals do not simply passively maintain these assumptions, but are constantly engaged in a joint enterprise aimed at sustaining this familiarity.[6] In all of these studies, the emphasis is on "the human production of common worlds of meaning as the only axis on which dialogue rotates."[7]

But is that all there is to the experience of the other? Is it really imperative constantly to assume that our fellow human beings are fundamentally identical to us? After all, as Z. D. Gurevitch has argued, "Under this principle, if a dialogue is to take place, strangeness as a phenomenon of everyday interaction must be considered negatively, namely, as that part of an encounter that must be constantly 'assumed away' by the participants."[8] Thus, we are left with a world in which people are classified either as familiar or as strangers. And, even more problematic, these studies suggest that it will be simply impossible to bridge the communication gap with those deemed strangers. Yet, as Georg Simmel noted long ago, the stranger is never truly distant,[9] so there will need to be some way of bridging gaps short of assuming away strangeness altogether.

To seek an alternative formulation, we might turn to political philosophy. Hannah Arendt, for example, offers a different way of conceptualizing the encounter with the stranger. Instead of assuming commonality, she seeks, in "Understanding and Politics," the quality that "makes it bearable . . . to live with other people, strangers forever, in the same world, and makes it possible for them to bear with us."[10] Note that for Arendt the task is how to "bear with" strangers, even while recognizing that they will forever be strange.[11] Significantly, this task is very different from the more intimate communication relationships studied in the sociological literature discussed above. After all, if strangers are "forever strange," their strangeness cannot be overcome through psychological assumptions; a different strategy is necessary.

Arendt's strategy for bearing with strangers is more than just mutual indifference and more than just toleration as well. It "involves a mental capacity appropriate for an active relation to that which is distant,"[12] which Arendt locates in King Solomon's gift of the "understanding heart."[13] Understanding, according to Arendt, "is the specifically human way of being alive; for every single person needs to be reconciled to a world into which he was born a stranger and in which, to the extent of his distinct uniqueness, he always remains a stranger."[14] And what does "understanding" entail for Arendt? This is a bit difficult to pin down, but she makes clear that it is not gained through direct experience of the other, and it is not just knowledge of the other.[15] Instead, understanding starts from the individual situated apart from others. Thus, instead of "feeling your pain," understanding involves determining what aspects of the pain people feel has to do with politics, and what politics can do to resolve our common dilemmas. Moreover, "Understanding can be challenged and is compelled to respond to an alternative argument or interpretation."[16] In short, understanding in Arendt's formulation looks a lot less like empathy and a lot more like judging.[17]

This more distanced conception of the encounter with the stranger appears to have something in common with Iris M. Young's vision of "unassimilated otherness," which she posits as the relation among people in the ideal "unoppressive city."[18] Young envisions ideal city life as the "'being-together' of strangers."[19] These strangers may remain strangers and continue to "experience each other as other."[20] Indeed, they do not necessarily seek an overall group identification and loyalty. Yet, they are open to "unassimilated otherness."[21] They belong to various distinct groups or cultures and are constantly interacting with other groups. But they do so without seeking either to assimilate or to reject those others. Such interactions instantiate an alternative kind of community,[22] one that is never a hegemonic imposition of sameness but that nevertheless prevents different groups from ever being completely outside one another.[23] In a city's public spaces, Young argues, we see glimpses of this ideal: "The city consists in a great diversity of people and groups, with a multitude of subcultures and differentiated activities and functions, whose lives and movements mingle and overlap in public spaces."[24] In this vision, there can be community without sameness, shifting affiliations without ostracism.

This discussion does not, of course, even scratch the surface concerning the myriad ideas and writings available about the encounter between Self and Other. Yet, for our purposes, we can at least establish one possible dichotomy that might be useful. At the most general level, the analyses discussed above suggest that, in responding to the other, we can pursue at least two possible strategies, which are very different from each other. We can seek commonality and assume away perceived difference, or we can acknowledge entrenched difference and attempt to bridge gaps. As we will see, each of these strategies has its analogue in law.

Conflicts Doctrines

The previous section discussed two distinct strategies for encountering the stranger. We can either work to make the other more familiar, or we can seek Arendt's form of understanding within a realm of unassimilated otherness. These strategies are also played out, I believe, in law's encounter with the other. In a world of multiple normative communities, law will inevitably become a forum for disputes involving differing underlying norms. To address such conflicts, we see two principal responses. Law either seeks commonality or it seeks procedures for mediating across difference.

Seeking commonality appears in the push for legal harmonization. Here, we see efforts to enact uniform rules, create multilateral treaties, and forge agreements on normative standards. Implicit in these efforts is the approach to difference described by Schutz and Garfinkel above. We assume that all normative communities share important commonalities, we de-emphasize difference, and we seek shared understanding through the encounter. A second approach is more similar to the one taken by Arendt and Young. Here, we assume that multiple normative communities will remain strangers to each other, but then seek forms of public discourse to mediate the encounters among strangers, without assimilation or enforced commonality. And, of course there is always a third option: the complete annihilation of difference through the hegemonic imposition of a dominant norm. This is what Robert Cover famously referred to as the jurispathic approach, in which courts (sometimes necessarily) "kill off" opposing norms in favor of a dominant one.

The legal doctrines traditionally grouped together as conflict of laws—jurisdiction, choice of law, and judgment recognition—are, at least potentially, examples of the second approach. These doctrines are the mechanisms for opening up areas of legal debate among strangers. Here, I briefly summarize each doctrine in turn and suggest that, although they have historically been deeply enmeshed both with ideas about territoriality and state prerogative, conflicts doctrines could be deployed to consider broader notions of community affiliation, nonstate norms, and interactions with the Other.

A. Jurisdiction

The assertion of jurisdiction has conventionally been linked to coercive power. If a community can literally seize a party (or its assets), then that party is usually deemed to be within the community's jurisdiction. As such, jurisdiction has historically been tied to physical territory. Anyone within the territorial borders was subject to jurisdiction; anyone outside of them was not. In this scenario, the territorially distant stranger is conceptualized as forever strange and therefore not even a part of the legal dialogue.

However, this pure territorialist vision has proven to be unsupportable in a world where territorially distant forces can so readily create local harms. With regard to the Internet, for example, since 1995 courts have developed as many as eight distinct tests in an attempt to apply the U.S. Supreme Court's jurisdictional framework to web-based contacts.[25] When one sees that much change in a common-law doctrine over such a short period of time, it is a sign that courts aren't comfortable with the paradigm they are using. At the same time, there are now approximately 125 international institutions, all asserting jurisdiction and issuing decisions that have some effect on state legal authorities,[26] though those effects are sometimes deemed binding, sometimes merely persuasive, and often fall somewhere between the two. And we frequently see transnational assertions of jurisdiction in matters relating to international human rights, cross-border commercial interactions, environmental harms, mass torts, and even bankruptcies.

Moreover, it has become a truism to observe that we are increasingly affected by activities and decisions that take place far from us in a spatial sense.[27] Such deterritorialized effects have always been present to some extent, of course. One need only look at the history of empire to realize that the strings of governance were often pulled by far-off rulers. But at least in the premodern world such political arrangements, perhaps because of the slow pace of transportation and communications, rarely meant strong centralized control of distant realms. Rather, the social construction of space was organized around many centers, with a patchwork of overlapping and incomplete rights of government.[28] And, although cross-border interaction obviously is not a new phenomenon, in an electronically connected world the effects of any given action may immediately be felt elsewhere with no relationship to physical geography at all.

Indeed, the globalization of capital, the movement of people and goods across borders, the reach of global corporate activity, the impact of worldwide nongovernmental organizations (NGOs), and the development, in recent decades, of these various international or transnational tribunals all make it far more likely that local communities will be affected by activities and entities with no local presence. As a thought experiment, one can imagine an "effects map," in which one identifies a territorial locality and plots on a map every action that has an effect on that locality.[29] Five hundred years ago, such effects would almost surely have been clustered around the territory, with perhaps some additional effects located in a particular distant imperial location. A hundred years ago, those effects might have begun spreading out. But today, while locality is surely not irrelevant, the effects would likely be diffused over many corporate, governmental, technological, and migratory centers.

This deterritorialization of effects is felt on an everyday, intuitive level. For example, the "local" shopping mall is not experienced as truly local at all; nearly "everyone who shops there is aware that most of the shops are chain stores," identical to stores elsewhere, and that the mall itself closely resembles innumerable other malls around the globe.[30] Thus, while experiencing a "local" place, we recognize the absent forces that structure our experience. Such forces include the steady decline in local ownership of public spaces, which can itself be linked to the globalization of capital.[31]

Similarly, we may feel the growing significance of "remote" forces on our lives, whether those forces are multinational corporations, world capital markets, or distant bureaucracies. As John Tomlinson has observed: "[P]eople probably come to include distant events and processes more routinely in their perceptions of what is significant for their own personal lives. This is one aspect of what deterritorialization may involve: the ever-broadening horizon of relevance in people's routine experience."[32] And, of course, those with less power to influence the processes of globalization—those forced to cross borders for work, those bankrupted through global competition, those affected by environmental degradation, and many others—experience this deterritorialization in even more insidious ways. Moreover, though the effects may often seem to flow in only one direction (industrialized centers affecting nonindustrialized peripheries), one need only consider migratory labor patterns and immigration, the rapid spread of diseases like the avian flu, and the bidirectional impact of labor outsourcing to realize that deterritorialization affects us all.

This deterritorialization of effects has inevitably had an impact on jurisdictional doctrine and practice and will undoubtedly continue to do so. Instead of simply ignoring the Stranger or treating that stranger as a spatially distant Other (as the territorialist vision does), the assertion of jurisdiction is best viewed as a mechanism that opens up an opportunity for negotiation across distance. Moreover, we can uncouple the idea of jurisdiction as solely a tool of territorially based enforcement power from the more capacious understanding of jurisdiction as a discursive space. Of course enforcement power (and who controls it) is important. But ultimately enforcement depends on whether those who assert jurisdiction can rhetorically persuade those who possess coercive power (the police force, the military) to enforce the judgment issued. Thus, the essence of law is that it makes aspirational judgments about the future, the power of which depends on whether the judgments accurately reflect evolving norms of the communities that must choose to obey them. If this is so, then we might view extraterritorial or nonstate lawmaking as substantially similar to state lawmaking within territorial bounds. Accordingly, it is not only the state that might assert jurisdiction, but any community that purports to use the language of law to articulate norms as a group. Acknowledging community affiliations that exist apart from the nation-state therefore becomes crucial. And by analyzing the social meaning of our affiliations across space, we can think about various alternative conceptions of community:[33]

Subnational communities. These include political identifications more local than the nation-state, such as provinces, states, towns, and voting districts, or affiliations that form around specific functions or activities, such as water regions, geographical areas, block associations, bowling leagues, religious institutions, and schools. Others include commonalities that derive from a purported ethnic identification that is not coterminous with the nation-state, such as Basques in Spain, Sikhs in India, Tamils in Sri Lanka, or even white supremacist militias in the United States. Interestingly, while historically considered subnational, many of these affiliations are increasingly transnational as well.

Transnational communities. These are communities of interest that cut across nation-state boundaries. Perhaps the most important transnational force in recent years has been the multinational corporation itself. In addition, we see international monetary funds, free trade regions, global commodities markets, and a nascent international civil society that includes nongovernmental organizations such as the Rockefeller and Soros foundations, Amnesty International, Oxfam, and Greenpeace, as well as business and trade union networks and cooperative efforts of government actors including banking regulators, law-enforcement officials, intelligence agencies, judiciaries, and other local authorities. And a darker example of transnational affiliation, of course, is the development of transnational terrorist organizations such as Al Qaeda.

Supranational communities. Whereas transnationalism binds people to communities of interest *across* territorial borders, *supranationalism* asserts the primacy of governing norms that exist *above* the nation-state. Perhaps the most obvious example of such affiliation is the United Nations, which insistently invokes an overarching narrative of world community. Another that has drawn considerable attention in recent years is the effort to construct a European identity operating beyond the individual nation-states on the Continent. And the World Trade Organization and other trade-related tribunals create a supranational community of interest regarding commercial activity.

Most important, if jurisdiction is in part about the assertion of community dominion over a distant actor, then courts must consider the nature of the community that has allegedly been harmed, the relationship of the dispute to that community, and the social meaning of asserting dominion over the actor in question. Accordingly, the jurisdictional inquiry becomes a site for discussion both about the nature of community affiliation and the changing role of territorial borders. The precise contours of the jurisdictional norms that would develop from this process are impossible to predict and would undoubtedly evolve over time. The crucial point, however, is that these discussions could no longer be truncated by a formulaic test that simply counts contacts with a geographical territory and therefore bears scant relationship to the core questions underlying the social meaning of jurisdiction. In a more free-wheeling jurisdictional inquiry, law functions as a site for discourse among strangers across both physical and normative space.

B. Choice of Law

In a dispute involving actors from two or more communities, the choice-of-law question revolves around which governing norms will apply to that dispute. As with jurisdiction, this question has often been resolved by reference to territory, allowing courts to sidestep more nuanced evaluations of conflicting normative systems. Thus, one venerable choice-of-law approach, known as "vested rights," seeks to locate all disputes spatially by identifying the physical location of the essential act that is deemed to constitute the cause of action. Applying the vested rights approach, judges look to the place of the tort,[34] or the place of contracting,[35] or the location of the property at issue.[36] Having "localized" the cause of action, only the state where the cause of action "vested" could apply its law to the dispute.[37] Such localization effectively avoids any consideration of multiple norms or the relationship between the familiar and the strange because it places all disputes within a familiar, territorially delineated framework.

However, as with jurisdiction, the single-minded focus on territoriality has proved to be problematic. Indeed, it is difficult to justify why the territorial location of only one event in a complicated set of transactions should determine the law to be applied. For example, in the oft-discussed case of *Alabama Great Southern Railroad v. Carroll*,[38] an employee was injured when a train coupling failed. The vested rights theory held that the relevant law was of the state where the injury occurred.[39] However, given that the negligence took place elsewhere, the choice of the place of accident seems arbitrary. Similarly, it may be difficult to determine when and where an injury takes place (for example in a toxic tort case), and again the state where the person happens to be when the first symptoms appear seems relatively unimportant.[40] Yet, under the vested rights approach such a determination is the *only* relevant factor in choice-of-law analysis. Thus, even if one agreed that territorialism should be the criterion for choice of law, it is not at all clear how best to choose the appropriate territorial nexus, and the mechanical vested rights rules seem substanceless.

Moreover, the focus on territoriality in choice-of-law, as with jurisdiction, ignores important nonterritorial factors, such as community affiliation. For example, in a pure territorialist system, two parties who are domiciled in one state could avoid a local contract rule by crossing the border, entering into the contract, and returning, thereby taking advantage of the foreign law.[41] This is not at all hypothetical in the modern world of off-shore regulatory havens, where corporations frequently attempt to avoid various forms of governmental control by changing their territorial location. A purely territorial approach, therefore, will have difficulty coping with a modern world where transactions and transportation across borders are so frequent. Indeed, although vested rights analysis treats as transcendental truth the idea that the state has complete and unchallenged authority within its own sphere and that no state, therefore, may meddle in another state's "local" affairs, we live today in a far more fluid world of jurisdictional assertions across territorial borders and entities that cause significant impact in far-away locations. A purely territorial choice-of-law rule is unlikely to be satisfying in such a world. Instead, we need to acknowledge that people may have multiple community affiliations beyond simply their territorial location at a particular moment in time, and therefore it might be appropriate for nonlocal law to apply to their transactions, at least under some circumstances.

Finally, it is worth noting that almost all choice-of-law approaches start from the premise that only one community's law could ever apply to any particular transaction, thereby ignoring the reality that, in a complex multistate transaction, the norms of multiple communities are obviously implicated. In order to avoid such limitations, choice-of-law regimes should recognize the possibility that norms of multiple states could apply to different parts of the dispute or that rules could ultimately be blended to account for the variety of normative systems implicated in a given transaction. Only such a hybrid, nonterritorial approach will allow for real engagement with the multiple communities and multiple norms implicated in encounters between the familiar and the strange.

C. Judgment Recognition

The final element of this three-pronged negotiation between Self and Other is the question of when one community should recognize and enforce a prior ruling of another community. A pure territorialist might answer, "Never." After all, what if the prior judgment was based on an entirely different set of governing norms? Why should such a ruling be enforced? And yet, often foreign judgments *are* recognized and enforced. Indeed, under the Full Faith and Credit Clause of the U.S. Constitution,[42] a valid judgment issued by one state must be enforced by every other state even if the judgment being enforced would be *illegal* if it had been issued by the enforcing state in the first instance.[43] And even judgments of foreign countries are routinely enforced by U.S. courts.[44]

Indeed, while the decision to enforce a judgment surely will be less automatic when the judgment at issue was rendered by a court whose governing norms are less familiar, the important point is that the decision to enforce a foreign judgment is fundamentally different from the decision to issue an original judgment, and it should not be treated as equivalent.[45] This is because judgment recognition implicates an entirely distinct set of concerns about the role of courts in a plural order. Thus, courts might consider the independent value of participating in an interlocking legal system, where litigants cannot simply avoid unpleasant judgments by relocating. Moreover, deference to other community judgments is likely to have long-term reciprocal benefits. Particularly when the parties have no significant affiliation with the forum state, there is little reason for a court to insist on following domestic public policies in the face of such competing values. As Judge Cardozo has observed: "We are not so provincial as to say that every solution of a problem is wrong because we deal with it otherwise at home."[46]

This is not to say, of course, that foreign judgments should always be enforced. Indeed, even employing a more cosmopolitan pluralist approach, one would expect that judges might sometimes interpose local public policies where they would not in the domestic state-to-state setting. But if we acknowledge the importance of the intersystemic values effectuated by strong judgment recognition, we will necessarily reject the idea that a court is simply *unable* to enforce a judgment just because such a judgment could not have been issued by the court in the first instance. Thus, there will always need to be engagement with the foreign statement of norms; one could not simply reject the foreign as simply alien and therefore automatically beyond consideration.

Conflicts among Norm-Generating Communities

At the very least it seems to me that sociolegal scholars and those seeking to understand law and globalization should turn their attention to the legal skirmishes involving jurisdiction, choice-of-law, and judgment recognition. For it is in those skirmishes that we see battles over conceptualizing territorial borders, sovereignty, and the relationship between Self and Other played out. In addition, by attending to changes in legal doctrine in these areas over time, we will glimpse the tectonic societal shifts that these legal rules both reflect and create.

But beyond simply their importance as windows on cultural change and the negotiation of difference, conflicts doctrines, I believe, can usefully help us think about a plural world where multiple state and nonstate entities generate norms, and where people with multiple community affiliations interact and create harms across territorial boundaries. Indeed, conflicts of law is a potential site for the sort of understanding across difference that Arendt and Young describe. This is because a conflict-of-laws decision, if taken seriously, neither assumes away difference nor annihilates difference through the jurispathic act of rejecting one normative commitment in favor of another one. Instead, we could use conflicts doctrines to more seriously engage foreign norms. And even when the alternative norms are so far beyond the pale that they cannot in the end be followed, using a conflicts framework means that such a decision will always be the exception, not the rule, and will need to be accompanied by an overriding normative commitment. Thus, even when acting jurispathically, decisionmakers will at least be engaging with the alternative norm and offering a strong normative justification for rejecting it.

To explore how a conflicts framework might work, I provide some examples, beginning with more conventional cases involving the interaction of state communities with each other and then considering a variety of conflicts issues raised by the norms of nonstate communities: religious communities, international communities, and ethnic communities. In each of these instances, the point is not to employ doctrine to "solve" conflicts disputes for all time. Rather, I hope to show simply that it might, at least at times, be fruitful to consider these debates through a conflicts lens, particularly when that lens takes seriously questions of community affiliation and the possibility of nonstate lawmaking.

A. State Communities

An exclusive focus on territorial location tends to lend conflicts disputes an air of unreality. Witness, for example, the bizarre claim of the U.S. government that federal courts have no jurisdiction over military detention facilities in Guantanamo Bay, Cuba, despite the fact that the facility is completely controlled by U.S. military personnel operating at the behest of the U.S. government.[47] And though the U.S. Supreme Court ultimately rejected that extreme claim to "foreignness" from U.S. law,[48] the Court's ruling might have been based on the particular circumstances of sovereignty over Guantanamo, rather than a more general understanding that U.S. court jurisdiction can be asserted over U.S. government–run detention facilities, no matter where they are located spatially.

Indeed, as in the Guantanamo case, territorial location is often largely irrelevant to the actual dispute, and yet, as discussed previously, territory takes on inflated significance in the various conflicts inquiries. For example, in the celebrated case involving France's efforts to prosecute Yahoo! for allowing French citizens to download Nazi memorabilia and Holocaust denial material,[49] location was a red herring. As an initial matter, Yahoo! conceded that the French court could assert jurisdiction over Yahoo.fr, Yahoo!'s French subsidiary, but insisted that jurisdiction was inappropriate over Yahoo.com. Yet that distinction was immaterial to Internet users because anyone wishing to access the proscribed materials could just as easily type "yahoo.com" as "yahoo.fr" into their browsers, thereby circumventing any restrictions placed on yahoo.fr. Likewise, though the parties and the court focused on minutiae such as the physical location of Yahoo!'s web servers (an arbitrary and easily changeable detail) or the safety deposit box housing the share certificate indicating Yahoo.com's ownership of Yahoo.fr, none of those elements addressed the core question of whether Yahoo! should be deemed within the dominion of France. Thus, a territorial analysis tends to preclude any engagement with the fundamental questions surrounding how best to negotiate normative differences among strangers.

Moreover, an analysis based on territoriality often results in stalemate. Thus, Yahoo! argued that the French assertion of jurisdiction was impermissibly extraterritorial in scope, that such extraterritorial censoring of U.S. web content would run afoul of the First Amendment of the U.S. Constitution, and that the French assertion of jurisdiction was therefore an improper attempt by France to impose global rules for Internet expression.[50] Yet, the extraterritoriality charge runs in both directions. If France is *not* able to block the access of French citizens to proscribed material, then the United States will effectively be imposing First Amendment norms on the entire world. Indeed, we should not be surprised that as the Internet itself becomes less U.S.-centered, a variety of content norms will begin competing for primacy.[51] And though geographical tracking software might seem to solve the problem by allowing websites to offer different content to different users, such a solution is probably illusory because it would still require the sites to analyze the laws of all jurisdictions to determine what material to filter for which users.[52] Cross-border environmental[53] and trade regulation[54] disputes raise similar issues.

In contrast, a more nuanced analysis of multiple norms and multiple community affiliations would suggest piercing the corporate form and analyzing Yahoo!'s substantive connections to French customers and the global Internet market, which were numerous.[55] Thus, the French court's ultimate assertion of jurisdiction can be justified on those grounds (though significantly they were not the stated basis of the judgment). But whatever the ultimate result, it seems clear that the territorial formalisms with which the debate was fought simply cannot provide a rational basis for making jurisdictional judgments.

In other circumstances, the reliance on territorial location actually results in a nonsensical outcome. Take another Internet case, involving a website with the domain name www.barcelona.com.[56] In that case, Mr. Joan Nogueras Cobo ("Nogueras"), a Spanish citizen, registered barcelona.com with the Virginia-based domain name registrar, Network Solutions. Subsequently, Nogueras formed a corporation under U.S. law, called Bcom, Inc. Despite the U.S. incorporation, however, the company had no offices, employees, or even a telephone listing in the United States. Nogueras (and the Bcom servers) remained in Spain. The Barcelona City Council asserted that Nogueras had no right to use barcelona.com under Spanish trademark law and demanded that he transfer the domain name registration to the City Council. The Fourth Circuit, though, ruled against the city, applying U.S. trademark law because the domain name was registered with a U.S. registrar company.

Using a cosmopolitan framework, this case should have gone the other way because the dispute concerns a Spanish individual and a Spanish city fighting over a Spanish domain name that itself refers to a Spanish city. The idea that this dispute should be adjudicated under U.S. law because of where the domain name registry company is or because the Spanish citizen created a dummy corporation in the United States does not take into account what is really going on. A U.S. court taking a cosmopolitan approach, therefore, would need to be restrained and not assume that U.S. trademark law should apply extraterritorially.

Similar principles should apply to judgment recognition. Thus, a community should not simply reflexively apply its own public policies to a dispute if that dispute has no substantive connection to the community and it was already adjudicated elsewhere. Consider *Telnikoff v. Matusevitch*,[57] a case decided in 1997 by the Maryland Supreme Court. This was a libel action between two British citizens concerning writings that appeared in a British newspaper. After a complicated sequence of proceedings in the United Kingdom, a jury ruled for the plaintiff and ordered damages. However, Matusevitch moved to Maryland and subsequently sought a declaratory order that the British libel judgment could not be enforced in the United States, pursuant to the First Amendment. The Maryland Supreme Court ultimately ruled that, because British libel law violates the speech-protective First Amendment standards laid out by the U.S. Supreme Court in *New York Times v. Sullivan* and its progeny,[58] the British judgment violated Maryland public policy and could not be enforced. Yet, as discussed earlier, the decision to enforce a foreign judgment is very different from the decision to issue a judgment in the first place. And particularly in a case such as *Telnikoff*, where the parties had no significant affiliation with Maryland, there was little reason for a court to insist on following domestic public policies in the face of such competing conflicts values.

Finally, we can recognize how thinking only in terms of territory and sovereignty can blind us to significant discursive processes that an assertion of jurisdiction can enable, even when that assertion is not literally "successful." For example, in July 2003, Spanish judge Baltasar Garzón sought extradition from Argentina of dozens of Argentines for human rights abuses committed under the Argentine military government in the 1970s.[59] In addition, Garzón successfully sought extradition from Mexico of one former Argentine Navy captain who was accused of murdering hundreds of people.[60] In the wake of Garzón's actions, realist observers complained that such transnational prosecutions were illegitimate because Argentina had previously conferred amnesty on those who had been involved in the period of military rule, and therefore any prosecution would infringe on Argentina's sovereign "choice" to grant amnesty.[61]

But the amnesty decision was not simply a unitary choice made by some unified "state" of Argentina; it was a politically contested act that remained controversial within the country.[62] And the Spanish extradition request itself gave then-President Nestor Kirschner more leverage in his tug-of-war with the legal establishment over the amnesty laws. Just over a month after Garzón's request, both houses of the Argentine Congress voted by large majorities to annul the laws.[63] Meanwhile the Spanish government decided that it would not make the formal extradition request to Argentina that Garzón sought, but it did so based primarily on the fact that Argentina had begun to scrap its amnesty laws, and the accused would therefore be subject to domestic human rights prosecution.[64] Accordingly President Kirschner could use Spain's announcement to increase pressure on the Argentine Supreme Court to officially overturn the amnesty laws.[65]

Ultimately, the Argentine Supreme Court did in fact strike down the amnesty laws, thus clearing the way for domestic human rights prosecutions.[66] Not only was the pressure exerted by Spain instrumental in these efforts, but it is significant that the Argentine Court cited as legal precedent a 2001 decision of the Inter-American Court of Human Rights striking down a similar amnesty provision in Peru as incompatible with the American Convention on Human Rights and hence without legal effect. So, in the end, the "sovereign" state of Argentina made political and legal choices to repeal the amnesty laws just as it had previously made choices to create them. But in this change of heart we can see the degree to which transnational legal pronouncements, even if they are without any literal constraining effect, may significantly alter the domestic political terrain.[67] This complex dance between foreign discursive norms and domestic ones is at the heart of any dialogic understanding of the legal relationship between Self and Other.

B. Religious Communities

Turning from state-to-state conflicts to the assertions of nonstate normative communities, we can first consider religious communities, which, of course, have historically provided some of the strongest challenges to state-based lawmaking. Indeed, the Treaty of Westphalia—widely viewed as the document that ushered in the era of the modern nation-state—was designed in large part to limit the influence of religious communities and their leaders. To this day, the ways in which state governments either accommodate or resist religious practices are among the most contentious issues such governments encounter in the negotiation between Self and Other, familiar and strange.

Here, I explore two well-known cases in which the U.S. Supreme Court was forced to determine how state-based law-making would interact with the norms of a religious community. First, in *Bob Jones Univ. v. United States*, the Court addressed an IRS decision to deny tax-exempt status to a religious school that interpreted Christian scriptures to forbid "interracial dating and marriage."[68] Second, in *Employment Div., Dept. of Human Resources of Oregon v. Smith*, the question was whether a general state statute forbidding certain narcotics should be applied to an Indian tribe's religious practice that included the use of peyote.[69] To my mind, viewing these conflicts as choice-of-law questions makes the analytical framework more coherent (though, it should be noted, no less difficult).

Turning to *Bob Jones*, the Internal Revenue Service had interpreted Section 501(c)(3) of the Internal Revenue Code, which gives tax-exempt status to qualifying charitable institutions, to apply to schools only if such schools have a "racially nondiscriminatory policy as to students." Accordingly, the IRS denied tax exemption to Bob Jones University, which had not admitted blacks at all until 1971 and had admitted them thereafter but had forbidden interracial dating, interracial marriage, the espousal of violation of these prohibitions, and membership in groups that advocated interracial marriage. Crucial to the case was the fact that the university grounded its rule not on racial attitudes but on biblical scripture. The school therefore considered the exclusion of interracial dating to be a principal tenet of its religious community. Nevertheless, although the text of section 501(c)(3) did not speak to racial discrimination at all, the Supreme Court upheld the IRS determination, finding the service's interpretation of the code provision to be permissible.

Robert Cover, in his article *Nomos and Narrative*, has famously criticized the reasoning of the *Bob Jones* decision, even while agreeing with the Court's result. According to Cover, the Court assumed "a position that places nothing at risk and from which the Court makes no interpretive gesture at all, save the quintessential gesture to the jurisdictional canons: the statement that an exercise of political authority was not unconstitutional."[70] In particular, Cover argued that, by grounding its decision on an interpretation of the Internal Revenue Code, the Court had sidestepped the crucial constitutional question of whether Congress could grant tax exemptions to schools that discriminated on the basis of race. This was a problem for Cover because he believed that if a state legal authority were going to "kill off" the competing normative commitment of an alternative community, it should do so based on a profound normative commitment of its own.[71] By avoiding the constitutional question, Cover complained, the Court had disserved both the religious community—whose normative commitments would be placed at the mercy of mere public policy judgments—and disserved racial minorities—who "deserved a constitutional commitment to avoiding public subsidization of racism."[72]

In contrast, had the clash between the university's religious rule and the IRS code, or between the religious rule and the U.S. Constitution, been viewed as a choice-of-law decision, two aspects of the case would have been clarified. First, the Court would have analyzed and defined the relevant community affiliations at stake. Second, the Court would have been forced to grapple with the strength of its commitment to the principle of nondiscrimination, just as Cover urged. As a result, instead of simply asserting federal law, a conflicts analysis encourages negotiation among the different norms advanced by different communities.

A cosmopolitan pluralist vision of conflict of laws recognizes that people and groups hold multiple community affiliations and takes those affiliations seriously. Thus, when a nonstate legal practice is largely internal and primarily reflects individuals' affiliation with the nonstate community, the practice should be given more leeway than when the state itself is part of the relevant affiliation. In this case, the issue at stake was a tax-exemption, a quintessentially state matter. Indeed, Bob Jones University was asking for a particular benefit for charitable organizations that was contained in the U.S. tax code. Therefore, for these purposes the place of the university within the nation-state was the most salient tie, making application of the federal law more justifiable. In contrast, as we shall see, other nonstate normative commitments do not implicate the nation-state so directly.

Moreover, even if the relevant community tie were largely with the religious community itself, certain norms might be held so strongly by the nation-state community that such norms would be applied *regardless* of the community affiliation. In choice-of-law analysis, this is usually called the public policy exception, and it allows courts to refuse to apply foreign law that would otherwise apply, if those legal norms are sufficiently repugnant. But as noted previously, application of the public policy exception is rare, both as a normative and descriptive matter. Thus, if a court asserts such an exception, it must justify the use of public policy grounds by reference to precisely the sorts of deeply held commitments that Cover envisioned. In the *Bob Jones* case, for example, it might be that the nation-state's deep commitment to eradicating racial discrimination would independently justify overriding the religious norms, regardless of the community affiliation analysis.

Accordingly, a cosmopolitan pluralist approach would not simply throw the claim of protected religious insularity to the mercy of political or bureaucratic judgments. Taking the ban on interracial dating seriously as law and performing a choice-of-law analysis would create the obligation to engage in crucial line-drawing. And while the community affiliation and public policy exception analyses *in this case* might justify application of state law, that will not always be the case.

Consider, by way of contrast, *Employment Div., Dept. of Human Resources of Oregon v. Smith*, in which the Supreme Court refused to extend First Amendment protection to the religious use of peyote.[73] Here, unlike the tax exemption at issue in *Bob Jones*, the Indian tribe was not negotiating its relationship with the state; rather the use of peyote was part of a purely internal religious practice open primarily (or exclusively) to members of that community. Thus, a choice-of-law analysis based on community affiliation might well result in deference to the nonstate norm. Moreover, the normative commitment to drug enforcement is perhaps better characterized as a governance choice than as an inexorable normative command. As such, the public policy exception is arguably less appropriate in this context than when addressing racial discrimination. Applying these principles, a cosmopolitan pluralist choice-of-law analysis might well have permitted the religious practice in *Smith*.

In the end, however, I am less concerned with the particular outcome than with the analytical framework. Conceiving of these clashes between religious and state-based norms in conflicts terms reorients the inquiry in a way that takes more seriously the nonstate community assertion. As a result, courts must wrestle both with the nature of the multiple community affiliations potentially at issue and with the need to articulate truly strong normative justifications for not deferring to the nonstate norm. Both consequences make the choice-of-law decision a constructive terrain of engagement among multiple normative systems, rather than an arm of state government imposing its normative vision on all within its coercive power.

Of course, this vision is not unproblematic. Two related objections immediately present themselves. First, a choice-of-law rule that tends to defer to nonstate norms when they implicate only internal community affiliation might be seen to rest on the often-criticized distinction between public and private action. Indeed, the idea of deference in this context might come to look like the classic state deference to family privacy or autonomy.[74] And just as family privacy was often invoked to shield domestic violence and gender hierarchy, so too may deference to "internal" community norms become deference to fundamentally illiberal norms.

Second, as in the family context, we may make a mistake by assuming that the nonstate community at issue is monolithic. Indeed, it may be that some members of the relevant community would prefer to have the *state* norm applied to their situation. As Judith Resnik has noted, Cover's vision of multiple norm-generating communities did not address the problem of conflict "*within* [such] communities about their own practices and authoritative interpretations."[75] Yet, such "contestation from within,"[76] which is likely to occur along the fault lines of power hierarchies within the community, is an almost inevitable part of community norm creation. Thus, the choice-of-law question becomes, in part, a question of whose voices within a community are heard by which speakers of nation-state power.

As to the concern that too much deference to "private" norms within a community will overly empower illiberal communities, it is important to remember that, because of the public policy exception, these norms, if sufficiently abhorrent, need not be applied by the state authority. After all, a lynch mob may also be a statement of community norms, but it need not for that reason necessarily be embraced. The object of a choice-of-law analysis is not to blindly follow nonstate community norms, but to ensure that if a state asserts its own norms it does so self-consciously. Indeed, simply acknowledging the state's jurispathic power does not necessarily mean that we must reject all exercises of that power.[77] Even Cover recognized the utility of a state court's speaking in "imperial mode" at least sometimes.[78] He noted that, when judges kill off competing law by asserting that "*this one* is the law," they may do violence to the competing visions, but they also enable peace both because too much law is too chaotic to sustain and because some laws are simply too noxious to be applied.[79] The point then is simply to make sure that the imposition of imperial, jurispathic law is not done blindly or arrogantly, but with intentionality and a respect for the other sources of law-making that are being displaced.[80] A conflicts analysis at least opens space for such self-consciousness and care.

More difficult is the problem of how to respond to Resnik's arguments about inevitable conflicts within a nonstate community concerning the content of that community's norms. Certainly the existence of substantial disagreement within the community might be factored into the decision of whether or not to apply the state norm. Thus, if some substantial portion of the nonstate community were clamoring for the application of *state* law, such clamoring might blunt somewhat the need to defer to the nonstate norm.

More important, in thinking about how to address disputes within a nonstate community, we must distinguish between two types of challenges. One concerns the proper understanding of what the content of the community's law *actually is* and the other concerns what that law *ought to be*. For example, in *Santa Clara Pueblo v. Martinez*, a woman who was a member of an Indian tribe challenged her tribe's refusal to consider her children to be tribal members.[81] She did so, however, not based on an argument that the tribe had improperly interpreted its own community law (which based tribal membership on the father's tribal membership, not the mother's). Instead, she argued that the tribe's law was inconsistent with a federal equal protection statute. Thus, the case did not present a contestation about the content of the community's norms; it merely raised a choice-of-law issue about whether the tribal law or the federal statute should govern. And however difficult the resolution of that choice-of-law question might be, it does not raise the conundrum of how to determine the appropriate content of the nonstate norm in the first place.

Finally, in those relatively infrequent situations when the actual content of the nonstate norm *is* at issue, courts can seek evidence to determine that community's governing norm. Historical documentation, anthropological testimony, and evidence of ongoing practice might all be relevant. And again, to the extent that there are concerns that the nonstate norm is the product of hierarchy, those concerns can be factored into the choice-of-law inquiry itself; they do not render it impossible to determine the content of the norm.

C. International Communities

As discussed previously, a conflicts perspective encourages negotiation among Self and Other, local and distant, familiar and strange. Sometimes the distant and unfamiliar Other will be embodied in the norms asserted by international bodies. Adopting a pluralist framework allows scholars to consider the impact of such international norms without endless debates about whether in fact such norms should count as "law." Because legal pluralism turns the gaze to an analysis of how such norms actually affect behavior on the ground, we can focus not on abstract questions of legitimacy, but on empirical questions of efficacy. The important point for legal pluralism, after all, is what people come to believe and with what commitment.

Accordingly, there is nothing inherently illegitimate, from a pluralist point of view, about a state-sanctioned court considering norms articulated in an international forum. To the contrary, one can think of the potential conflict between a state norm and an international one as again raising a conflict-of-laws question. And, even when a court does actually decide to defer to an international norm, the court might be seen not as thwarting the democratic will of the local polity, but as effectuating a broader domestic governmental interest in being part of an interlocking and smoothly functioning global legal system. In order to explore these issues further, I will briefly address two recent cases and analyze them from a conflicts perspective.

In *Torres v. State of Oklahoma*, the Oklahoma Court of Criminal Appeals was forced to decide how much weight to give to a decision issued by the International Court of Justice (ICJ).[82] Torres, a Mexican national, had been arrested in 1993, convicted of murder, and sentenced to death. After the Oklahoma Court of Criminal Appeals affirmed Torres's conviction on direct appeal, Torres filed a habeas petition in federal court, complaining for the first time that the Oklahoma authorities who arrested him had failed to inform him of his right to have the detaining officials contact the Mexican consulate if he so wished. This right is contained in the Vienna Convention on Consular Relations (Vienna

Convention), of which the United States is a signatory.[83] The federal courts denied habeas relief on the Vienna Convention issues, applying both Oklahoma's procedural default rule (because the Vienna Convention claim had not been raised in state court) and the federal Antiterrorism and Effective Death Penalty Act's requirement that habeas relief not be granted unless the claimant can prove prejudice. The U.S. Supreme Court denied certiorari, with two justices writing separately to express concern about the Vienna Convention violation.[84]

Subsequently, Mexico, on behalf of some fifty Mexican nationals on death row in various U.S. states (including Torres), filed a Vienna Convention case against the United States in the ICJ. Thus, the conflict-of-laws question for the Oklahoma Court of Criminal Appeals was what, if any, consideration to give to the ICJ case. At first, it seemed, very little. On March 2, 2004, even though the ICJ case was still pending, the Oklahoma Court of Criminal Appeals set Torres's execution date for May 18, 2004. However, on March 31, 2004, the ICJ issued its decision, concluding that, in its arrest, detention, trial, and sentencing of the Mexican nationals, the United States had violated its obligations under the Vienna Convention.[85] Significantly, although Mexico had argued that the convictions in all of the cases should be annulled, the ICJ determined, in deference to U.S. judicial process, that the defendants need only be afforded "review and reconsideration" to determine the extent to which each particular defendant had been prejudiced by the respective Vienna Convention violations.[86] The ICJ further concluded that the various procedural default rules initially relied upon by the federal courts in *Torres* themselves violate the Vienna Convention to the extent that they precluded such "review and reconsideration."[87]

With Torres's execution date approaching, the conflict-of-laws decision was particularly stark: continue to adhere to its previous affirmance and ignore the ICJ order, or treat the order as a relevant decision entitled to recognition. Finally, on May 13, 2004, just five days before Torres's scheduled execution, the Oklahoma Court of Criminal Appeals, by a 3 to 2 decision, stayed the execution and remanded the case for an evidentiary hearing to determine, in part, whether Torres was "prejudiced by the State's violation of his Vienna Convention rights."[88] The governor commuted Torres's sentence to life in prison without parole later that day.

Although some argued that the Oklahoma court's deference to the ICJ decision was inappropriate and diminished the autonomy of the Oklahoma courts, looking at the decision from a conflicts perspective helps to clarify the issues at stake. After all, as noted previously, United States courts routinely enforce judgments issued by foreign tribunals. As far back as 1895, in *Hilton v. Guyot*, the U.S. Supreme Court made clear that comity "is the recognition which one nation allows within its territory to the legislative, executive or judicial acts of another nation, having due regard both to international duty and convenience, and to the rights of its own citizens, or of other persons who are under the protection of its laws."[89] The Second Restatement of Conflict of Laws codified this idea, noting that a "judgment rendered in a foreign nation . . . will, if valid, usually be given the same effect as a sister State judgment."[90] Moreover, validity is based only on whether the court that rendered judgment had proper personal jurisdiction over the parties and utilized procedures that were not inherently unfair.[91]

In addition, while courts enforcing foreign judgments (as opposed to domestic ones) have applied a public policy exception to avoid enforcing particularly egregious rulings, the exception has been construed very narrowly. Accordingly, courts refuse to enforce only "where the original claim is repugnant to fundamental notions of what is decent and just in the State where enforcement is sought."[92] Likewise, the UN Convention on the Recognition and Enforcement of Foreign Arbitral Awards and the Uniform Foreign Money-Judgments Recognition Act require that a U.S. court enforce a judgment or arbitral award unless there is fraud or if doing so would be repugnant to the public policy of the enforcing forum. Thus, in most recognition of judgments cases, "[c]ourts consistently have enforced foreign judgments even if they would have refused to entertain suit on the original claim on grounds of public policy."[93]

Moreover, thinking of *Torres* using a judgment recognition frame encourages courts to consider the normative community that the ICJ decision represents. This normative community, significantly, includes the United States. Indeed, the Optional Protocol to the Vienna Convention, which makes the ICJ the venue to consider all "[d]isputes arising out of the interpretation or application" of the convention, was not only ratified but also drafted (and championed) by the United States in the first place.

Thus, as Judge Chapel wrote in a special, unpublished concurrence to the Oklahoma Court of Criminal Appeals' decision,[94] the United States freely and consensually signed and ratified the Vienna Convention, including the Optional Protocol, creating binding, contractlike legal obligations between the United States and other state parties. The Court of Criminal Appeals was therefore "bound by the Vienna Convention and Optional Protocol" and was obligated "to give effect" to both. And the ICJ decision, because it was a "product of the process set forth in the Optional Protocol" deserved, according to Judge Chapel, the Court of Criminal Appeals' "full faith and credit." By conceiving of the ICJ decision's force in conflicts terms, Judge Chapel was able to stave off concerns about encroachments on local state sovereignty.

Turning to the private law context, under Chapter 11 of the North American Free Trade Agreement (NAFTA), we face the prospect of international panels reviewing the judgments of domestic courts.[95] And though these NAFTA panels lack formal authority over the domestic courts they review, they do have the power to assess damages against federal authorities for violations of the trade agreement, even if those violations occurred in the context of a domestic court judgment. Thus, we again see plural sources of normative authority: the domestic court that issued an initial judgment, the NAFTA tribunal that reviews this judgment for fidelity with the principles of the treaty, and the federal authorities who, in response to pressure from the NAFTA tribunal, may in turn put pressure on the domestic court.

For example, in *Loewen Group v. United States*, a NAFTA tribunal reviewed the proceedings of the Mississippi courts concerning contract and antitrust claims brought by a local entity against a Canadian corporation.[96] The tribunal criticized the trial as "so flawed that it constituted a miscarriage of justice amounting to a manifest injustice as that expression is understood in international law."[97] In addition, the tribunal criticized the $400 million punitive damages, and even the compensatory damages, as "grossly disproportionate" to the damage actually suffered.[98] And while in the end the NAFTA panel refrained (on standing grounds) from assessing damages against the United States, there is little reason to think that liability in similar situations will not be imposed in the future.

Thus, the question becomes: how will a domestic court, faced with a multinational dispute, respond both to the NAFTA precedents already in place and the threat of possible NAFTA panel review? Robert Ahdieh has argued that we are likely to see, over time, a dialectical relationship form between the domestic and international tribunals, in which both courts pay attention to each other's interpretations and, while not literally bound by each other's decisions, develop a joint jurisprudence partly in tandem and partly in tension with each other.[99]

Although Ahdieh doesn't identify it as such, the sort of hybrid jurisprudence he envisions can be conceptualized as part of a cosmopolitan pluralist choice-of-law approach. Recognizing multiple community affiliations and multiple sources of norms, courts adopting a cosmopolitan pluralist perspective will seek to develop rules that reflect, as well as possible, the multiple values implicated. In this respect, a cosmopolitan pluralist choice-of-law methodology borrows from the so-called substantive law method associated in the 1970s and 1980s with Arthur von Mehren[100] and Friedrich Juenger,[101] but most recently championed by Graeme Dinwoodie.[102]

Dinwoodie notes that courts in ordinary domestic disputes often must generate common-law rules or glosses on legislative enactments.[103] Indeed, any time a court adjudicates a dispute that does not involve a single governing rule the judge must select among possible models. For example, a court asked for the first time to adjudicate a question of contract formation where the parties communicated telephonically might draw on rules developed for face-to-face negotiations as well as those applicable to negotiations via postal mail. As Dinwoodie points out, a court may consider both rules, but is not required simply to choose one or the other; instead the court is likely to blend principles from each set of rules. Likewise, Dinwoodie argues, a court in a multistate dispute should not consider itself bound to choose one state's law over the other in toto; it should instead be free to craft a hybrid rule that reflects the interests of the multiple states and parties involved. Again, considering such hybridity forces courts to grapple with the multiple normative orders in play, thereby surfacing the interactions across different communities and different perspectives, rather than simply choosing one order while ignoring all others.

D. Ethnic Communities

Finally, a cosmopolitan pluralist perspective on conflict of laws would take seriously the fact that even citizens of a nation-state may have strong ethnic ties with a "homeland" that are sufficiently significant to warrant application of the ethnic group norm rather than the state-based one. The relevant question in such cases would be whether the applicable community affiliation is more appropriately deemed to be the community of current residence or the ethnic identity.

For example, Anupam Chander has written about the fact that many members of the Indian-American diaspora purchase bonds issued by their home country of India.[104] The purchase of these bonds obviously reflects the ongoing tie these members of the Indian diaspora feel for their "homeland." Thus, using a cosmopolitan pluralist framework, one might argue that, even when these bonds are purchased in the United States, the purchases should be governed by Indian, rather than U.S., securities laws because the bond sale reflects a substantive (and voluntary) tie between the purchasers and the Indian government.

Of course sometimes, particularly in multiethnic states with uncertain or unstable political sovereignty, we may see dueling legal systems operating among different ethnic populations within the same territorial space. Indeed, some of the classic pluralist literature focused on the interaction of colonial and indigenous legal systems in the African colonies. More recently, Elena Baylis has written about the two parallel court systems currently operating in Kosovo, one Serbian and the other largely Kosovar Albanian and controlled by the UN Interim Administration Mission in Kosovo.[105] Baylis notes that, "[f]or the people of Kosovo these parallel systems create legal uncertainty and conflict on a basic, day-to-day level."[106] Because the systems do not recognize each other's judgments and do not share court files, parties must register land titles, births, deaths, marriages, and divorces, and pursue even run-of-the-mill civil matters in both courts, leading to conflicting judgments, speculation, and arbitrage. Meanwhile, criminal suspects may also face trial in both courts.

As Baylis observes, Kosovo's parallel courts present in an acute form a problem facing many divided societies:

> How, for example, should Mexico treat decisions from Zapatista courts? What about the judgments of religious authorities in Iraq, Pakistan, Nigeria, or France? How can long divided societies like the Greek and Turkish administrations in Cyprus incorporate each other's judicial determinations if they are eventually unified?[107]

Significantly, while bringing to justice those accused of the worst human rights abuses has long been the focus of international law scholars and activists, the day-to-day operation of these plural legal systems and their resolution of more ordinary disputes may be just as important to the local population and may be an even more crucial element in the rebuilding of postconflict societies.

Interestingly, although Baylis (like Ahdieh) does not identify the problem as one involving conflict of laws, she offers a solution grounded in a cosmopolitan pluralist conception of judgment recognition. While acknowledging that the competing claims to sovereignty in Kosovo are fundamentally political (or military) problems, she points out that, in real practical terms, the parallel courts have issued legal decisions for many years now and will continue to do so. Thus, "[as] long as people in Kosovo continue to rely on those decisions, past or present, whether those judgments can and should be recognized and enforced are legal questions that must be addressed."[108] And significantly, in a world of plural norm creation, it is not necessary for courts to recognize each other's actual *legitimacy* or claims to *sovereignty* to recognize each other's legal *judgments*, at least in the mine run of cases. Indeed, as Baylis argues, such negotiation of difference could actually provide a foundation for political compromise on the broader question of sovereignty.

Of course, in a land of intense interethnic rivalry and contest, some judgments may so reek of ethnic favoritism that enforcing the judgment will be anathema. But that is simply a more extreme form of the trade-off between finality and public policy that is always part of any judgment recognition calculus. "Subjecting judgments to increased levels of scrutiny to ensure their fairness inevitably introduces delays and unpredictability in their enforcement, in rough proportion to the complexity of the procedures and the stringency of the tests employed for that purpose."[109] Accordingly, a cosmopolitan pluralist vision of judgment recognition, as discussed previously, will take seriously the systemic value of having a functioning, interlocking judicial system, and therefore deny recognition only in those rare cases where the judgments are so tainted by bias or so contrary to local policy that they cannot be followed. And even then, the general norm of recognition would require explanation of, and justification for, any deviations from this norm.

Conclusion

Again it must be emphasized that viewing these disputes through a cosmopolitan pluralist conflicts lens will not "solve" the intractable problem of plural communities with plural norms. Indeed, in a plural world, eradicating normative conflict is not only impossible, it is undesirable. In the interaction between Self and Other, I follow Arendt and Young in accepting that we are strangers forever, living in a space of unassimilated otherness. Thus, I believe that conflict-of-laws doctrines are best understood not as seeking harmonization and convergence among the world's legal regimes. Rather, I view conflicts as both a celebration of and negotiation of difference. Accordingly, even if, as some have suggested, the nation-state legal regimes of the world are increasingly converging and developing a "world law,"[110] we would still need conflicts thinking so as to acknowledge and accommodate nonstate norms that may operate outside of this harmonization process. Moreover, we would need conflicts as a way of emphasizing important normative differences that remain among the peoples of the world, rather than seeking homogenization.

Adopting a conflicts framework, we can turn the gaze to the discursive interaction among a wide variety of norm-generating communities that are based on the entire panoply of multiple overlapping affiliations and attachments people actually experience in their daily lives, from the local to the global (including some affiliations not based on territory at all). In this vision, a jurisdictional assertion is part of an international and transnational process of community definition and norm creation. Moreover, the state need not only be seen as a jurispathic force that imposes its law and eradicates all others. Instead, the state, through a broader commitment to the governmental interest in being part of a functioning and interlocking global legal order, might actually be jurisgenerative, enabling recognition of, discussion about, and even deference to nonstate norms, at least some of the time.[111] And even when deference is impossible (because substantive agreement about norms is impossible), we may at least be able to develop a legal language in which the negotiation of difference can take place. As Stuart Hampshire has written, although we inevitably disagree about values, we might sometimes reach provisional compromises about procedures.[112] Therefore, we may find ways to "bear with" each other, as Arendt hoped, without needing to assume away normative difference. In any event, given an increasingly intertwined global legal system, where communities cannot avoid encountering strangers both within and without, law's potential role as a site for communication across difference grows ever more important.

Notes

An earlier version of this Essay was presented in April 2006 at Amherst College. I thank participants in that session for many useful comments, and I acknowledge the outstanding research assistance I received from Paul Johnson, Michelle Querijiero, and Gavan F. Meehan.

1. I have attempted to map this legal terrain in several previous articles. See Paul Schiff Berman, "Towards a Cosmopolitan Vision of Conflict of Laws: Redefining Governmental Interests in a Global Era," *University of Pennsylvania Law Review* 153 (2005): 1819; Berman, "From International Law to Law and Globalization," *Columbia Journal of Transnational Law* 43 (2005): 485; and Berman, "The Globalization of Jurisdiction," *University of Pennsylvania Law Review* 151 (2002): 311; see also Berman, *Law Beyond Borders: Jurisprudence in a Hybrid World* (New York: Cambridge University Press, 2011).

2. My discussion here relies heavily on Z. D. Gurevitch, "The Other Side of Dialogue: On Making the Other Strange and the Experience of Otherness," *American Journal of Sociology* 93 (1988): 1179.

3. See Alfred Schutz, *On Phenomenology and Social Relations*, ed. H. R. Wagner (Chicago: University of Chicago Press, 1970); Schutz, *Collected Papers I: The Problem of Social Reality*, ed. Maurice Natanson (The Hague: Martinus Nijhoff Publishers, 1962); Schutz, "The Stranger: An Essay in Social Psychology," *American Journal of Sociology* 49 (1944): 499.

4. Schutz, *On Phenomenology and Social Relations*, 181.

5. See Gurevitch, "The Other Side of Dialogue," 1180 (summarizing arguments in Schutz, *The Problem of Social Reality*).

6. See Harold Garfinkel, "Studies of the Routine Grounds of Everyday Activities," *Social Problems* 11 (1963): 225.

7. Gurevitch, "The Other Side of Dialogue," 1180.

8. Ibid., 1181–82.

9. See, generally, Georg Simmel, "The Stranger," in *The Sociology of Georg Simmel*, ed. K. H. Wolff (New York: Free Press, 1950).

10. Hannah Arendt, "Understanding and Politics (The Difficulties of Understanding)," in her *Essays in Understanding: 1930–1954*, ed. Jerome Kohn (New York: Harcourt Brace, 1994), 322.

11. In focusing on Arendt's idea of "bearing with strangers," I draw from the analysis in Phillip Hansen, "Hannah Arendt and Bearing with Strangers," *Contemporary Political Theory* 3 (2004): 3.

12. Ibid.

13. Arendt, "Understanding and Politics," 322.

14. Ibid., 308.

15. See ibid., 310–13.

16. Jean Bethke Elshtain, "Judging Rightly," *First Things* 47 (1994): 49 (reviewing Arendt, "Understanding and Politics").

17. Arendt, "Understanding and Politics," 313.

18. See Iris Marion Young, "The Ideal of Community and the Politics of Difference," in *Feminism/Postmodernism*, ed. Linda J. Nicholson (New York: Routledge,1990), 300, 317, 319. ("Our political ideal is the unoppressive city.")

19. Ibid., 318.

20. Ibid.

21. Ibid., 319.

22. Young resists using the word "community" because of the "urge to unity" the term conveys, but acknowledges that "[in] the end it may be a matter of stipulation whether one chooses to call" her vision "community"; ibid., 320. See also Jerry Frug, "The Geography of Community," *Stanford Law Review* 48 (1996): 1047, 1049. ("Unlike Young, I do not cede the term community to those who evoke the romance of togetherness.")

23. See Young, "The Ideal of Community and the Politics of Difference," 319 (positing that a group of strangers living side by side "instantiates social relations as difference in the sense of an understanding of groups and cultures that are different, with exchanging and overlapping interactions that do not issue in community, yet which prevent them from being outside of one another").

24. Ibid.

25. These tests include: (1) finding jurisdiction everywhere a website can be viewed; (2) finding jurisdiction only where content is uploaded; (3) finding jurisdiction only where servers are located; (4) finding jurisdiction anywhere effects are felt; (5) basing jurisdiction on number of web "hits"; (6) basing jurisdiction on the degree to which the website in question is commercial and interactive; (7) finding jurisdiction if a website "targets" a jurisdiction; (8) basing jurisdiction on whether the site is "of local character" or if instead it is meant for a more general audience. Berman, "The Globalization of Jurisdiction," 412–23. For a discussion of jurisdiction doctrine concerning the internet, see ibid., 512–14; Michael A. Geist, "Is There a There There? Toward Greater Certainty for Internet Jurisdiction," *Berkeley Technology Law Journal* 16 (2001): 1345.

26. See Cesare P. R. Romano, "The International Judiciary in Context: A Synoptic Chart," *The Project on International Courts and Tribunals*, HTTP://WWW.PICT-PCTI.ORG/PUBLICATIONS/SYNOPTIC_CHART/SYNOP_C4.PDF.

27. See, for example, Arjun Appadurai, "Disjuncture and Difference in the Global Cultural Economy," in Appadurai, *Modernity at Large: Cultural Dimensions of Globalization* (Minneapolis: University of Minnesota Press, 1996), 27, 27–29 ("[T]oday's world involves interactions of a new order and intensity. . . . [W]ith the advent of the steam-

ship, the automobile, the airplane, the camera, the computer, and the telephone, we have entered into an altogether new condition of neighborliness, even with those most distant from ourselves"). See also, for example, Anthony Giddens, *Runaway World: How Globalization Is Reshaping Our Lives* (New York: Routledge, 2000), 24–37 (pointing to the increased level of trade, finance, and capital flows, and describing the effects of the weakening hold of older nation-states); Saskia Sassen, *Globalization and Its Discontents: Essays on the New Mobility of People and Money* (New York: New Press, 1998) (analyzing globalization and its economic, political, and cultural effects on the world).

28. See, for example, John Gerard Ruggie, "Territoriality and Beyond: Problematizing Modernity in International Relations," *International Organization* 47 (1993): 139, 149, (noting that premodern states were not based principally on territorial sovereignty and that, instead, medieval Europe was in some ways an archetype for "nonexclusive territorial rule," with its "patchwork of overlapping and incomplete rights of government" inextricably superimposed and tangled, quoting Joseph R. Strayer and Dana C. Munro, *The Middle Ages* [New York: Appleton-Century-Crofts, 1959], 115; and Perry Anderson, *Lineages of the Absolutist State* [London: New Left Books, 1974], 37, respectively).

29. This thought-experiment is derived from David G. Post, "Against 'Against Cyberanarchy,'" *Berkeley Technology Law Journal* 17 (2002): 1365, 1371–73.

30. Giddens, *The Consequences of Modernity* (Stanford, CA: Stanford University Press, 1990), 140–41.

31. See John Tomlinson, *Globalization and Culture* (Chicago: University of Chicago Press, 1999), 107–8.

32. Ibid., 115.

33. For further discussion of these multiple forms of community, see Berman, "The Globalization of Jurisdiction," 472–95.

34. Restatement (First) of Conflict of Laws §378 (1934) ("The law of the place of wrong determines whether a person has sustained a legal injury").

35. Joseph H. Beale, *A Treatise on the Conflict of Laws*: Volume 2, *Choice of Law* (New York: Baker, Voorhis, 1935), 1091 ("The question whether a contract is valid . . . can on general principles be determined by no other law than that which applies to the acts, that is, by the law of the place of contracting. . . . If . . . the law of the place where the agreement is made annexes no legal obligation to it, there is no other law which has power to do so").

36. See ibid., 938 (finding that immovable property, "being unable to be taken away from the state in which [it is located], must always in the last analysis be governed by the laws of that state").

37. Ibid., Volume 1, *Jurisdiction* (New York: Baker, Voorhis, 1935), 64 ("[T]he chief task of the Conflict of Laws [is] to determine the place where a right arose and the law that created it").

38. 11 So. 803, 803–4 (1892).

39. See Restatement (First) of Conflict of Laws §386 (1934).

40. See, for example, Lea Brilmayer, *Conflict of Laws: Foundations and Future Directions* (Boston: Little, Brown, 1991), 20–22 (discussing such difficulties).

41. This scenario is discussed in Brainerd Currie, *Selected Essays on the Conflict of Laws* (Durham, NC: Duke University Press, 1963), 88.

42. See U.S. Constitution Art. IV, §1 ("Full Faith and Credit shall be given in each State to the public Acts, Records, and judicial Proceedings of every other State. And the Congress may by general Laws prescribe the Manner in which such Acts, Records and Proceedings shall be proved, and the Effect thereof").

43. See, for example, *Baker v. Gen. Motors Corp.*, 522 U.S. 222, 233 (1998) (making clear that there is no public policy exception to the full faith and credit due judgments); see also, for example, *Estin v. Estin,* 334 U.S. 541, 546 (1948) (noting that the Full Faith and Credit Clause "ordered submission . . . even to hostile policies reflected in the judgment of another State, because the practical operation of the federal system, which the Constitution designed, demanded it"); *Milwaukee County v. M.E. White Co.,* 296 U.S. 268, 277 (1935) ("In numerous cases this court has held that credit must be given to the judgment of another state, although the forum would not be required to entertain the suit on which the judgment was founded"); *Fauntleroy v. Lum,* 210 U.S. 230, 237 (1908) (holding that the judgment of a Missouri court is entitled to full faith and credit in Mississippi even if the Missouri judgment rested on a misapprehension of Mississippi law).

44. In most areas of law, U.S. courts have generally enforced foreign judgments as a matter of comity. See Mark D. Rosen, "Exporting the Constitution," *Emory Law Journal* 53 (2004): 171, 176 (noting that, since the nineteenth century, "the United States has been at the vanguard of enforcing foreign judgments"). Indeed, as far back as 1895, in *Hilton v. Guyot,* the U.S. Supreme Court made clear that comity "is the recognition which one nation allows within its territory to the legislative, executive or judicial acts of another nation, having due regard both to international duty and convenience, and to the rights of its own citizens, or of other persons who are under the protection of its laws." 159 U.S. 113, 164 (1895). The Second Restatement codifies this idea, noting that a "judgment rendered in a foreign nation . . . will, if valid, usually be given the same effect as a sister State judgment." Restatement (Second) of Conflict of Laws §117, cmt. c (1971). Moreover, validity is based only on whether the court that rendered judgment had proper personal jurisdiction over the parties and utilized procedures that were not inherently unfair. Restatement (Second) of Conflict. . . . §92.

45. U.S. courts enforcing foreign judgments (as opposed to domestic ones) have sometimes applied a public policy exception to avoid enforcing particularly egregious rulings, but the public policy exception has been construed very narrowly. See Rosen,

"Exporting the Constitution," 177–79 (surveying U.S. case law on enforcement of foreign judgments). Accordingly, courts usually refuse to enforce only "where the original claim is repugnant to fundamental notions of what is decent and just in the State where enforcement is sought." Restatement (Second) of Conflicts of Law §117 cmt. c (1971). Likewise, the UN Convention on the Recognition and Enforcement of Foreign Arbitral Awards Art. V and the Uniform Foreign Money-Judgments Recognition Act §4(B)(2)-(3) requires that a U.S. court enforce the judgment or arbitral award unless there is fraud or if doing so would be repugnant to the public policy of the enforcing forum. Thus, in most recognition of judgments cases, "[c]ourts consistently have enforced foreign judgments even if they would have refused to entertain suit on the original claim on grounds of public policy." Rosen, "Exporting the Constitution," 178–79.

46. *Loucks v. Standard Oil Co.*, 120 N.E. 198, 201 (N.Y., 1918).

47. See Brief for the Respondents, at *11–12, *Rasul v. Bush*, Nos. 03-334, 03-343, 2004 WL 425739 (March 3, 2004).

48. See *Rasul v. Bush*, 542 U.S. 466 (2004).

49. T.G.I. Paris, UEJF et Licra c/ Yahoo! Inc. et Yahoo France (May 22, 2000), http://www.juriscom.net/txt/jurisfr/cti/tgiparis20000522.htm.

50. See ibid. (November 20, 2000), http://www.juriscom.net/txt/jurisfr/cti/tgiparis20001120.pdf. As Greg Wrenn, associate general counsel for Yahoo!'s international division, put it: "We are not going to acquiesce in the notion that foreign countries have unlimited jurisdiction to regulate the content of U.S.-based sites." Carl S. Kaplan, "Experts See Online Speech Case as Bellwether," *N.Y. Times*, January 5, 2001, available at http://www.nytimes.com/2001/01/05/technology/05CYBERLAW.html?pagewanted=print.

51. See Joel R. Reidenberg, "Yahoo and Democracy on the Internet," *Jurimetrics Journal* 42 (2002): 261 (arguing that the French *Yahoo!* decision signals that the Internet regulatory framework "must recognize values adopted by different states" and can no longer be dictated by primarily U.S.-based technical elites).

52. Indeed, one member of an expert panel appointed by the Yahoo! court to explore the feasibility of geographical filtering subsequently argued that such filtering, though technically feasible, would impose a tremendous burden on services such as Yahoo! because such services would be required "to maintain a huge matrix of pages versus jurisdictions to see who can and can't see what." Ben Laurie, "An Expert's Apology," (November 21, 2000), http://www.apache-ssl.org/apology.html.

53. See, for example, Rebecca M. Bratspies and Russell A. Miller, eds., *Transboundary Harm in International Law: Lessons from the Trail Smelter Arbitration* (Cambridge: Cambridge University Press, 2006); Philippe Sands, "Turtles and Torturers: The Transformation of International Law," *New York University Journal of International Law and Politics* 33 (2001): 527, 535–36.

54. See, for example, Richard W. Parker, "The Use and Abuse of Trade Leverage to

Protect the Global Commons: What We Can Learn from the Tuna-Dolphin Conflict," *Georgetown International Environmental Law Review* 12 (1999): 1–13.

55. See Berman, "Towards a Cosmopolitan Vision of Conflict of Laws," 1878; Reidenberg, "Yahoo and Democracy on the Internet," 267.

56. *Barcelona.com, Inc. v. Excelentisimo Ayuntamiento de Barcelona,* 330 F.3d 617 (4th Cir. 2003).

57. 702 A.2d 230 (Md., 1997).

58. 376 U.S. 254 (1964).

59. See Larry Rohter, "Argentine Congress Likely to Void 'Dirty War' Amnesties," *N.Y. Times*, August 21, 2003, A3 (recounting Garzón's extradition request).

60. Emma Daly, "Spanish Judge Sends Argentine to Prison on Genocide Charge," *N.Y. Times*, June 30, 2003, A3 ("In an unusual act of international judicial cooperation, and a victory for the Spanish judge Baltasar Garzón, Mexico's Supreme Court ruled this month that the former officer, Ricardo Miguel Cavallo, could be extradited to Spain for crimes reportedly committed in a third country, Argentina").

61. See David B. Rivkin, Jr., and Lee A. Casey, "Crimes outside the World's Jurisdiction," *N.Y. Times*, July 22, 2003, A19 (noting that Argentina had granted amnesty to Cavallo and arguing that "Judge Garzón is essentially ignoring Argentina's own history and desires").

62. The Argentine army, for example, made known its desire for amnesty for human rights abuses through several revolts in the late 1980s. The Argentine Congress granted amnesty after one such uprising in 1987. Joseph B. Treaster, "Argentine President Orders Troops to End Revolt," *N.Y. Times*, December 4, 1988, Section 1, 13 (describing an army revolt in Buenos Aires).

63. "Congress Scraps 2 Amnesty Laws," *Chicago Tribune*, August 21, 2003, 8; "Lower House Votes to End Amnesty Laws," *Chicago Tribune*, August 13, 2003, 8.

64. Elizabeth Nash, "Garzón Blocked over 'Dirty War' Extraditions," *Independent*, August 30, 2003, 14; see also Al Goodman, "Spain Blocks Trial of Argentines," CNN.com, August 29, 2003, http://www.cnn.com/2003/WORLD/europe/08/29/spanish.argentina/index.html (quoting the Spanish attorney for the victims saying that the Spanish government's decision sends a "powerful message" to Argentina's Supreme Court to overturn the amnesty laws).

65. Héctor Tobar, "Judge Orders Officers Freed," *Los Angeles Times*, September 2, 2003, 3 ("President Nestor Kirchner used Spain's announcement to increase pressure on the Argentine Supreme Court to overturn the amnesty laws that prohibit trying the men here").

66. Corte Suprema de Justicia [CSJN], 14/6/2005, "Simón, Julio Héctor y otros s/ privación ilegítima de la libertad, etc." causa No. 17.768, S.1767.XXXVIII (Arg.), available at http://www.mpf.gov.ar/MPF2/Novedades/Simon.pdf. See also "Argentina: Amnesty

Laws Struck Down," *Human Rights Watch,* June 14, 2005, available at http://www.hrw.org/en/news/2005/06/14/argentina-amnesty-laws-struck-down.

67. For further discussion of various ways in which international law exerts significant impact on states by altering both legal consciousness and the relative power of domestic political actors, see Berman, "Seeing Beyond the Limits of International Law," *Texas Law Review* 84 (2006): 1265, reviewing Jack L. Goldsmith and Eric A. Posner, *The Limits of International Law* (Oxford: Oxford University Press, 2005).

68. 461 U.S. 574 (1983).

69. 494 U.S. 872 (1990).

70. Robert M. Cover, "*Nomos* and Narrative," *Harvard Law Review* 97 (1983): 4, 66.

71. See ibid., 52–60.

72. Ibid., 67.

73. 494 U.S. 872 (1990).

74. See, for example, Frances E. Olsen, "The Myth of State Intervention in the Family," *University of Michigan Journal of Law Reform* 18 (1985): 835, 836–37.

75. Judith Resnik, "Living Their Legal Commitments: Paideic Communities, Courts, and Robert Cover," *Yale Journal of Law and the Humanities* 17 (2005): 17, 27 (emphasis added).

76. Ibid., 27.

77. See ibid., 25.

78. Cover, "*Nomos* and Narrative," 13–14.

79. Ibid., 53.

80. See Resnik, "Living Their Legal Commitments," 25 ("[Cover] wanted the state's actors . . . to be uncomfortable in their knowledge of their own power, respectful of the legitimacy of competing legal systems, and aware of the possibility that multiple meanings and divergent practices ought sometimes to be tolerated, even if painfully so").

81. 436 U.S. 49 (1978).

82. *Torres v. State (Torres II),* No. PCD-04-442, 2004 WL 3711623 (Okla. Crim. App. May 13, 2004) (order granting stay of execution and remanding case for evidentiary hearing). My analysis of this case is indebted to Janet Koven Levit, "The Supreme Court, Constitutional Courts and the Role of International Law in Constitutional Jurisprudence: A Tale of International Law in the Heartland: *Torres* and the Role of State Courts in Transnational Legal Conversation," *Tulsa Journal of International and Comparative Law* 12 (2004): 163.

83. "Vienna Convention on Consular Relations and Optional Protocol on Disputes," April 24, 1963, TIAS no. 6820, 21 U.S.T. 77.

84. *Torres v. Mullin,* 124 S. Ct. 919 (2003) (Stevens, J., respecting the denial of the petition for certiorari) and 540 U.S. 1035 (2003) (Breyer, J., dissenting from the denial of the petition for certiorari).

85. See *Avena and Other Mexican Nationals (Mex. v. U.S.)*, 43 I.L.M. 581, March 31, 2004. For a useful summary of the ICJ decision, see Dinah L. Shelton, "Case Concerning Avena and Other Mexican Nationals (Mexico v. United States). 43 I.L.M. 581 (2004). International Court of Justice, March 31, 2004," *American Journal of International Law* 98 (2004): 559.

86. *Avena and Other Mexican Nationals,* 619 (para. 139).

87. Ibid., 619–24 (para. 139–53).

88. *Torres v. State* (Torres II), *1.

89. 159 U.S. 113, 164 (1895).

90. Restatement (Second) of Conflict of Laws §117, cmt. c (1971).

91. Ibid., §92 (1971).

92. Ibid., §117, cmt. c (1971).

93. Rosen, "Exporting the Constitution," 178–79.

94. See *Torres v. State (Torres II)*, *2–3 (Chapel, J., concurring).

95. See Canada-Mexico-United States, "North American Free Trade Agreement," December 8, 1992, Art. 1135, 32 I.L.M. 605, 646 (1993) (outlining remedies available under Chapter 11) [hereinafter NAFTA].

96. *Loewen Group v. United States,* ICSID Case No. ARB(AF)/98/3, 42 I.L.M. 811 (NAFTA Ch. 11 Arb. Trib. 2003). Publicly released documents on all NAFTA disputes are available online at http://www.naftalaw.org.

97. Ibid., 819.

98. Ibid., 829.

99. See Robert B. Ahdieh, "Between Dialogue and Decree: International Review of National Courts," *New York University Law Review* 79 (2004): 2029.

100. See, for example, Arthur Taylor von Mehren, "Special Substantive Rules for Multistate Problems: Their Role and Significance in Contemporary Choice of Law Methodology," *Harvard Law Review* 88 (1974): 347, 371 (arguing that by adopting a substantive approach, "choice of law theory and practice could . . . take a large step toward resolving the ancient conflict between the objectives of aptness and of decisional harmony"); see also von Mehren, "Choice of Law and the Problem of Justice," *Law and Contemporary Problems* 41, no. 2 (Spring 1977): 27, 43 (suggesting that "functional . . . approaches" to choice of law issues achieve "a higher quality of . . . justice" than more traditional choice-of-law methods).

101. See, for example, Friedrich K. Juenger, *Choice of Law and Multistate Justice* (The Netherlands: Martinus Nijhoff Publishers,1993) (calling for the adoption of a substantive approach based on qualitatively evaluating conflicting laws to bring predictability and uniformity to conflicts thinking).

102. See Graeme B. Dinwoodie, "A New Copyright Order: Why National Courts Should Create Global Norms," *University of Pennsylvania Law Review* 149 (2000): 469, 542–71.

103. See ibid., 548.

104. See Anupam Chander, "Diaspora Bonds," *New York University Law Review* 76 (2001): 1005.

105. Elena A. Baylis, "Parallel Courts in Post-Conflict Kosovo," *Yale Journal of International Law* 32 (2007): 1.

106. Ibid., 3.

107. Ibid., 4.

108. Ibid.

109. Ibid., 5.

110. See, for example, Harold J. Berman, "World Law: An Ecumenical Jurisprudence of the Holy Spirit," Emory University School of Law Public Law and Legal Theory Research Paper Series, Research Paper No. 05-4 (February 2005): 5, available at http://ssrn.com/abstract=666143 ("[It] is obvious that there cannot be a world community without a body of world law to maintain both order and justice among its different constituents"); Berman, "World Law," *Fordham International Law Journal* 18 (1995): 1617–22; see also Berman, "Is Conflict-of-Laws Becoming Passe? An Historical Response," Emory Public Law Research Paper No. 05-42 (December 2005): 44, available at http://ssrn.com/abstract=870455 ("[W]ill increasing harmonization of the civil and criminal law of the nation-states of the world substantially reduce the scope of that branch of law that we call conflict-of-laws?").

111. In this sense, my argument may expand on Cover, who arguably did not see a jurisgenerative role for the state. See Robert C. Post, "Who's Afraid of Jurispathic Courts?: Violence and Public Reason in *Nomos and Narrative*," *Yale Journal of Law and the Humanities* 17 (2005): 9, 14 ("Ultimately *Nomos and Narrative* denies the state a role in jurisgenesis because it is skeptical of the possibility of a jurisgenerative politics"). But see Resnik, "Living Their Legal Commitments," 26 ("[U]nlike Robert Post, who reads Robert Cover as turning 'quite palpably away from the state' when he focused on the violence done in the name of court orders, I read Cover as endlessly fascinated with the interactions between the state and paideic communities—and with the potential for such interactions themselves to be jurisgenerative moments") (footnotes omitted).

112. See generally Stuart Hampshire, *Justice Is Conflict* (Princeton: Princeton University Press, 2000).

Who's the Stranger?
Jews, Women, and Bastards in *Daniel Deronda*

HILARY M. SCHOR

George Eliot's 1876 novel *Daniel Deronda* stands as one of the most impressive and most challenging examples of nineteenth-century fictional realism. It is also a novel with an impressive number of strangers—those who simply appear unannounced, after the fashion of many fictional characters; those who are sojourners in a strange land; those who exist outside the community of full English rights and identities, like Jews; those who cannot inherit or own property (not only Jews, but married women or bastards); and those who may begin with coherent legal, social, psychological identities, only to feel themselves increasingly estranged, both from society and themselves, as the novel progresses. Such is the case of the novel's heroine, Gwendolen Harleth, who moves through a plot that strips her of social power only to lend her a powerful sense of moral responsibility; the opposite, in some ways, is true of the novel's hero, Daniel Deronda. Daniel begins the novel with a sense of alienation he cannot quite name, but believes to be his own bastard status. He comes to identify himself increasingly with the Jewish characters with whom he has become entangled, and (learning himself to be a Jew by perfectly legitimate birth) takes up a mission to the Holy Land where he will become, like the Egyptian born Moses, a kind of enlightened leader, a law-giver, to his new-found people.[1] These two characters come together in a plot that itself entangles questions of legal and social identity, romantic desire, and a nameless longing for identity and home, a plot that seems to call out for a discussion of law, fiction, and the stranger.

It is not clear, however, where such a discussion ought best to begin. I began this essay with a set of assumptions that now seem to me somewhat naive, and yet I have found them hard to abandon. I assumed that the question of justice at the heart of law must be most fully engaged by the story of the stranger—

that societies are judged by the way they treat strangers, and that the law in turn is challenged by the questions the stranger asks of it. Similarly, I believed that strangers were at the heart of the novel as a genre, for the novel needs to *conjure* the stranger to exist. I would have said (and again, I am not sure that I was wrong) that the realist novel consists of little beyond the meeting of strangers, the rendering of strangers familiar, and the decision, at the end of any novel, to estrange someone else, to make an ending happy by putting someone outside of it. To the extent that the novel is no less governed by "laws" than the society in which it is written, locating the stranger is a powerful way of understanding the way fiction works, and works within its culture. But when I began this essay I expected, as a literary critic, to find that the law simplified and novels complicated—that it was easy in Victorian Britain to know who the stranger was, and what to say to him; that it was the novel that made strangeness, in a word, interesting. This, for better or worse, has turned out not to be true. *Daniel Deronda* opens with what George Eliot calls, on its opening page, "the make-believe of a beginning,"[2] and goes forward with that same fictional self-consciousness, playing games with form, with character, with the interweaving of plot, to make us aware of the difficulty of "placing" any of its characters absolutely. But it is equally difficult to come to terms with different kinds of strangeness before the law in George Eliot's England, and in asking myself these questions, I have turned variously to the laws governing the inheritance of property, discussions of Married Women's Property laws, and, most unexpectedly, parliamentary debates on the status of "Jewish aliens" and their political "emancipation." *Daniel Deronda*, as a novel, looks forward with strangely utopian fervor to the promised land of Zionist redemption, the mysterious and unnarated East, and that question has fascinated recent critics of the novel,[3] but it also looks forward to as-yet unscripted forms of female emancipation and to new forms of fictional possibility; both the novel and the law are far more interesting, and far more complicated, than I might have imagined.

Any discussion of so long and rich a novel is haunted by the questions it could not fully engage, and in thinking through the questions this essay raises, I have been conscious of the larger conversations about emigration, emancipation, and nationhood; they will play a part in my argument. But my discussion here will focus on two distinct kinds of strangers, those who are in some way outside the law's full dispensation of rights, and those who are estranged by their own consciousness, something seen as a peculiarly modern, and peculiarly liberal, problem in the nineteenth century. I will begin by restoring to *Daniel Deronda* a lost piece of the historical debate that surrounds it, the debate in Britain in the nineteenth century over the emancipation of the Jews. Coming to *Daniel Deronda* from the parliamentary discussion of expanding legal and civic rights allows me to read what is usually read as "two novels," Gwendolen's and Daniel's stories, as a single novel obsessed with foreignness, alienation, and estrangement; it also, unexpectedly, allows me to pay particular attention to the way the plot of bastardy, as the most explicit plot of illegitimation in the Victorian novel, crosses the lives of both Daniel and Gwendolen, forcing on them a new consciousness of (self-)estrangement. This focus has the advantage of freeing the novel from the assumption that the later George Eliot had no interest in the liberal questions of identity and subjecthood that fascinated her in earlier years, but I do not mean this reading to be a purely political intervention in literary history. I want use the complex *formal* entanglement of Daniel's and Gwendolen's stories, the novel's experiments with the forms of realism, as a way of engaging more deeply with the question of the stranger, of asking, of the array of foreigners, sojourners, and legal nonpersons who pass through the novel, "Who's the stranger?"

Strangers in the House

A Victorian thinking about strangers would have begun with the Bible, with the central message that "You were strangers in a strange land"; with the evangelical imagining of African slaves as the new Israelites; with anxieties about usury and strangers; with "Ruth amid the alien corn," the modern individual conceived as an exile.[4] The writings of Emmanuel Levinas and Jacques Derrida have lately reminded us, powerfully, that early stories of the Bible are obsessed with questions of hospitality and welcome, and the question of how we are to greet the stranger.[5] The Bible, like Homer's *Odyssey*, is fascinated by the unexpected visitor, often an angel or (in Homer) a god in disguise, who either bears welcome news (as when an angel tells Sarah that she will give birth to Isaac, and "Sarah laughs," or when Athena arrives to tell Telemachus that his father will return) or who conducts a kind of test of the host. Lot's visit from the angel, like the visit to Abraham before him, saves the Jewish people—in this case, saving Lot and his family from the destruction of Sodom and Gomorrah. But this obsession with the stranger also reflects the postexilic nature of much of the Bible: written as the Jewish people are forming themselves as a nation in exile, these stories reflect back constantly on the nature of estrangement. The most significant verses of the Bible in the chapters of law that discuss strangers (Exodus, Deuteronomy, Numbers) are all reminders of the exile in Egypt: "[F]or you were strangers in a strange land," they say, and they call out for generous treatment of strangers. Laws govern everything from whom strangers can marry to how they can enter the Temple; what they can eat, and which feasts they must be invited to join; when they can rest, and when they can work. But there is no single category of "stranger," no single kind of person, to whom the text refers. Rather, there are varieties of strangers, and this suggests immediately some of the difficulty in what we will come to recognize as a persistent anxiety about stranger-recognition.[6]

The biblical treatment of the stranger enters modern law at the same juncture at which Daniel's and Gwendolen's plots initially meet, and where Jews first enter the novelistic world of *Daniel Deronda*: in the laws governing usury.[7] No biblical passage distinguishing between the "brother" and the "stranger" has drawn more attention than the passage in Deuteronomy that states, "You shall not lend upon interest to your brother, interest on money, interest on victuals, interest on anything that is lent for interest. To a foreigner [*nokri*] you may lend upon interest, but to your brother you may not lend upon interest; that the LORD your God may bless you in all that you undertake in the land which you are entering to take possession of it" (Deut. 23:19–20). This passage begins as a protection of the tribe: a man in desperate straits will borrow money, and you must not take advantage of his poverty and desperation by charging him interest. No such law protects the stranger, however, and hence the historical link between Jews, non-Jews and usury—a link nowhere explicitly disavowed by the Bible. But the modern peregrinations of this injunction create a very different story of "brothers" and "strangers," one with important implications for the attempt in the nineteenth century to distinguish between subjects and aliens. In Benjamin Nelson's classic analysis of the history of what he calls "the wandering Hebrew commandment in the Western Christian world," he notes that in medieval Christian analysis, and in the radical elements of German reformation, the injunction was to be reread, in the light of the New Testament, as enjoining us to treat all people as brothers—hence, to charge usurious interest to no one, for no one is truly a stranger. But to the more conservative Protestant reformers (Calvin and Luther among them) that revision of the prohibition was, as Nelson recounts, "an invitation to social revolution and anarchy." These premodern (and protocapitalist) theorists of usury moved the argument in a different direction: rather than extending the law against usury to others, they released members of the "tribe," in this case Protestants, to charge interest to "brothers." Or, to quote from Nelson's account, "Western morality after Calvin reaffirmed the vocabulary of universalism, refused to concede that God could authorize or equity allow us to treat the Other differently from the Brother, assimilated the Brother to the Other, and eventuated in the Universal Otherhood." In his stunning summary: "In modern capitalism, all are 'brothers' in being equally 'others.'"[8]

By the time Blackstone writes his commentaries in the eighteenth century, as modern England is being given a legal identity, not only is the redemption of usury complete, but the world has been turned into a world of strangers. This is a problem to which I will return. But we might note at this moment merely that while usury is redeemed, usurers are not, and it is as usurers that Jews enter not only *Daniel Deronda* but English law. Anxieties about Jews and usury were present at the expulsion of the Jews from England in 1290, and resurfaced in the seventeenth century when Cromwell first explored the possibility of the return of the Jews in 1649; it was as money-lenders that they returned to England in 1656, following the invitation of Charles II who, while still a king in exile (at the end of the Protectorate following the English revolution), needed the money of Dutch Jewish merchants to sponsor his own return. But the distrust of Jews as not only typical (and dangerous) modern subjects, but emblematic of strangeness that cannot be absorbed into society, persists in English public life. In the parliamentary debates over the Jewish disabilities, one member remarked that the Jews under discussion were not "the hereditary inhabitants of this our England."[9] Rather, "the remotest ancestors of the present generation of Jews came into England less than 200 years ago; they came here *for their own profit*, for their own convenience," and they should not thus be granted "a share in the government of England" (emphasis added). They cannot, "as true Jews, be amalgamated with us . . ."—and here the discussion of the strangeness of the stranger, the alienation of the usurer, comes to be central to the broader nineteenth-century debate over who "shares" in the "government of England." In the wave of reform that overtook England in the 1820s and 1830s, and continued through a series of Reform Bills, extensions of property rights and the suffrage, as well as debates over Poor Law, Marriage and Divorce laws, each inching forward of the law seemed to raise not only new issues but new groups of subjects, edging toward emancipation. Each in turn raised precisely this question—who are "the hereditary inhabitants of this our England?" Jews, like married women and like bastards, might appear to share in the nation, but precisely what they cannot do is inherit it.[10]

The case of the Jews is not, then, anomalous, but suggests the outlines of every such move toward full legal emancipation.[11] Jewish emancipation is a fascinating story in its own right, for it is far from an obvious story of persecution or even total alienation. After the return of the Jews, there were no specific laws crafted to exclude Jews from public life—indeed, one attempt to create such a law brought, instead, an order of council from the king declaring them under his protection. There were also, however, no legal bills to restore to them rights taken away by acts in the pre-expulsion period. Despite persistent legal rhetoric that all infidels in law must be considered as "perpetual enemies," Jews had been confirmed in the free exercise of their religion and had been recognized as subjects in the law courts. Jews were able to serve as witnesses in a court of law, were free to sue, and were free to marry under their own rites. It was less clear if Jews were able to own land, but throughout the eighteenth and early nineteenth centuries Jews did in fact own and purchase lands; in 1846 the question was clarified by the removal of the older laws (both dating from the thirteenth century, before the expulsion) that had led to the extended legal debate.[12]

But if there were not explicit prohibitions within the law, what one found instead, covering the ground of English law like so many thorny bushes, were "disabilities"—that is, areas where ordinary rights could not be permitted to Jews because these rights and civic activities were hedged in by oaths requiring either status as a Christian or adherence to the 39 Articles of the Church of England.[13] Among these rights were such things as admission to the legal profession, attendance at public schools, attendance at the universities, inclusion in the franchise, and the ability to hold parliamentary and national offices. The first specific efforts to extend full citizenship to Jews followed hard upon the two great liberatory pieces of legislation that began the age of reform: the repeal of the Test and Corporation Acts in 1828, and the Act of Catholic Emancipation in 1829. The former allowed Protestants who were not members of the Church of England to serve in municipal corporations or hold Crown offices; the latter allowed similar privileges to Catholics. Both, in short, challenged the authority of the Church of England—though her authority was hardly revoked absolutely, for the two universities, Oxford and Cambridge, continued to require the Oath of Supremacy (the subscription to the 39 articles) for all degrees, and hence, continued to wall out Dissenters and Catholics, as well, of course, as Jews and Quakers, the two groups not legitimated by the previous acts. As this suggests, however, the two important acts of the 1820s not only prepared the way for the Reform Bill of 1832, which extended voting rights for the first time to copyholders and leaseholders (essentially enfranchising the middle class and a not insignificant number of working class men), but suggested an end to the absolute hold of the Church of England on political rights in the realm—and, to interested liberals, suggested that it was only a question of logic to extend these votes to Jews.[14]

Thus, the emancipation of the Jews, a political struggle that took place over the next thirty years, follows a common pattern in nineteenth-century legal debate: if x, why not y? And it is precisely this almost inevitable growth of rights that alarmed opponents of the repeal of Jewish disabilities: what would follow, what would come next? Two specific, very different kinds of threats presented themselves. One is a simple question of expanding citizenship, and in this way we are not surprised to see members of Parliament, in the debate in 1830, asking, "If Jews, why not Mahometans?" Or, to make a more pungent example of this fear of encroaching voters, as one Member of Parliament did, "Why not wives?" or, as another added, "Who knew but they might have a Mary Wollstonecraft to adorn the benches of that House?" Precisely the seeming reasonableness of the liberal case caused conservatives to tremble: where, exactly, would liberals draw the line, and, as the same anxious member asked, "What was Liberalism? . . . Liberalism was just egotism."[15]

But the other anxiety conjured by the expansion of Jewish rights suggests the broader aspect of this debate, one that returns us to the deeper concerns that hover over the encroachment of strangers on the community: would this mean an end to the community, in the form of the nation, itself? As the debate took form around Jews, would permitting Jews to vote end England's status not only as a Christian nation but as a nation that followed God? Jews, not uncharacteristically, stand in English parliamentary debates as examples not only of themselves, but of creeping modernity, a world in which secular concerns will repeatedly trump religious ones and, in which, in the absence of a common faith ruling the polis, we will live in a world of no faith at all. If we admit the Jews to the state, then the state loses meaning—or, put another way, without the Jews acting as strangers before the law, all the law becomes strange, unfamiliar, uncommunal. Without strangers, no state. Or, put another way, without Jewish disabilities, we are all strangers. Dr. Thomas Arnold, in arguing against Jewish emancipation in the 1830s and 1840s, and in strong contradistinction to his son Matthew's later conception of all of English culture as a balance between "Hebrew and Hellene," sounded this note more strongly than any. "The Jews are strangers in England, and have no more claim to legislate for it than a lodger has to share with the landlord in the management of his house. . . . For England is the land of Englishmen, not of Jews."[16] If the lodgers are running the house, then no one will ever truly be at home.

This is a problem rehearsed throughout the nineteenth century, increasingly so as waves of immigrants come to England in the light of unrest first in the 1840s and then in greater numbers at the turn of the century. But nowhere is this debate more troubling than when it arises around questions not of religious or national difference, but of what we might call domestic estrangement: particularly the suggestion that within a family, within a "home," individual members might have different interests, and might indeed require separate representation before the law. This question took on particular pungency when feminists in the 1850s challenged the law of coverture, the laws that stated that "husband and wife were one person in law, and that person was the husband." With the suggestion that wives might have individual rights over their own property ("separate" property, as the law called it) came the possibility that wives might in other ways emancipate themselves—and more than that, it brought a challenge to the question of the way throughout English law rights of property and inheritance in turn determined political rights, particularly the right to vote. If the great reform acts increasingly extended the suffrage to men of less property, first to the middle class and then deeper into the working class, what was the logic that kept women of property from voting?[17] And, to shift the logic around, if property determined one's civic status, what were the implications of forcing married women to live under a regime in which they could not write a will, control the money they inherited, or own their own land, business, or personal possessions? From either side of the mirror (either the challenge to the relationship between property and the vote, or the challenge to the relationship of disability and gender), the relationship between women, property, and civic identity was increasingly unstable.

Part of the story I am tracing here is the seemingly inevitable progress from discussions of property rights to enfranchisement to rights of self-representation. This is in some ways a comforting story about strangers and the law—about the plight of "sojourners" or (as Sir Edward Coke said, referring to Jews) "enemy aliens." By the time the parliamentary crisis was resolved for Jewish members of Parliament, it seemed clear that Jews were (contra Mr. Arnold) English, and the rest of the legal solution would follow; but notice how odd it seems to write a similar sentence about women: would one want to say of English wives that only with the full rights to property with the passage of the Married Woman's Property Act of 1893 or with the accession to the vote in 1919 did they become something other than strangers in the eyes of the law? Would one draw similar conclusions from the debates over bastards in the 1830s when, with the enormous transformations of the English Poor Laws of 1834, for the first time "inheritance" and obligation for bastards went not with fathers but with mothers; where the state removed from the now-responsible mothers the ability to make a claim on fathers for arrest or support; where, in essence, the uncertainty of paternity became the *inability* to make a claim of kinship? Like the alienated wife or the alien Jews, the uncertainty of fatherhood before the law became another sign (or is it source?) of anxiety about just who the stranger was—or raised the even more troubling possibility that, in this dizzying new world of reform, there were only (relationships between) strangers. Given this anxiety, it is no wonder that the novel as well has trouble accounting for its strangers.

A Novel of Strangers

Novels love to sort strangers. It is a little-discussed secret of novels how much they exist simply to sort everybody—for what is a plot, but a way of moving people, property, and desires around, switching couples like so many cars riding down a railway track; moving inheritances; fulfilling some wishes and frustrating others, until everyone falls into place at the end? Which is another way of saying that novels love the law almost as much as they do strangers—but that both aliens and the explicit apparatus of the law must be expelled by the end of the novel, to maintain strenuously the fiction that not man's law but the law of the heart has written the ending, and that the strangers we have come to love will be rewarded, and those we have come to distrust will be sent along their way, far from the home that the novel has made of the world.

These are craven generalities, but they suggest at the least what I want to argue in what follows: that the realist novel, when confronting the legal disabilities of the strangers I have so far been considering, is being pushed to its explanatory limits. We are accustomed by now to thinking about the way a thinking woman exists uneasily within nineteenth-century mechanisms of plotting—from at least Jane Eyre forward, through such resistant, curious heroines as Isabel Archer and Sue Bridehead, the question of what to do with an independent woman has metaphorically kept the novel on its toes, pushing at the constraints of the marriage plot and the tidy assignment of property and persons. What I want to argue for *Daniel Deronda*, and for George Eliot at the end of her fiction-writing career, is that the explicit dis-ease of debates of legal dispensations of alien persons entered into the novel-writing machinery with particular emphasis in Eliot's work. Where others have seen in *Daniel Deronda* a conservative impulse, one that backs away from the liberal promise of "emancipation" and moves backward, resealing Gwendolen Harleth within female domesticity, I see a sustained engagement with precisely the concerns of liberal debate I have just outlined: who is to be a person; who is to inherit; how many strangers can a society absorb before it is (fatally, perhaps) altered; and what will happen if strangeness, rather than being contained or ghettoized, increasingly makes its way toward the family hearth and the domestic center. *Daniel Deronda*, most often read simply as a novel that looks toward the utopian promise of a Zionist homeland, seems to me at the same time a novel that looks toward the unsettling of the home by unhappy strangers.

It is worth rehearsing the plot of *Deronda* briefly, to recount just how many strangers populate its pages. Daniel himself is a lovely, foreign-looking English lad, raised by Sir Hugo Mallinger, with no idea who his parents are, and a yearning after his absent mother. In the absence, in fact, of any information about his birth, he assumes that he is a bastard and that Sir Hugo is his father; all his curiosity centers entirely around the mother, creating in him a rare sensitivity to lost women, a sensibility that will be quite convenient as the plot advances. When we meet Daniel, he is a grown man, and is watching a beautiful woman gamble in Leubronn, a seedy watering place in Europe; the woman he is watching is Gwendolen Harleth, a serpentine seductress who, despite her relative lack of importance in the world, imagines herself always on a world-historical stage, and expects life to offer her dramatic possibilities, which (given her limited experience and even patchier education) consist largely of, as she describes it, doing only what she likes, and never doing what she doesn't like.[18] These two characters meet and exchange glances with no expectation that they will matter to each other, but as Daniel watches, Gwendolen begins to lose at the roulette wheel; when she is forced to pawn her jewelry to return quickly to England, Daniel redeems it for her, and sends it to her with a note saying that "a stranger who has found Miss Harleth's necklace" begs to return it to her.

The novel could not be more explicit about the importance of strangeness to the plot, but this is, so far, very much business as usual—strangers must meet for a plot to get underway, for the constant repetition of the familiar can never generate a narrative.[19] *Deronda* goes further, thematizing strangeness through a series of introductions, not only the repeated re-meeting of Gwendolen and Daniel under complicated circumstances, but through the introduction of those most convenient "tokens" of strangeness, Jews. While reflecting on his own feelings of loss and alienation, Daniel has seen a beautiful, foreign-looking woman staring at the river from the banks of the Thames; as he rows past her, he sees her drench her cloak with water and plunge herself in. He saves her, only to discover that "I am a stranger. I am a Jewess"—the woman, Mirah, has fled a vicious father and the threat not merely of a life in the theater but of prostitution, and come to England to find her lost mother and brother. Thinking, as always, "Perhaps my mother was like this one," Daniel saves her, bringing her to friends who will take in the beautiful Jewish stranger—and, in time, he comes not only to marry her, but to discover that his mother was in fact "like this one," in at least one (significant) way. His mother, though no hesitant, retiring girl, but rather an amazingly successful singer and actress, was "a Jewess," and now, as she faces her own death (clearly a novelistic punishment for abandoning her son to pursue her vocation), she has returned to her heritage, not for herself but for her son. Legitimate after all, and a kind of Jewish prince, with a casket of letters and mysterious jewels awaiting him, Daniel is free not only to marry the lovely Mirah but to pursue his own destiny, to bring together a nation of exiles, to give to them what the English have, a sense of united purpose and common heritage.

This is the "Jewish plot" of *Daniel Deronda*, and it is one that readers have disliked to the point of elision—F. R. Leavis famously rewrote the novel as "Gwendolen Harleth," and attempted to publish this version as one "liberated" from *Daniel Deronda*.[20] But as even he went on to note, it is difficult to disentangle the one story from the other, and our attention to the contemporary legal debates might suggest why that is. For Gwendolen's plot is also a story of aliens, exiles, and bastards—and in her case, her own guilt in rendering landless those she has contracted to protect. It is this anxiety about disinheriting others that first draws her to the (allegedly) bastard son, Daniel. When Daniel meets Gwendolen in Leubronn, he has already met the lost heroine Mirah, though (such is the novel's intricacy of structure, built on a series of forward-moving and flashback scenes) we will not "see" their meeting for quite some time. Gwendolen similarly has already met, and fled from, her eventual husband, Henleigh Grandcourt, who is the nephew and heir of Daniel's guardian, Sir Hugo Mallinger. Grandcourt, that is, is not only Gwendolen's suitor, but the man everyone assumes has taken the place of the (rightful, if illegitimate) heir, Daniel. Gwendolen was about to accept Grandcourt's marriage proposal, when she came upon his former mistress, Lydia Glasher, in a glade at the village archery event. Lydia appeared, "a stranger . . . unmistakably a lady, and one who must once have been exceedingly handsome" with two of her four illegitimate children, and said to Gwendolen, "I left my husband and child for him nine years ago. Those two children are his. . . . My husband is dead now, and Mr Grandcourt ought to marry me. He ought to make that boy his heir." Gwendolen, shaken to her core, promises that she will not marry Grandcourt, will not "interfere with your wishes," and she flees not only the scene but the country, with this vision before her, "as if a ghastly vision had come to her in a dream and said, 'I am a woman's life'" (128). But at the moment she meets Daniel, she learns that her family has lost all their money. Faced with a life of servitude as a governess and the bitter impoverishment of her mother and sisters, Gwendolen breaks her word to Lydia and agrees to marry Grandcourt.

This entangling of Gwendolen with the bastardy plot is the novel's most daring move. From the moment she accepts Grandcourt's proposal, until the book's end, Gwendolen has the thing she least needs: a moral conscience, one that repeatedly estranges her from herself and moves her toward Daniel, the text's most prominent bastard. She is haunted first by her own act of dispossession, having taken what she believes belonged to another woman, and second by her husband's vicious treatment of her, stirred on not only by his casual sadism, but by his pleasure in recognizing how little she wanted to marry him, and how powerfully she is drawn to Daniel. Daniel, attracted in turn by Gwendolen's visible suffering and her spiritual struggles, finds himself as interested in her misery as he is in Mirah's loveliness and his own search for identity, just as Gwendolen sees in what she (and everyone else) presumes to be Daniel's bastardy and disinheritance the visible sign of the wrong that she has been brought to do. The climax of the plot (and of the entanglement) comes at Genoa, where Daniel has come to meet his mother and learn the secret of his birth, and Grandcourt has brought Gwendolen to take her away from England and Daniel. Yet again, strangers come together in the mysteries of plot; as Daniel leaves his mother following their final meeting, he comes across Gwendolen at the docks, as bedraggled as Mirah was many chapters ago, having survived a boating accident in which Grandcourt drowned, and Gwendolen was, for a terrifying moment, unable or unwilling to reach out to save him. In an unexpected reversal, Daniel is unable to save her, either. Everything in her plot has led her to expect that he will fall in love with her, marry her, and restore to her a heroine's destiny; she is in painful ignorance of the other destiny coming toward him, that he will become a Jew, marry Mirah, and travel to the Holy Land. Gwendolen will remain behind, chastened and subdued ("I have been a cruel woman, and I have been punished") but, as she and the novel repeatedly reassure us, a better person for having known Daniel. In the final sorting of strangers, Gwendolen will return to live with her mother and sisters, and Grandcourt's (and Sir Hugo's) estate will, in turn, pass to Lydia Glasher's son. Bastards and Jews, in short, will inherit the earth; Gwendolen will have enough money to live on, and the possibility of moral justification, but the novel gives us no sense that any other happiness will come her way.

Several things will be clear even from so brief a summary. In the interweaving of its plot and its deliberate jumbling of the time frame of the novel, *Daniel*

Deronda is a deeply estranging text. It keeps readers aware not only of how little we know but how little the characters know of each other. This is, as I have suggested, particularly clear in the Gwendolen portion of the text—Gwendolen can have no idea not only that Daniel has a separate destiny, but that he has become caught up in the lives of Jews. Like most of the Christian characters, Gwendolen regards Jews as "eccentrics," pawnbrokers, and old clothesmen—to the extent that they, as a people, have not died out since the time of the Old Testament, or at most Sir Walter Scott.[21] And she is of course not wholly wrong—Eliot's depictions of the Jews range from the noble, Sephardic family Mirah eventually rejoins to the more vulgar, jolly, but definitely down-at-heel Cockney Jews with whom Mirah's brother resides; Daniel heaves quite a sigh of relief when his porcelain love-interest is not related to them, and readers are clearly expected to follow suit. But Gwendolen's inability to imagine that Daniel could be a Jew, that he could marry a Jew, suggests a deeper critique of the Victorian imagination—that there is strangeness in our midst, and we travel our own plots in such perfect oblivion only at our own risk. All the work of the plot, looked at in this way, is to get Gwendolen to realize that that which seems strange to her is reality to someone else—and will enter her own life, however little she might wish it.

But Gwendolen's plot suggests another kind of strangeness, that of domestic relations and even of romantic love; the sense that the man who seems to be a perfect English gentleman (polite, withdrawn, genteel) might be the most vicious stranger of all. We can trace this through the movement of the word stranger through Gwendolen's perspective. At first, the stranger is Deronda, whom she observes in the novel's opening scene; then it is his self-signature, his willed anonymity, when he returns her necklace, an open secret. Next, Grandcourt, whom she has already seized upon as a possible suitor, is introduced by the narrator as "the prefigured stranger," who shocks Gwendolen when he suddenly appears; then it is Grandcourt's mysterious manservant, Lush ("Who this stranger was she did not care much to know"), but only a short time later, she meets Lydia Glasher, introduced as the "whole figure of a stranger." The relationship between these three strange figures is unclear to Gwendolen—in part because, as a sheltered young woman, she cannot know the real mysteries of men's secret, erotic life, and in part because it is in the interest of all three to conceal parts of their past from her. Grandcourt is "strange" to her, till the end, because she cannot understand the compound of power and erotic laziness that creates him—or, as the narrator says, he was "a handsome lizard of a hitherto unknown species, not of the lively, darting kind. But Gwendolen knew hardly anything about lizards . . ." (115). Gwendolen's education is her growing awareness of how much of the world lies beyond her knowledge—for, as she says to the Jewish musician Klesmer, when she inquires about going on the stage, "Of course I cannot know how things go on about theatres. But I thought that I could have made myself independent. I have no money, and I will not accept help from anyone" (221). It is after this scene of humiliation that, for the first time, Gwendolen sees herself as a stranger:

> For the first time since her consciousness began, she was having a vision of herself on the common level, and had lost the innate sense that there were reasons why she should not be slighted, elbowed, jostled—treated like a passenger with a third-class ticket. (223)

That sense of ordinariness is for Gwendolen her own estrangement. The alienation that others feel in her throughout (as one character says, after Gwendolen's marriage, "A stranger might suppose that she had condescended rather than risen. I always noticed that doubleness in her" [468]) becomes increasingly her sense about herself, until the climactic moment of the novel, when she watches Grandcourt drown. As she says, in the scene where she confesses to Daniel, "I was like two creatures. I could not speak . . . . He was struck—I know nothing—I only know that I saw my wish outside me" (592; 596). As the novel has progressed, as Gwendolen has lost legal status and (propertied) independence, she has perversely struggled into another form of independence, but that has meant becoming a stranger to herself, to the degree that we might also posit consciousness itself as estrangement, not only seeing oneself from the outside but seeing one's own mind fully lighted, illuminated, externalized, as if the self were being simultaneously translated or subtitled. Here, Gwendolen Harleth, here is your wish . . .

The remarkable movement of strangeness and strangers across Gwendolen's story might direct us to several conclusions about fiction, strangers, and the law—for, to point out only the most obvious, the law is of no use to Gwendolen in her miserable marriage, nor does it reach out to punish her for the drowning death of her husband, and (though we might want to quarrel with this ourselves) it is clear that George Eliot thinks the law is right in both instances. In what ways, though, does this instability of strangers, beyond the necessary movement of strangers in fiction from unknown to intimate to people from whom we must separate, permeate the entire novel? How do these various forms of strangeness (those linked to gender, to race, to property or to political relationships, and those linked to a strangely alienated, modern self) bump up against each other in the novel? And, finally, what do strangeness and the law have to do not just with fiction, but with fictions of justice? Is there, finally, nothing for the law to do in the novel but watch, powerless to help or hinder?

The Novel and the Law

Daniel Deronda has always seemed to me like the setup of a very bad joke: "A Jew, a bastard, and a woman walk into a room . . ." We might expect the novel to turn up an illegitimate Jewish girl just to solve the puzzle ("look; they're all the same person!")—and yet, it quite deliberately doesn't, and in fact goes on naming people closer and closer to the heart of Victorian culture as the strangers. Over the hundreds of pages the novel consumes, the following people are called strangers: potential spouses, potential lovers, drowning Jewesses, booksellers' assistants, an English gentleman looking to pawn his father's ring, former lovers, your unknown grandfather's best friend, some guy you meet in a Prague synagogue on the Sabbath, your secret adversary, your own mother (who knew?) and your future husband's former mistress, the mother of his children. Strangeness is not quite (or not only) estrangement, and it is not quite foreignness, and is not quite a question of distance, but it presents a constant challenge to characters and readers: I am strange; what will you make of me? For Daniel, who will cheerfully lay claim to the strangeness of his inheritance at the end of the novel, foreignness is a kind of blessing, in part (as his mother points out to him) because he still has the enormous benefit of being an English gentleman, of being an Etonian and a Cambridge man, of having read law and learned of the world, and having enough property behind him to float whatever fantasies of redemption he chooses to entertain. For Gwendolen, the consequences of estrangement are, very different, and for that reason, the novel invokes two very different ideas of the law.

The form of law we were most intent on following at this essay's opening, the progress of emancipation through parliamentary reform, is nowhere explicitly mentioned, but (like Daniel's Englishness, which allows him to assume Jewishness in the forms he wishes, and only those forms), a notion of rights and privileges underwrites much of the book's own emancipatory (indeed, messianic) leanings. Law is very much the road not taken for Daniel—when he moves to London, after his years at university, he is reading law "in deference to Sir Hugo's wish, and to fence off idleness, . . . [though] this apparent decision had been without other result than to deepen the roots of indecision" (157). It is Sir Hugo who wishes that "[y]ou might make yourself a barrister—be a writer—take up politics. I confess that is what would please me best" (149), and Sir Hugo who repeatedly brings up Parliament, even at the moment when Daniel learns who his mother is, and that he is a legitimate heir to some Zionist dream. If you had been my son, says Sir Hugo, you should have been "future master of the Abbey instead of my fine nephew, and then you would have seen it necessary for you to take a political line" (531). We can in fact see Daniel's voyage into the promised land as precisely his escape from these responsibilities of gentlemanly politics—it is at the moment that the narrator describes Daniel's "indecision" in the face of the law that Mirah floats into the water in front of him, as if to save him from the seriousness of politics, creating instead the Romance that comes with the dream of a new Palestine.

But it is not possible that George Eliot could separate Daniel's story from the thirty-year debate over Jewish emancipation, or that Sir Hugo's constant references to parliamentary representation could not be understood as part of the Jewish question, any more than she could silence the extensive public debate over women's rights. While scholars have pointed out that Eliot's interest in the messianic plot of Zionism is more in keeping with Protestant Evangelicals (who longed for the return of Jews to Palestine) than the desires of English Jews (who longed simply for political, civic, and economic rights), I think they have been too quick to assume that she didn't, precisely, want to register the importance of these rights for Jews and others throughout the novel. We can imagine much of Eliot's interest outside the novel: she was an editor of the *Westminster Review* at the time of the parliamentary debates, when the review ran several articles on the question; her lover, George Henry Lewes (widely rumored to be Jewish) took a strong interest in the questions, and her earlier novels (both *Middlemarch*, with its perhaps-Jewish hero, Will Ladislaw, and *Romola*, which ends with the heroine floating into a community of isolated Jews, refugees from the Spanish Expulsion) show a rare sensitivity to these issues. The 1870s, the decade in which Deronda was written, saw a renewal of debates over "the Jew" in Benjamin Disraeli's "Eastern Question," the problem of foreign policy that seemed to many within Britain to propose "a Jewish war." That war is nowhere in *Daniel Deronda*, where the world-shattering conflict against which the characters' fates are measured is the American Civil War, but parliamentary debates over the other "Jewish question" (or "the woman question") are hardly unthinkable. Within the novel, whenever Jews and women are mentioned, Parliament tugs at their sleeves. When Catherine Arrowpoint, the talented heiress whose estate borders Gwendolen's mother's house, announces that she is going to marry the musician Klesmer—"a gypsy, a Jew, a mere bubble of the earth" (210)—her father announces:

> "It will never do to argue about marriage, Cath," said Mr Arrowpoint. "It's no use getting up the subject like a parliamentary question. We must do as other people do. We must think of the nation and the public good."
>
> "I can't see any public good concerned here, papa. People had better make a new sort of public good by changing their ambitions." (211)

Victorian novels were often very quick to point out the difference between the way they asked questions and those who "got up" subjects like a parliamentary question, but at a time when a novelist was a prime minister (or is it that the prime minister was a novelist?) it wasn't so easy to tell the difference—as Trollope, entitling his "Jewish novel" *The Prime Minister*, certainly noticed.[22] But we should note again that the central characters of this novel (bastards, married women, Jews) were precisely the subject of parliamentary questions—and note again the novelist's sympathy for at least one of her heroines and her questions at this moment.

Catherine Arrowpoint, clearly the most admirable character in this novel and the one closest to Eliot's own story, is an heiress, plain, talented, independent-minded, well-educated, and about to marry a Jewish musical genius—it is no large stretch for her to imagine "getting up" a parliamentary question. Indeed, her defiance of social roles and her proposal of marriage to the eccentric Klesmer remind us of both Eliot herself and the feminist reformers she admired. Gwendolen Harleth, we might hypothesize, is about as likely to take up a parliamentary question as the Jews to establish a homeland in Palestine—although, as I will suggest at the essay's end, these two visionary resolutions are not as far off as we might expect from the novel's rhetoric. But let us ask what happens if we take seriously Mr. Arrowpoint's challenge—is there a feminist argument about marriage in this novel? The question of reform of the marriage laws, and of other versions of the woman question, was certainly in the air while George Eliot was writing *Daniel Deronda*. By the 1870s, England had seen extensive debates over divorce and child custody laws, marital violence, women's property, and female suffrage. Of these, only the divorce laws had seen any real modifications, and those only to protect the rights of mothers, for real access to divorce (divorce with remarriage) remained limited to wealthy people—and for women, limited to those who were the victims of multiple marital crimes (not just adultery, but adultery compounded by cruelty, incest, bigamy, or bestiality). No one knew this better than George Eliot, or more accurately, to free her from her pseudonymous self, Marian Evans, who was (at the time she wrote all of her fiction) living with a married man, George Henry Lewes, who was unable to win a divorce from his wife, Agnes, having initially accepted several of her illegitimate children as his own, and (on her repeated and quite impressive production of illegitimate children) not having any legal grounds for repudiating them or her. Gwendolen Harleth, of course, would have known far less of the legal disabilities of women—but the point of this novel is, of course, that she will learn them all too well.[23]

Gwendolen's plot is very much the plot of female ambition, but it has no place in the world in which she lives. The narrator compares her to her male contemporaries "when they felt a profession too narrow for their powers": "Because her education had been less expensive than theirs, it did not follow that they should have wider emotions or a keener intellectual vision" (234–35). As Daniel notes, at his most scornful, "She has a dreary lack of the ideas that might help her . . . . She was clearly an ill-educated, worldly girl" (354). We, who have followed Gwendolen's progress, can certainly see her dreariness, but we know more about her "worldliness"—it is illusory; imperfect; the result particularly of her terrible education, an education (which Eliot notes with equal scorn) entirely of novels and dreams. Like any heroine, Gwendolen has only one real choice, the choice of whom to marry (the third book of the novel is called "Maidens Choosing"), but that freedom to choose, as the novel makes clear, is itself an illusion: "Again she seemed to be getting a sort of empire over her own life. But how to use it? Here came the terror. . . . Where was the good of choice coming again?" (247). What exactly is the terror? It is, remember, the confrontation with Lydia Glasher, the sense that marrying Grandcourt means dispossessing another; the realization that Gwendolen cannot make her own fate, or can make it only by taking it from someone else.

What Eliot grants Gwendolen, and it is here that the novel begins to draw on a very different sense of law than that of parliamentary reform or legislation, is the sense that she can be a legal person—that, despite the laws of the land, she can make promises and keep them, a fascinating description of what it means to be a legal subject, one fully able to contract. Gwendolen lacks any other visible forms of (legal) power. As the novel nears its end, as Gwendolen finds herself incapable of extricating herself from Grandcourt, she begins to imagine that she might divorce or leave him, that she might "insist on separation." But that, says the narrator, "is as about as practicable as to give him a pliant disposition" (515). This merely confirms the sense of Grandcourt's power that we have had since we first met him—a power marked, in one of the most chilling scenes in the book, when he goes to threaten Lydia Glasher into returning his mother's jewels to his new wife, and he looks at her "as if any stranger were opposite to him, instead of a woman quivering with a suspense which every word and look of his was to incline toward hope or dread." Gwendolen, it would seem, cannot threaten Grandcourt, because his powers of estrangement are always going to be greater than hers—how can you separate yourself from someone who holds himself entirely separate, in no way responsible for (or bound to) you, except in that he possess you utterly. Eliot's answer is an extraordinary one: it is to return to Gwendolen a sense of herself as precisely a legal agent, a person, someone capable of forming a contract. When she agrees to marry Grandcourt, "Yes came as gravely from Gwendolen's lips as if she had been answering to her name in a court of law"; later, when she realizes that having married him in full knowledge of her promise to Lydia, "Her capability of rectitude told her again and again that she had no right to complain of her contract or to withdraw from it" (515). And despite our feeling that Gwendolen had very few choices indeed when she agreed to marry Grandcourt, it remains astonishing that she feels herself "contracted." An irate reader will find herself more than annoyed at this moment (for what is it, but an excuse to stay in a bad marriage), and yet the terms in which the argument is made are remarkable for this moment: a wife remains a person, and her word, her assent, however constrained, is her own.

It is this sense of subjecthood, of self-ownership rather than dispossession, that Gwendolen holds on to at the book's conclusion, when she learns that (as she had been warned) Grandcourt has left his estate to Lydia's son, and left only a small allowance to Gwendolen. No reader need be bothered by the anxiety that Grandcourt has developed a sense of justice at last, for Sir Hugo tells us plainly that, had Gwendolen borne an heir, the estate would have reverted to her and her son, and Lydia would have been returned to the smoky house and the pittance of an allowance. Not fairness, but a sense of his own importance (and the importance of any small, male replica of himself) has motivated Grandcourt to the last. (Lizard, indeed.) Gwendolen, on the other hand, tries to impose her own sense of justice—wanting, to the end, to make up for what she has taken from Lydia, she asks Daniel if she can keep only enough for her mother to live on; no, he says, it would cause pain to others to insist on an arbitrarily small sum; better to take the inheritance and live quietly on it. And this Gwendolen agrees to—but her attempt to imagine another form of law (of quiet subsistence) seems to me one of the book's small movements toward justice.

Where, then, can the heroine stand before the law? I want to propose two answers to that question, the first (coming out of the novel's character field) will remain where we are now, in the realm largely of private law. The second, to which I will turn in a moment, comes out of the novel's formal revolutions, and will turn us back to the larger question of formal, public law with which I began.

I have said that there is no Jewish female bastard in the novel, but that is not quite right. In some ways, there are two—for Daniel himself, although he turns out to be a legal heir after all, is repeatedly described as small, beautiful, feminine, and (strikingly) having the "same blending of child's ignorance with surprising knowledge which is oftener seen in bright girls" (141). But Daniel rejects a female inheritance—just as he turns from his mother, with her unwilling maternity and willed strangeness, so he turns from Gwendolen's passion and anger, turning toward a Jewish brotherhood with Mordecai (the "stranger" he met while looking for Mirah's family) and the dream of a fraternal homeland.

Daniel's mother, however, poses a different kind of illegitimacy—or perhaps I mean a different model of legitimacy, one that might cry out for a different kind of justice, that of the illegitimate, outside-the-law daughter. In some ways, she has willingly placed herself outside the tribe and its laws—by claiming the exemption of genius, she has left the laws of her people behind, only to see them written on her in the suffering of her (fatal) illness. Yet in other ways, she invokes the law's legitimacy when we least expect it. Where Daniel has imagined himself (as Gwendolen has imagined him) the bastard son, somehow born of an illegitimate mother, dispossessed and stranded (as Grandcourt's son is) in a family of sisters, all of them without an inheritance, the Princess carries a different story. When she meets with Daniel to give him his grandfather's message, she returns him to the fraternity of dead Jews, offering him a paper inheritance, the casket of documents that return him to the tribe, that render him at once stranger (Jew) and family, no longer an estranged (modern) subject.

But the Princess also offers her own cry of rage at the injustice done to her, continuing to describe herself as separate from the law, asking a very different question of the law. Repeatedly, she describes the constraint of Jewish daughterhood: "He only thought of fettering me into obedience"; "I was to be what he called 'the Jewish woman' under pain of his curse"; "I was to adore the wisdom of such laws [keeping women from prayers]"; "You can never imagine what it is to have a man's force of genius in you, and yet to suffer the slavery of being a girl . . . a woman's heart must be of such a size and no larger, else it must be pressed small, like Chinese feet" (540–41). As she deliberately invokes her own part in the larger plot of inheritance the novel traces, she claims: "He wished I had been a son; he cared for me as a makeshift link." Like Gwendolen resisting the demands of other people's wills, the Princess Halm-Eberstein makes a different claim on the law:

> He never thought of his daughter except as an instrument. Because I had wants outside his purpose, I was to be put in a frame and tortured. If that is the right law for the world, I will not say that I love it. (567)

What, we might ask, is a form of the law that an intelligent, passionate woman might love? The Princess raises the question, but it hangs over Gwendolen, tortured and resistant as she is, for the rest of the novel; more than a single character, however, it is the form of the novel that answers it.

A New Law for Strangers: Fiction after All?

Much of this essay has been concerned with legal debates over subjects in England in the nineteenth century—and with the way these debates both enter and are repressed in a seemingly antilegalist novel, *Daniel Deronda*. I have tried to trace a biblical language of strangeness within English law, and illuminate that oddest of concepts, the "sojourner" within, the alien in our midst. I have outlined a series of public debates (largely, but not exclusively, parliamentary) that riveted England in the nineteenth century, a process that gradually (and certainly more quickly for some than others) expanded the realm of rights; and I have tried to account in some ways for a persistent attraction toward legal language and forms in George Eliot's fiction, even as her interest in law skitters between the law of property, contract, political representation, and inheritance—and the way in which Jews, bastards, and women themselves travel between these very different (but somehow metaphorically linked) legal "dispensations." But what, exactly, does the novel in particular offer? I want in my conclusion to suggest that it may be through her experiments in fictional form, rather than in any explicit echoes of social or political debate, that George Eliot is most able to address the questions of law, persons, and justice that concern me here.

As I suggested earlier, *Daniel Deronda* has a highly elaborate time frame, one that persistently distances the reader, that reminds us of what characters do and do not know about each other, that tests our expectations of readerly conventions. The novel begins *in media res*, with an unnamed woman gambling and an unnamed man watching her, asking himself "Was she beautiful, or wasn't she?" That is the opening sentence of the novel, and it announces that this book will be a radical questioning of the basic grounds of knowledge—that each time we look at a stranger, we are thrown back on what we think of the world, and we are very often (in fact, nearly always) wrong. "Are you English?" "Are you my mother?" "Am I a Jew?" Knowledge, as I have been arguing, is hard come by in this novel, and accidents of timing (when we meet; where we are coming from and where we are going) repeatedly tangle the plot, the characters, and the readers in false expectations, false deductions, false hopes. Daniel's and Gwendolen's plots do not keep to the same pace—nor do the two characters know equal amounts about each other's lives. Daniel keeps from

Gwendolen the secret of his meeting with Mirah, his encounter with Mordecai, the mystery of his own birth, his discovery of his mother and his own identity. (Even his name, he—and we—learn, is not "real," but one his mother has given him, from a deceased branch of his father's family; Gwendolen never knows his "real" name.)

We can read this divergence of their plots, the trickery of their entanglement and the misapprehensions into which Gwendolen falls, as an extended reverie on the nature of coincidence, that staple of melodrama and Dickensian realism. We can read it as yet another way of impressing on poor Gwendolen the limits of her little world, and the pathos of her belief that she is important within any grand scheme of existence. We can read it as a clever game that Eliot is playing with her readers—both congratulating us on our recognition of the roles of genre, and tricking us repeatedly, so that we, like the characters, are unsure of what to read, how to read, what will happen next.

Or, I would argue, we could read the discontinuous time scheme back into the political concerns of the novel, and see in it yet another plot of emancipation, one in which, eerily, George Eliot was yet again more prescient (and more radical) than we might have expected. Again, let us look at what does happen in the novel: the bastard inherits; the Jews get a messiah; why shouldn't women get feminism and legal recognition? The evolutionary force of the novel, the same inevitable movement of change that led England's Jews through their emancipation, is moving women forward as well: a world historical movement, from estrangement and alienation to a promised land, redeeming the lost world of contract, in Gwendolen's final promise to Daniel: "It shall be better with me because I have known you." Why shouldn't Gwendolen, like first Mordecai and then Daniel, be the prophet of a new promise for women?

In this way, the discontinuity of the plots offers us a different reading entirely. Gwendolen and Daniel have each met their spouses before they meet each other, but while Daniel is on the right path, Gwendolen is not. Coming after the legal emancipation of the Jews, Daniel's discovery of his heritage *can* be a promise of a fuller life, of fuller nationhood, for Jews and for himself as a Jew, at once inside and outside of England.

Gwendolen, to say the least, cannot imagine such a life for herself—nor can Lydia Glasher; nor can the Daniel's mother, the Princess Halm-Eberstein. But that is not to say that George Eliot cannot imagine one for her. The author of

Daniel Deronda, the colleague of brilliant young feminists, the illicit "wife" of George Henry Lewes, was hardly to be contained by existing laws governing women—and, just as she was writing her proto-Zionist novel with the memory of the legal battles over Jewish emancipation in her head, so she is writing, I would argue, with fore-knowledge of the battles over female emancipation and their eventual success equally vivid in her imagination. We might in that way look back at the reform of English law: in the face of "customary" law, a "common" law that reflects facts as people have always known them ("Jews are strangers"; "wives exist only under their husbands' legal protection"), the reforms of the 1830s and beyond proposed a different, formal structure of law, the law of statute that can rewrite, can overleap existing common law, expectations, and customs. Such a law has already extended, at the time of the novel's writing, to the Jewish disabilities, now largely though not entirely a thing of the past; what if we read the book's conclusion as secure in the faith that women's emancipation, that further leap over custom and expectation, is about to come next?

What I am arguing is that *Daniel Deronda* traces the process by which people who seem initially to be at home (however uneasily) in their culture—Jews, women, bastards—come gradually to see themselves as estranged within it. The novel, despite its avowedly conservative elements, takes place under a general dispensation of legal solutions—property rights; voting rights; rights of full representation—and it traces a moment when one group (Jews) has achieved most of that, and women almost none of it. But it also sees legal rights as only part of the process of larger emancipation—an utopian moment it both registers and subtly resists. That is, I want to argue that nowhere does *Deronda* entirely disavow the process of legal recognition of strangers—the moment when rights are fought for, earned, granted, achieved, however one chooses to view the process. Daniel himself might make light of Parliament, but it is not clear that George Eliot does the same. But neither does the novel entirely put its faith in legal solutions, for the emancipation of the Jews (their freedom to be fully endowed, liberal subjects, part of the polis) has not brought them to the promised land either. What then does it aspire to for its female subjects?

The novel may seem to end with Gwendolen Harleth returning to the English countryside, a sadder but better member of the English race: I would argue that it ends with her sense of the almost deliberate alienation of women under English law, the sense (which we saw most profoundly in Lydia Glasher's battles with her former lover, Gwendolen's demon husband) that under English property and marital arrangements, it is women who are the most entirely estranged. And as this novel so brilliantly showed, there is no more powerful challenge to justice, than someone who has just realized she is a stranger among us. This challenge, as Daniel's plot suggests, will take place first on the field of law, though it will not take place exclusively there; like Daniel's plot, it may take its plunge, eventually, into the unknown. Gwendolen Harleth, at home at Glasdene at the novel's end, surrounded by her mother and sisters, with the bitterness of self-knowledge and her new-found sympathies for ordinary women's lives, might be the woman who will, finally, speak for these strangers, and her struggle might not begin and end with the reform of the law. The novel, with its ability to play with plot, possibilities, and the laws of fiction, might be the place where such fantasies of justice can, for at least the space of reading, hold out the promise of a new world, of a law that makes the world more rather than less open to new identities; of a law that an intelligent woman could love.[24]

Notes

1. It is Freud's Moses, of course, who comes before us as an Egyptian prince. See Michael Ragussis, *Figures of Conversion: "The Jewish Question" and English National Identity* (Durham: Duke University Press, 1995) for a provocative discussion of Deronda and Moses.

2. George Eliot, *Daniel Deronda* (Oxford: Oxford World's Classics, 1984), 3. Originally published in 1876.

3. F. R. Leavis, *The Great Tradition: George Eliot, Henry James, Joseph Conrad* (New York: New York University Press, 1964); Edward Said, "Zionism from the Standpoint of Its Victims," *Social Text* 1 (Winter 1979). Said's essay has dominated recent criticism of the novel, to the exclusion of almost every other question. An unusually well informed response, dwelling on the ambivalence of Eliot's depiction of the Jews in the novel, and on the absence of a British, Jewish Zionist movement within history, is Susan Meyer's "'Safely to Their Own Borders': Proto-Zionism, Feminism, and Nationalism in *Daniel Deronda*," *ELH* 60, 1993: 733–58. As Meyers notes, Zionism as a political movement came to life in the 1880s following the pogroms in Russia and Eastern Europe; it is hardly on the screen of British Jews in 1871, when Eliot wrote the novel. Among the best readings of Jewish questions in the novel are Catherine Gallagher, "George Eliot and Daniel Deronda: The Prostitute and the Jewish Question," in *Sex, Politics and Science in the*

Nineteenth Century Novel, ed. Ruth Bernard Yeazell (Baltimore: Johns Hopkins University Press, 1986); Ragussis, *Figures of Conversion;* and Irene Tucker, *A Probable State: The Novel, the Contract and the Jews* (Chicago: University of Chicago Press, 2000).

4. For a discussion of the evangelical debate, particularly over the economy of slavery, see Boyd Hilton, *The Age of Atonement: The Influence of Evangelicalism on Social and Economic Thought, 1785–1865* (Oxford: Oxford University Press, 1992).

5. See, in particular, Emmanuel Levinas, *Totality and Infinity: An Essay on Exteriority*, trans. Alphonso Lingis (Pittsburgh, PA: Duquesne University Press, 1969); Jacques Derrida, *Adieu to Emmanuel Levinas*, trans. Pascale-Anne Brault and Michael Naas (Stanford, CA: Stanford University Press, 1999); Derrida, *Of Hospitality*, trans. Rachel Bowlby (Stanford, CA: Stanford University Press, 2000).

6. There are three kinds of strangers in the Hebrew Bible: while the clan (the *mishpocha*) is clear, there is also the *ger* (the protected sojourner), the *toshab* (the resident stranger), and the *nokri* (the foreigner), and these categories carry with them not only different exclusions but different inclusions into the practices of the tribe. The *ger* seems to have been, originally, a stranger (or, as one text puts it, a "client") who resided in Palestine and put himself under the protection of the people among whom he resided; in later, postexilic usage, it appears to mean a proselyte or convert, one who observes the rules of the tribe, who "cleaves to the house of Jacob." But even in the earliest uses of *ger*, the sojourner who lived with a Hebrew family or clan, the stranger is ensured not only of protection against oppression but of the love of the natives. (*Gerim* could participate in all festivals, except the Passover—and even there, the stranger could participate if he agreed to be circumcised. This seems a rather heavy duty for an indifferent, at best, meal—but such are the demands of culture.) The *nokri,* by contrast, are heathens, and they are not usually protected by the same laws—but even there, the rules of hospitality obtain. The unconverted stranger (*nokri*) who seeks refuge from God (like Ruth) can become a part of the tribe—and, in the case of Ruth, the most famous stranger in the Old Testament can become the source of the Redeemer. For these passages, I have relied on the *Jewish Encyclopedia* (1901–6), now available on line at jewishencyclopedia.com. It has a remarkable richness of commentary, and has the advantage of being closer in time to what Eliot would have known or encountered in the rich study of Jewish learning that she carried out to write *Daniel Deronda*. My quotations are from both the King James Bible and the Revised Standard, though I have drawn on the latter only when I think the meaning is clearer. For more on Eliot and her Jewish studies, see William Baker, *George Eliot and Judaism* (Salzburg Studies in English Literature, Institut for Englische Sprache und Literatur, Universitat Salzburg, 1975); and a fascinating nineteenth-century account, David Kaufmann's *George Eliot and Judaism: An Attempt to Appreciate Daniel Deronda* (1888; reprinted New York: Haskell House, 1970).

7. For the best discussion of usury in the novel, see Gallagher, "George Eliot and

Daniel Deronda," who first pointed out that the plot of the novel arises when "a young man who thinks he has a mission to save wayward women turns out to have a mission to save a nation of usurers" (50).

8. See Benjamin Nelson, *The Idea of Usury: From Tribal Brotherhood to Universal Otherhood* (Chicago: University of Chicago Press, 1969), xix–xxv, for further discussion of these concepts. Nelson's examples are too rich to summarize here, but note in particular his reading of a masterful passage from Calvin, which claims that "usury is not now unlawful, except in so far as it contravenes equity and brotherly union. Let each one, then, place himself before God's judgement seat, and not do to his neighbor what he would not do to himself." Note the way the sternest biblical injunction against distinguishing between oneself and another has here become an alibi for charging "reasonable" interest (ibid., 79).

9. Hansard's Parliamentary Debates, December 16, 1847, 1263–64

10. Bastards, according to Blackstone, "are incapable of being heirs," because they are the son of nobody: "Being thus the sons of nobody, they have no blood in them, at least no heritable blood: consequently, none of the blood of the first purchaser." "Aliens, also, are incapable of taking by descent, or inheriting, for they are not allowed to have any inheritable blood in them." See Blackstone's *Commentaries on the Laws of England,* ed. George Sharswood (Philadelphia: J. B. Lippincott, 1908), bk. II, ch. 15, 246–47. Married women could inherit, but (except under well-crafted trusts) their inheritances became the property of their husbands; a married woman could write a will, but the husband could revoke it after her death.

11. The most thorough summary of Jewish legal history in England remains H. S. Q. Henriques, *The Jews and the English Law* (Oxford: Hart, 1908; reprinted Clifton, NJ: Augustus M. Kelley, 1974). Given the relatively unwritten quality of English law (the absence of a written constitution, for example), Jewish law must be pieced together through case history to a surprising extent, and Henriques's account makes for fascinating reading. Two highly useful summaries of the debate over Jewish Emancipation are M. C. N. Salbstein, *The Emancipation of the Jews in Britain: The Question of the Admission of the Jews to Parliament, 1828–1860* (Rutherford, NJ: Fairleigh Dickinson Press, Associated University Press, 1982); and Abraham Gilam, *The Emancipation of the Jews in England 1830–1860* (New York: Garland Publishing, 1982). For a broader survey, see Todd M. Endelman, *The Jews of Britain 1656 to 2000* (Berkeley: University of California Press, 2002); and David Feldman, *Englishmen and Jews: Social Relations and Political Culture 1840–1914* (New Haven: Yale University Press, 1994).

12. The debate over land is one of the most fascinating bits of arcana from the period: an eighteenth-century antiquarian named D'Blossiers Tovey, researching the "history and antiquities of the Jews in England" unearthed an ordinance from 1271 (54 and 55 Henry III) forbidding Jews to own land. Given that this ordinance had covered Jews

who had subsequently left the kingdom, it was unclear that it could govern Jews in the present day; there also arose significant disagreement on the technical writing of the ordinance, which also may have rendered it invalid. Jews did, as was frequently the case given their legal disabilities, continue to own and to purchase land—and in one telling incident, Chief Justice, Lord Ellenborough bought a freehold at Roehampton from Benjamin Goldsmid. This raises several intriguing questions, all of them (to my mind) better answered by literature than the legal debate we have: what did Tovey think, when his research at the Bodleian Library uncovered this distressing bit of legal history? To what extent did most buyers of land continue in blissful ignorance of their uneasy legal hold on their property? And finally, and it is the question that resounds throughout the debate over the disabilities, if the ordinance made virtually no difference "in reality," what difference did it make to the way English Jews felt about their residence in Britain—and why did it take so long, given other advances in law, for the instability to be rectified?

13. These oaths are survivors of the religious wars of the seventeenth century, following the English Civil War and reflecting anxiety over Catholics and loyalty to the pope; questions about the divided loyalty of Jews, and their allegiance to the (perhaps returning) Messiah are raised in the debate over the Jewish Disabilities Bills, but given the absence of a political equivalent to either the pope or the Holy Empire, they could not realistically raise the same anxieties, suggesting some of the more hysterical content of these "disabilities."

14. The extended debates over Jewish Emancipation make for compelling reading. As my summary suggests, they swirl around a few central issues: apart from the key question of religious liberty, Were Jews not loyal subjects?; Did they not already have many of these rights without the law?; and (as long as they were prepared to swear oaths of loyalty on their own beliefs) What logic was there in keeping them from civil rights they had otherwise earned by their participation in British society? The full scope of liberal arguments is best seen in Thomas Babington Macaulay's justly famous speech on "The Jewish Disabilities," reprinted in *Essay and Speech on Jewish Disabilities* (Edinburgh: Ballantyne, Hanson, 1909) as well as in his collected works. The objections are, of course, equally fascinating, ranging from William Cobbett's virulent attacks on Jewish moneylenders and urban blight (the association of Jewish rights with David Ricardo's theory of rents is one of the most interesting side-bars to this debate) to Christians who asserted that they would have no difficulty swearing an oath on their faith as Jews were Jews in power—where did the difficulty lie? Notions of Jewish exclusionism, of course, worked both for and against civil rights arguments—those in favor of the repeal of the disabilities pointed out that since Jews were not likely to proselytize, they were far less a threat than Catholics, newly emancipated in 1829, but opponents of emancipation argued (as indeed they had for Catholics) that Jews would not be loyal to the state, but to an absent, Jewish land. The scatter-shot nature of the debate in some ways anticipates

the piece-meal removal of the disabilities from English law; the most revealing of these was the compromise in 1858 on oaths sworn by members of Parliament. After Lionel Rothschild was elected to Parliament in 1847 (and elected another four times after that, before being allowed to serve), a series of bills in both houses attempted to allow him to take his duly elected seat by taking a nondenominational oath; repeatedly, the bill would pass the House of Commons only to be defeated in the House of Lords. Finally someone realized that no Jew was likely to be named to the House of Lords—at which point a compromise bill was proposed to allow each House to offer its own oath. The act passed in 1858, and Rothschild was allowed to take his seat in the Commons.

15. Hansard 95, December 17, 1847, 1379–80.

16. A. P. Stanley, *The Life and Correspondence of Thomas Arnold*, 2 vols. (London, B. Fellowes), 1958), vol. 2, 27–29. Quoted in Bryan Cheyette, *Constructions of 'The Jew' in English Literature and Society: Racial Representations, 1875–1945* (Cambridge: Cambridge University Press, 1993), 16. Thomas Arnold's views of England and Englishness are themselves fairly unusual, it should be noted.

17. This led John Stuart Mill to propose changing "men" to "person" in the Reform Bill of 1864—a simple, but absolutely radical, suggestion: if property is to determine the vote, fine, but then why should gender pose an insuperable barrier?

18. Gwendolen's desire echoes quite explicitly Matthew Arnold's critique of modern liberalism as the culture of "doing what one likes." Eliot's relationship to the argument Arnold makes in *Culture and Anarchy*, a series of essays expressing his horror at the second Reform Bill, seems to me quite vexed—not least in that she imagines a woman as the modern subject.

19. See, among others, Tzvetan Todorov, *The Poetics of Prose* (Ithaca, NY: Cornell University Press).

20. In a brilliant recent essay, Claudia L. Johnson has argued that Leavis (whose wife, Queenie, was Jewish, and who taught at the far-more-sympathetic-to-Jews university, Cambridge) turned against Daniel Deronda not out of anti-Semitism but out of a feeling that Eliot herself had turned against England, and against the redemptive plot of the "new heavens and new earth" that he saw at the heart of the Great Tradition. Put vulgarly, he shared too much Blake's project of "building the new Jerusalem/in England's green and pleasant land" to wish to see any hero sail off toward Palestine. See Johnson, "F. R. Leavis: The 'Great Tradition' of the English Novel and the Jewish Part," *Nineteenth Century Literature* 56, no. 2 (2001): 198–227.

21. When Daniel takes Mirah to the Meyrick family, he reports that they "would at once associate a lovely Jewess with Rebecca in 'Ivanhoe'" (165).

22. See Ragussis, *Figures of Conversion,* on the relationship of Disraeli, Trollope, and Eliot at this period.

23. The thirty-four-year-old Marian had moved in with Lewes in the early 1850s, a

scandalous relationship in theory, which in practice proved extremely sturdy and downright respectable. But its violation of Victorian codes of behavior found no sympathetic echo in the law—and very little among Marian's friends or relations. Interestingly, the women who continued to visit her when she began living with Lewes were Barbara Bodichon (herself illegitimate) and Bessie Rayner Parkes, two of the most forceful feminists of their day, and while she did not support female suffrage, Eliot did sign the petition for the Married Woman's Property act (though she also introduced a paragraph protecting husbands from their wives' debts) and eagerly supported women's education.

24. The author wishes to thank, among others, the members of the Program for Law, Jurisprudence and Social Thought at Amherst College for a highly stimulating workshop, and Austin Sarat and Martha Umphrey for the invitation to participate, as well as their hospitality; the commentators (Catherine Gallagher and Robert Post) as well as the participants at the conference "Literary Justice," sponsored by the Center for Law, History, and Culture at the University of Southern California; and her research assistants, Jennifer Conary and Nora Gilbert. Thanks also to Richard Menke, Ned Schantz, and Nomi Stolzenberg for their engaged readings of this essay and my other recent work on George Eliot; and Peggy Kamuf, for a timely conversation about Levinas.

Of Stranger Spaces

KENJI YOSHINO

Of Stereotypes and Clichés

To a scholar of antidiscrimination law, the title of this volume conjures the law's treatment of social outsiders—aliens, outlaws, and others whom the state has declared "strangers to its laws."[1] To a scholar of law and literature, the title evokes the law's banishment of literature—texts deemed too false, emotional, or seductive to contribute to governance.[2] Because I am both, the title invites speculation about the relationship between the people and discourses the law makes strange.

The connection between social outsiders and literary discourse finds etymological expression in the link between the words "stereotype" and "cliché." English receives these words from French, in which *stéréotype* refers to a printing plate, and *cliché* is the onomatopoeic click the plate makes while stamping out its numberless copies. Both words denote standardized substitutes for more individualized treatment. As those engaged in the practice of civil rights seek to disestablish stereotype, those engaged in the practice of literature seek to disestablish cliché.

No accident, then, that social outsiders have deployed the estrangement effects of literature to resist subordination. Writers such as Derrick Bell,[3] Paulette Caldwell,[4] and Patricia Williams[5] have used such "stories from the bottom"[6] to break down stereotypes about individuals. While I celebrate this deployment of law and literature, I believe it has stood too much for the whole. This essay will explore narratives that defamiliarize the state—the literature of utopia.

Of Utopias and Heterotopias

The *Oxford English Dictionary* defines "utopia" as "[a] place, state, or condition ideally perfect in respect of politics, laws, customs, and conditions."[7]

Because no such place exists, portrayals of it are perforce fictions. These two senses of the utopia—its perfection and nonexistence—are built into the word. In coining the neologism, Sir Thomas More drew on both *eutopia* (Greek for "good place") and *outopia* (Greek for "no place").[8] His successors would make the point in other ways, as when Samuel Butler dubbed his ideal state "Erewhon," an anagram of "nowhere."[9]

This definition is still broad, as it could include the Garden of Eden, Elysium, or the Land of Cockaigne. Yet as Ruth Levitas observes, most authors take utopias to be social orders of human contrivance, rather than products of divine or natural grace.[10] She observes that the scholarly commentary converges around five texts: Plato's *Republic*,[11] More's *Utopia*,[12] Francis Bacon's *The New Atlantis*,[13] Tommaso Campanella's *City of the Sun*,[14] and Etienne Cabet's *Travels in Icaria*.[15] In these texts, utopias are figured as spaces carefully cordoned off from the real world, often taking the form of walled cities (Plato's Republic,[16] Augustine's City of God,[17] Campanella's City of the Sun[18]) or as islands (the archipelago extending from More's Utopia[19] to Bacon's Bensalem[20] to Cabet's Icaria[21] to Huxley's Island[22]). More's Utopia is the clearest example of deliberate geographical isolation: Utopia was connected to the mainland until its ruler dug a channel to sequester it.[23]

Utopias invite comparisons through which our world is meant to suffer. More's Utopia is marked by harmony (fifty-four cities "large and splendid and having exactly the same language, customs, institutions, and laws");[24] common property (food is grown and distributed in common, and anyone can enter another's house);[25] humane work conditions (no one works more than six hours a day);[26] chastity (sex before marriage is prohibited);[27] pleasure (both of the body, as found in health, and of the mind, by practicing virtues and knowing one has the good life);[28] freedom of religion (with voluntary convergence around one);[29] free and common education (there is a scholar class, but anyone can enter it, and reading is deemed one of life's great pleasures);[30] few laws (the society runs on internal obedience to the moral code);[31] and peace (no war except, ostensibly, in self-defense or to defend or help others).[32] This vision defamiliarizes our world so it becomes available for contestation. As Paul Ricoeur puts it: "[The utopia] makes the actual world seem strange. Usually we are tempted to say that we cannot live in a way different from the way we presently do. The utopia, though, introduces a sense of doubt that shatters the obvious."[33]

So we return to ask, with added force, why literature that estranges the state is relatively absent as a subject of law-and-literature scholarship. The most obvious answer is that these utopias are fictional representations. Using such depictions as a guide to governance would—to borrow Richard Posner's phrase—"be like reading *Animal Farm* as a tract on farm management."[34] Some have done so. Cabet's *Travels in Icaria* led his French socialist disciples to found a real Icaria in the United States;[35] B. F. Skinner's *Walden Two* inspired the communal societies of Los Horcones in Mexico, Twin Oaks in Virginia, and East Wind in Missouri.[36] Yet the dramatic failure of these communities supports Posner. As Northrop Frye dryly maintains: "There have been one or two attempts to take utopian constructions literally by trying to set them up as actual communities, but the histories of these communities make melancholy reading."[37]

Even the progenitor of the genre did not make the mistake of conflating fiction with fact. Although More preached religious toleration in Utopia, he persecuted religious dissenters as lord chancellor of England.[38] As if to emphasize that Utopia was not his own island thinly disguised, More was careful both to compose and to publish *Utopia* abroad.[39] He also retained plausible deniability by putting the account in the mouth of Raphael Hythloday, whose surname means "speaker of nonsense."[40] The "man for all seasons," More was a realist as well as an idealist.

So the criticism that utopian fiction is unlikely to inform governance because it is fiction holds. Yet this criticism can be leveled at all literature. It therefore does not explain why the law-and-literature movement favors fiction that defamiliarizes the individual rather than the state. The question remains of why we are more likely to read Richard Wright's *Black Boy* to inhabit the "lives of distant others"[41] rather than to read More's *Utopia* to inhabit the mores of a distant state.

One tentative answer is that fiction is better at representing individuals than communities. Indeed, this is where the political and literary senses of the word "representation" slide apart. Literary representation is usually an individual act. Political representation—the creation of a community—is usually a collective act. When literature represents the claims of an individual, the slippage between literary and political representation may not be that great. But when literature "represents" a polity, the two usages are so distinct one wishes they were separate words.

Because literary representation differs so fundamentally from political representation, utopias fail as guides to governance. Literary utopias themselves make for "melancholy reading." As H. G. Wells notes in *Modern Utopia*, "Utopian speculations" are always attended by "a certain effect of hardness and thinness."[42] Lewis Mumford elaborates: "Isolation, stratification, fixation, regimentation, standardization, militarization—one or more of these attributes enter into the conception of the utopian city."[43] Peter Ruppert agrees that "[u]topias "appear to ignore difference, to reduce multiplicity and diversity, and to exclude choice, conflict, complexity, history."[44]

This dimension of utopias flows from the limited tolerance the unfettered individual imagination has for any deviation from its ideal of the good. Mumford captures this tragic egotism:

> [T]he abstract intelligence, operating with its own conceptual apparatus, in its own self-restricted field, is actually a coercive instrument: an arrogant fragment of the full human personality, determined to make the world over in its own oversimplified terms, willfully rejecting interests and values incompatible with its own assumptions, and thereby depriving itself of any of the cooperative and generative functions of life—feeling, emotion, playfulness, exuberance, free fantasy—in short, the liberating sources of unpredictable and uncontrollable creativity.[45]

Without any constraints to press against, the writer is placed in the posture of God in creating the world, but apparently without God's humility. Utopian fiction fails as art and as a plan of government because it is at best illiberal, and at worst totalitarian.

A closer look at More's *Utopia* reveals these pathologies. Although individuals need only work six hours a day, the state monitors their leisure time so it "is not wasted in debauchery and idleness."[46] The freedom of religion does not include the freedom to believe "that the soul dies with the body or that the world is ruled by mere chance."[47] The putatively peaceable Utopians conquer surrounding lands when their population grows.[48] Perpetual criminals become slaves.[49] The harmony of the society is ensured only by the homogeneity of its population, which remains faceless and nameless.

When more closely examined, the lawlessness of utopias also reveals a sinister aspect. The Houyhnhnms of *Gulliver's Travels*, whose social system Swift admires above all the rest, have only hortatory laws—compulsion is not needed on the Habermasian ground that no one "can disobey reason."[50] More's *Utopia* absolutely bans all lawyers as "clever practitioners and sly interpreters," preferring to have all citizens proceed *pro se*.[51] Scholars of utopias note the "antilegal tradition of the literary utopias."[52] Crane Brinton, for instance, states that "many modern utopias including the most widely known of all, that of Marx-Engels, do indeed have as a goal the 'withering away of the state,' the abolition of law, police, armies."[53]

Yet in their lawlessness, utopias often seem to share more with dystopias than with any world in which we would want to live.[54] In both *1984* and *Brave New World*, formal laws are unnecessary because citizens have been forced to internalize the appropriate codes of behavior.[55] Huxley wrote *Brave New World* as a response to Butler's *Erewhon* to show the dark side of the insinuating state. The individuals in these societies have no more freedom than characters in a novel.

The strictures placed on the human imagination may be enabling constraints not just as a matter of law, but as a matter of art. Poets who work with forms often describe how constraints stimulate rather than suppress creativity. Wordsworth's sonnet "Nuns fret not at their Convent's narrow room," compares the paradoxical freedom of the immured nun with that of the poet confined in the sonnet form. The poem performs the point that wise restraints can set us free, concluding with the following lines: "In truth, the prison, unto which we doom / Ourselves, no prison is: and hence to me, / In sundry moods, 'twas pastime to be bound / Within the Sonnet's scanty plot of ground: / Pleased if some Souls (for such there needs must be) / Who have felt the weight of too much liberty, / Should find short solace there, as I have found."[56] Enabling constraints can also be substantive. Great literature, like great law, arises out of the constraints of scarcity and conflict. This is why Dante's *Inferno* is so much more powerful than his *Paradiso*, and why Milton's *Paradise Lost* is so much more powerful than his *Paradise Regained*. Freed of both formal and substantive constraints, utopias are perhaps too free.

The law-and-literature movement may then be right to ignore utopian fiction, as such fiction seems consistently to fail on both political and aesthetic terms. I think that rejection would be premature. I could make a descriptive case that utopian thinking is an ineradicable dimension of human personality. As Manuel puts it, "[To] attack utopias is about as meaningful as to denounce dreaming. No great civilization has lived without them."[57] Or I could argue in more normative terms that to reject utopias is to reject a progressive human impulse. In Oscar Wilde's characteristically colorful argot: "A map of the world that does not include Utopia is not worth even glancing at, for it leaves out the one country at which Humanity is always landing. And when Humanity lands there, it looks out, and seeing a better country, sets sail. Progress is the realization of Utopias."[58] The challenge is to capitalize on the merits of the utopia without being overwhelmed by its demerits.

In the aegis-creating 1967 lecture (published in 1986) from which I draw my title, Michel Foucault takes up that challenge.[59] Foucault begins *Of Other Spaces* with the claim that the obsession of modernity has been with place: "I believe that the anxiety of our era has to do fundamentally with space, no doubt a great deal more than with time. Time probably appears to us only as one of the various distributive operations that are possible for the elements that are spread out in space."[60] Two spaces in particular draw his attention because they "have the curious property of being in relation with all the other sites, but in such a way as to suspect, neutralize, or invert the set of relations that they happen to designate, mirror, or reflect."[61] These two spaces are the utopia and what he dubs the "heterotopia."

Foucault's definition of utopia tallies with convention: "Utopias are sites with no real place. They are sites that have a general relation of direct or inverted analogy with the real space of Society. They present society itself in a perfected form, or else society turned upside down, but in any case these utopias are fundamentally unreal spaces."[62] Yet for Foucault, utopias are not the only sites that relate to all other sites while standing apart from all of them:

> There are also, probably in every culture, in every civilization, real places—places that do exist and that are formed in the very founding of society—which are something like counter-sites, a kind of effectively enacted utopia in which the real sites, all the other real sites that can be found within the culture, are simultaneously represented, contested, and inverted. Places of this kind are outside of all places, even though it may be possible to indicate their location in reality. Because these places are absolutely different from all the sites that they reflect and speak about, I shall call them, by way of contrast to utopias, heterotopias.[63]

The contrast is best elucidated through example. Foucault's instances of heterotopias are scandalously various, including cemeteries, Persian rugs, and ships. Unlike utopias, these sites exist in the real world. Yet like utopias, they represent some fundamental dimension of the human condition. A cemetery is a map of death, the place where none of us live but to which all of us will go; a Persian rug with a circle in the middle is a map of a garden with a fountain in the middle, which is in turn a map of the four-cornered earth with the omphalos in the middle; a ship is a map of the human imagination in that it is "a floating piece of space, a place without a place, that exists by itself, that is closed in on itself and at the same time is given over to the infinity of the sea."[64] Foucault ends the essay by asserting that the ship is the "heterotopia *par excellence*," because, like Wilde, he believes it represents the "greatest reserve of the imagination." Yet the heterotopian imagination contrasts with the utopian imagination in standing against the totalitarian state, rather than with it: "In civilizations without boats, dreams dry up, espionage takes the place of adventure, and the police take the place of pirates."[65]

The concept of heterotopia is gorgeously hopeful. It takes the reality of an object in the world as the enabling constraint that permits acts of imagination to remain in conversation with our actual lives. While many things can be imagined in a heterotopia, certain brute facts are non-negotiable. As Foucault points out, until the eighteenth century, the cemetery was placed in the heart of the city, next to the church, and bodies were buried en masse. Only in the early nineteenth century was the cemetery moved to the edge of the city to become a city in its own right where bodies were buried individually. Foucault posits that this physical shift reflected a spiritual one away from the belief in an immortal soul. When the dead body "became our only trace of our existence," it became important that everyone "had the right to her or his own little box for her or his own little personal decay."[66] Foucault disciplines his imaginative exercise with a respect for historical facts.

Just as More's book is the paradigmatic utopian text, Italo Calvino's *Invisible Cities* is the paradigmatic heterotopian one.[67] Published five years after Foucault's lecture, Calvino's novel features Marco Polo telling the emperor Kublai Khan about the cities he has visited on his travels. These cities are splendidly odd—one is a city where everything but the plumbing has fallen away; another is a city from which no one returns; still another is a city designed to fulfill all one's youthful desires but which can be entered only when one is old. These cities are not utopian in any classical sense. None is lofted up as ideal. Perhaps more important, the turn in the novel comes when we realize that Polo is describing one city, the city of Venice. The invisible cities are the many cities Venice contains, whether that be the piece of Venice that is its plumbing, the piece of Venice that is its death, or the piece of Venice that is its regret.

To a liberal's eye, at least, Calvino's heterotopia has advantages over More's utopia. It is antitotalitarian, diverse, and seems to open up possibility rather than to foreclose it. And from a literary perspective, Calvino's book far surpasses More's book in a way I attribute to the genres in which the authors are writing. *Invisible Cities* is a tribute to Venice, but one ennobled by its avoidance of both stereotype and cliché. Perhaps law-and-literature scholars should avert their eyes from utopias and train them on heterotopias.

Of Force and Fancy

Just as utopias scorn legal systems, legal systems scorn utopias. In Supreme Court opinions, the word "utopia" has a consistently negative cast. Sometimes the opinion's tone is millennarian: "More will not be asked by those who have learned from experience and history that government is at best a makeshift, that the attainment of one good may involve the sacrifice of others, and that compromise will be inevitable until the coming of Utopia."[68] At other times, the tone is monitory, praising the idealism of a position but underscoring its naivety: "The Court's effort to 'furthe[r] the ends of justice,' and achieve hoped-for utopian bliss may be admired, but it is far more likely to enlarge the evil."[69] At still other times, the tone is purely critical of the impracticality of the utopian ideal: "The aim in short is toward 'voluntariness' in a utopian sense, or to view it from a different angle, voluntariness with a vengeance. To incorporate this notion into the Constitution requires . . . a disregard of the very pragmatic concerns that alone may on occasion justify such strains."[70] Law, it seems, has no place for utopian thinking.

Indeed, it may seem that law has no place for any kind of imaginative thinking. Generally, an inverse relationship should obtain between force and fancy. If we exercise coercion over a fellow human being, we have an obligation to abstain from some forms of imagination. Because law is distinguished from other discourses by its violence, law presses that obligation upon us with particular insistence. This is one of the cardinal distinctions between law and literature.

Robert Cover begins his celebrated essay *Violence and the Word* in that knowledge: "Legal interpretation takes place in a field of pain and death."[71] Acts of legal interpretation "signal and occasion the imposition of violence upon others."[72] For this reason, legal interpretation is "bonded interpretation," which can never be understood apart from the violence it inflicts.[73]

To drive home the distinctive nature of law's violence, Cover compares it to literary violence. "The judges deal pain and death," Cover declares. "In this they are different from poets, from critics, from artists. It will not do to insist on the violence of strong poetry, and strong poets. Even the violence of weak judges is utterly real—a naive but immediate reality, in need of no interpretation, no critic to reveal it."[74]

Law's violence is its greatest generic constraint: "The gulf between thought and action widens wherever serious violence is at issue, because for most of us, evolutionary, psychological, cultural and moral considerations inhibit the infliction of pain on other people."[75] The restriction is indirect: It is not the violence itself, but our ethical posture when wielding violence, that shapes our speech. Seamus Heaney neatly captures this dynamic in his doubled phrase "the government of the tongue"[76]—when the tongue governs, it must be governed.

This inverse relationship between force and fancy is widely accepted. Like most constraints, it is most visible in the breach. Justice J. Michael Eakin of the Pennsylvania Supreme Court is known as the "rhyming judge" for waxing poetic in his opinions.[77] His dissent in a case involving a fake engagement ring consisted of a series of couplets, including: "A groom must expect matrimonial pandemonium / When his spouse finds he's given her cubic zirconium."[78] His lyricism drew the ire of the chief justice, who observed that "an opinion that expresses itself in rhyme reflects poorly on the Supreme Court of Pennsylvania."[79] Eakin remained unrepentant, observing that "[y]ou have an obligation as a judge to be right" but not "to be dull."[80] But even he conceded he would "never do it in a serious criminal case."[81] Law professor Stephen Gillers draws the same line: "A couplet here or there is fine, and judges should strive to use poetic devices in opinions to make them memorable and readable."[82] Yet Gillers also invokes law's violence as a constraint: "But a judge's opinions often cause pain. Rhyming diminishes the solemnity of the event and its seriousness to the litigants."[83]

I do not (here) challenge the inverse relationship between force and fancy.[84] Rather, I contest the assumption that law is always a field of force and literature always a field of fancy. I maintain that legal actors often deprive themselves of force precisely to engage in flights of fancy, forgoing coercion to permit themselves acts of imagination. We see this trade in many conventional legal genres: dissents, hortatory laws, dicta, legal scholarship, advisory opinions, cases raising issues of justiciability, and so on.

These acts of imagination are more heterotopian than utopian. Unlike the worlds imagined in utopian literature, the worlds imagined in legal discourse are routinely realized. So while dissents themselves have no coercive effect, over 130 dissents have been embraced by majority opinions.[85] Hortatory laws often become mandatory ones, such as Racketeer Influenced and Corrupt Organizations Act or Anti-Terrorism and Effective Death Penalty Act. And while dictum has no force on its own, it is notoriously hard to discern the line between dictum and holding, both internal to a particular opinion and in the use of that opinion as precedent.

Imagined legal worlds are heterotopias because they are always in argument with the real. They are anchored in and accountable to the world in a way in which literary utopias are not. For this reason, legal heterotopias do not share the "flatness and hardness" that characterize literary utopias. Because they do not give free rein to the unfettered egotistic imagination, they are more textured, diverse, changeful, colorful, and humane.

At the same time, these legal heterotopias function as countersites, where the law can reimagine the world without performatively enacting that vision as the world. Like literary heterotopias, legal heterotopias can exploit the virtues of utopian thinking without being entrapped by its vices. In the balance of this essay, I examine three different genres through which the law engages in acts of heterotopian imagination—dissents, hortatory laws, and dicta. I then briefly show how these three genres were key in the development of the concept of color blindness.

Of Dissents

In an essay titled *Law and Literature*, Justice Benjamin Cardozo recognizes the constraints force places on majority opinions: "The spokesman of the court is cautious, timid, fearful of the vivid word, the heightened phrase. He dreams of an unworthy brood of scions."[86] The coercive effect of his words disciplines his rhetoric: "The result is to cramp and paralyze. One fears to say anything when the peril of misunderstanding puts a warning finger to the lips."[87] To this point, Cardozo agrees with the Cover who wrote *Violence and the Word*.

Unlike the Cover of *Violence*, however, Cardozo explicitly recognizes that not all "legal interpretive acts" coerce. He contrasts "the spokesman of the court" with "the dissenter," who "has laid aside the rôle of the hierophant, which he will be only too glad to resume when the chances of war make him again the spokesman of the majority."[88] Cardozo goes on to observe that the dissenter's posture as "the gladiator making a last stand against the lions" gives him a concomitant rhetorical freedom: "We need not be surprised, therefore, to find in dissent a certain looseness of texture and depth of color rarely found in the *per curiam*. . . . Deep conviction and warm feeling are saying their last say with knowledge that the cause is lost."[89]

This claim—that dissents are often more literary in their style than majority opinions—has been rehearsed by modern scholars.[90] Yet the dissenter's freedom extends far beyond the ability to use colorful rhetoric. As Cardozo continues:

> The voice of the majority may be that of force triumphant, content with the plaudits of the hour, and recking little of the morrow. The dissenter speaks to the future, and his voice is pitched to a key that will carry through the years. Read some of the great dissents, the opinion, for example, of Judge Curtis in Dred Scott *vs.* Sandford, and feel after the cooling time of the better part of [a] century the glow and fire of a faith that was content to bide its hour. The prophet and the martyr do not see the hooting throng. Their eyes are fixed on the eternities.[91]

The dissenter's greatest permission is the permission to imagine a better world, to be the prophet of eternities.

Many attributes of heterotopias are attributes of dissents. Dissents are things in our world, spoken by legal actors whose pronouncements might become law on the morrow. At the same time, dissents do not have the immediate coercive effects we associate with law. They are spatially and temporally distinct from the majority opinion, operating as rhetorical islands distinguishable from the majority opinion, and focusing their attention on the future. Moreover, some capacity to dissent may be necessary to preserve the dignity of the judge. As the "great dissenter" William O. Douglas once observed: "The right to dissent is the only thing that makes life tolerable for the judge of an appellate court . . . .

It is the right of dissent, not the right or duty to conform, which gives dignity, worth and individuality to man."[92]

Perhaps most important, dissents defamiliarize the majority opinion. Chief Justice Marshall broke with the English tradition of issuing seriatim opinions to deliver the opinion of the court with one voice, discouraging concurrences and dissents.[93] Marshall sought to secure the authority of the Court by suggesting its rulings were inexorable.[94] At the urging of Thomas Jefferson, Justice William Johnson quickly brought the practice of dissent to the Court.[95] Nonetheless, the practice of dissent did not become commonplace until the New Deal era. Robert Post observes that "[j]ustices of the Taft Court felt presumptively obligated to join Court opinions, even if they disagreed with their content, so as to preserve the influence and prestige of the Court."[96]

That status quo is hard to recollect today. In describing the "collapse of the norm of acquiescence" on the Taft Court, Post observes that "[o]nce members of the Court began to regard 'growth' as 'the life of the law' . . . a Justice like William O. Douglas, perhaps the most consummate dissenter in the history of the Court, could affirm that 'philosophers of the democratic faith will rejoice in the uncertainty of the law and find strength and glory in it.'"[97] Dissents have been celebrated as ways of imagining alterities—of "enabl[ing] the law to admit new ideas and adapt old doctrines, exposing them to scrutiny and consideration both inside and outside the court."[98] Under this view, introducing new ideas without immediate effect smooths the course of the law: "[D]issent facilitates progression and change, and does so in a more open and less abrupt way than might occur in the absence of any ability to deliver such opinions."[99] Dissents have also been touted for their idealism: "Without the judicial dissent, 'boulders which are fused together with time-defying cement form a wall which could some day obstruct the passage of a needed road to the City of the Realized Hope of Man.'"[100]

Of Hortatory Law

It is often said that an unenforced law is worse than no law at all, as it not only is inefficacious in its own right but also undermines the rule of law.[101] As Albert Einstein commented: "The prestige of government has undoubtedly been lowered considerably by the Prohibition law. For nothing is more destructive of respect for the government and the law of the land than passing laws which cannot be enforced."[102] In fact, unenforceable law has been deemed oxymoronic—as James Garfield is alleged to have said, "A law is not a law without coercion behind it."[103]

So to some, hortatory laws, which merely "exhort" individuals to engage in or desist from certain practices, will seem inherently suspect. They may escape the criticism that they undermine the rule of law, if—unlike Prohibition—they disclaim any intent to coerce. Yet they may still raise ontological problems, as coercion is seen to be a definitional component of the law.

If hortatory laws are so troublesome, we might ask why they are so widespread. Legislative resolutions are commonly enacted to articulate ideals that are unenforceable at the time. Sometimes, however, such resolutions are subsequently codified into hard law. Senate Resolution 1861 first articulated the substance of the Racketeer Influenced and Corrupt Organizations Act of 1970.[104] Senate Resolution 735 became the Antiterrorism and Effective Death Penalty Act in 1996.[105] As we will see, cases sometimes issue their holdings with enough ambiguity to move from the realm of coercion to exhortation. "Soft" international law, such as the "law of nations," is also viewed as hortatory. And of course, various declarations, ranging from the Declaration of Independence to the Universal Declaration of Human Rights, can be seen as instances of the genre.

In the realm of hortatory law, the Universal Declaration of Human Rights stands as the most powerful instance of a legal heterotopia. The declaration was self-consciously adopted without binding obligations, presented instead as a "common standard of achievement for all peoples and all nations" toward which "every individual and every organ of society" should "strive."[106] The declaration's lack of immediate coercive effect clearly permitted it to be loftier in its aspirations. This disjuncture between force and fancy led to varying predictions about its prospects. "Many regarded it as a milestone in the history of freedom, but to others it seemed to be just a collection of pious phrases—meaningless without courts, policemen, and armies to back them up."[107] International law scholar Hersch Lauterpacht commented that the declaration would have "no legal force and, probably only inconsiderable moral authority."[108] Eleanor Roosevelt, however, had more confidence, "due in part to her lively sense of the Declaration of Independence as a bright thread running through American history."[109] Maybe because of her faith

> the State Department explained the U.S. view of the Declaration's nature and purpose by referring to what Abraham Lincoln had said about the assertion of human equality in the Declaration of Independence: "They [the drafters] did not mean to assert the obvious untruth, that all were then actually enjoying that equality, nor yet, that they were about to confer it immediately upon them. In fact they had no power to confer such a boon. They meant simply to declare the *right* so that the *enforcement* of it might follow as fast as circumstances should permit.
>
> "They meant to set up a standard maxim for free society which should be familiar to all: constantly looked to, constantly labored for, and thereby constantly spreading and deepening its influence and augmenting the happiness and value of life to all people, of all colors, everywhere."[110]

By tying these two declarations together, Roosevelt suggested that sometimes individuals must live *under* ideals before they are forced to live *up* to them.

History richly vindicated Roosevelt's confidence. The declaration now exerts "moral, political, and legal influence far beyond the hopes of many of its drafters."[111] It quickly became a model for new constitutions and human rights instruments enacted in the post–World War II period.[112] Similarly, "[t]he most impressive advances in human rights—the fall of apartheid in South Africa and the collapse of the Eastern European totalitarian regimes—owe more to the moral beacon of the Declaration than to the many covenants and treaties that are now in force."[113] "Legally, politically, and morally, the Universal Declaration remains even more significant today than when it was adopted nearly a half-century ago."[114]

Of Dicta

Of the three genres considered here, dicta might be the hardest legal genre to dub heterotopian. Unlike dissents and hortatory laws, dicta do not clearly satisfy the tenet that heterotopias are distinct spaces. No trench divides dictum from holding—making that distinction is one of the tasks of the legal interpreter.[115] The consequence of this distinction is that holding counts as binding precedent, while dictum does not: "The rule has always been that a dictum is not binding as a precedent."[116] A wrinkle is that while a dictum "is not binding under the doctrine of stare decisis, . . . so-called dicta are often followed."[117]

Nonetheless, it fairly can be said that a dictum is less coercive on the parties before it than the holding of the case. And so it can also be said that dictum is the place within the majority opinion where judges can imagine better worlds. Footnote four of *United States v. Carolene Products* is the most famous instance.[118] It is most familiar history that the Court at first repeatedly struck down Franklin Delano Roosevelt's New Deal legislation.[119] This led FDR to lash out with his Court-packing scheme, which forced the Court to adopt a much more deferential posture to federal legislation.[120] The holding of *Carolene Products*, which upheld the Filled Milk Act against both Commerce Clause and Substantive Due Process challenges, was a show of judicial obeisance.[121]

Yet Justice Stone retained an ace for the Court in the opinion's famous fourth footnote. The footnote maps out three circumstances in which the Court will be less likely to presume constitutionality: (1) when legislation is within a specific prohibition of the Constitution; (2) when "legislation restricts political processes"; and (3) when legislation reflects "prejudices against discrete and insular minorities."[122]

The significance of this footnote has far surpassed the significance of any other part of the opinion, including its holding.[123] In this footnote, the Court articulates nothing short of a new theory of judicial review.[124] In the second and third sections of the footnote, the Court describes circumstances in which the legislative process is marked by flaws. In stepping in to correct those flaws, the judiciary is not incurring a legitimacy deficit, but curing a legitimacy deficit on the part of the legislature.[125] Footnote four provides a way for future courts to surmount the countermajoritarian difficulty.

Carolene exemplifies how dictum permits courts to outline in idealized strokes the nature of the regime they wish to endorse. If the Court had not been permitted to write dicta, it is hard to imagine the case that would have permitted Justice Stone to pen the words of his immortal footnote.

Of Color Blindness

I have argued that dissents, hortatory laws, and dicta are all forms of legal utopian imagining necessary to the development of the law. To underscore that point, I will demonstrate that the principle of racial color blindness has relied on these three genres for its doctrinal elaboration. The dissent in *Plessy*, the hortatory law of *Brown*, and the dicta in *Grutter* are all instances of the legal heterotopian imagination at work.

The concept of color blindness entered U.S. equal protection jurisprudence through a dissent. In *Plessy v. Ferguson*,[126] the Supreme Court validated the principle of "separate but equal," upholding a Louisiana law requiring whites and African-Americans to ride in separate cars. Homer Plessy's lawyer, Albion Tourgée, made the argument to the Court that justice was color blind.[127] The sole dissenter, Justice Harlan, enshrined that language in the United States Reports: "There is no caste here. Our Constitution is color-blind."[128] As Alan Barth states: "Harlan foresaw those evils before they became generally apparent. He spoke as a seer, before his time—before the time was ripe for the acceptance of what he saw."[129]

Harlan's sweeping dissent was vindicated, of course, in *Brown v. Board of Education*.[130] It may seem odd to call the most canonical U.S. opinion of all time merely "hortatory," but a good case can be made that *Brown v. Board of Education* had such dimensions. In *Brown I*, the Court categorically declared that "separate educational facilities are inherently unequal."[131] *Brown I*, however, did not require the states to implement that holding immediately, stating that the Court would defer fashioning a remedy until the next year. Then in *Brown II*, the Court stated that desegregation should occur with "all deliberate speed."[132] This formulation has been criticized for permitting massive foot-dragging by the Southern states.[133] Yet I see it as a stroke of genius. By explicitly permitting the inevitable resistance, the Court retained its own legitimacy. And in denuding its holding of some of its force, the Court was able to articulate it with crystalline purity.

The Supreme Court recently wrestled with the topic of color blindness in a 2003 case concerning affirmative action. In *Grutter v. Bollinger*,[134] the Court upheld the constitutionality of a race-conscious admissions program adopted by a state law school. Nonetheless, Justice O'Connor, writing for the majority, included some fascinating dictum about how "race-conscious admissions policies must be limited in time":[135]

> We take the Law School at its word that it would like "nothing better than to find a race-neutral admissions formula" and will terminate its race-conscious admissions program as soon as practicable. . . . We expect that 25 years from now, the use of racial preferences will no longer be necessary to further the interest approved today.[136]

Here color blindness is still touted as an ideal, just not one attainable in the present. O'Connor's vision is not just prophetic, but Mosaic. Even at the time the opinion was written, one certainty about the Court in 2028 was that it would be a Court on which O'Connor would no longer sit. Just as Moses pointed his people toward a promised land he could not inhabit, O'Connor is pointing her Court toward a heterotopia she cannot enter.[137] Her tone is elegiac, as if her generation is too fallen to see justice done.

O'Connor's heterotopian vision is not my own. The world she imagines seems utopian in buying its harmony at the price of homogeneity. But I nonetheless believe that it is important for the justices to engage in such acts of imagination. O'Connor is forcing herself to outline what she views the endpoint of affirmative action to be. Although the twenty-five years has been interpreted by some to be "a biblical 40," we can see in her numeric precision a good-faith attempt to argue with the real.

The history of color blindness, then, is a history of nonbinding opinions that trade their force for fancy to imagine better worlds. Notice that while this narrative is one about imaginatively furthering civil rights in the courts, it has nothing to do with "stories from the bottom." What is being estranged is not the individual, but the state.

Of Poets and Legislators

"Poets are the unacknowledged legislators of the world!" cries Percy Bysshe Shelley at the end of his *Defense of Poetry*.[138] George Oppen administers the corrective that poets are not so much "the unacknowledged legislators of the world" so much as "the legislators of the unacknowledged world."[139] On Oppen's formulation, poets are the legislators (perhaps the gods) of the utopias they create. Their jurisdiction, however, does not extend into the acknowledged world—the utopias they rule are literary, not legal. This essay seeks to give something back to Shelley. In all the ways they imagine heterotopias, lawmakers are poetic in their aspirations. To that extent, poets are indeed the hitherto unacknowledged legislators of an acknowledged world.

Notes

1. *Romer v. Evans*, 517 U.S. 620 (1996).

2. See, generally, Kenji Yoshino, "The City and the Poet," *Yale Law Journal* 114 (2005): 1845.

3. Derrick Bell, *Faces at the Bottom of the Well: The Permanence of Racism* (New York: Basic Books, 1992).

4. Paulette Caldwell, "A Hair Piece: Perspectives on the Intersection of Race and Gender," *Duke Law Journal* 41 (1991): 397.

5. Patricia Williams, *The Alchemy of Race and Rights* (Cambridge: University of Harvard Press, 1991).

6. See, for example, Daniel Farber and Suzanna Sherry, "Telling Stories out of School: An Essay on Legal Narratives," *Stanford Law Review* 45 (1993): 807.

7. *The Oxford English Dictionary*, 2nd ed. (1989), s.v. "Utopia."

8. *The Oxford English Dictionary*, 2nd ed. (1989), s.v. "Eutopia." Sir Thomas More, *Utopia*, trans. Clarence H. Miller (New Haven: Yale University Press, 2001).

9. Samuel Butler, *Erewhon*, ed. Peter Mudford (1872; London: Penguin Books, 1985).

10. Ruth Levitas, *The Concept of Utopia* (Syracuse: Syracuse University Press, 1990).

11. Plato, *The Republic of Plato*, ed. and trans. Allan Bloom (New York: Basic Books, 1991).

12. More, *Utopia*.

13. Francis Bacon, *The New Atlantis*, in *Three Early Modern Utopias: Utopia, New Atlantis, Isle of Pines*, ed. Susan Bruce (1627; New York: Oxford University Press, 1999).

14. Tommaso Campanella, *The City of the Sun: A Poetical Dialogue*, trans. Daniel J. Donno (1623; Berkeley: University of California Press, 1981).

15. Etienne Cabet, *Travels in Icaria*, trans. Leslie Roberts (1840; Syracuse: Syracuse University Press, 2003).

16. Plato, *Republic*.

17. St. Augustine, *The City of God against the Pagans*, ed. and trans. R. W. Dyson (c. 426; Cambridge: Cambridge University Press, 1998).

18. Campanella, *The City of the Sun*.

19. More, *Utopia*, 53.

20. Bacon, *The New Atlantis*.

21. Cabet, *Travels in Icaria*.

22. Aldous Huxley, *Island* (New York: Harper and Brothers, 1962).

23. More, *Utopia*, 53.

24. Ibid.

25. Ibid., 54–55, 57.

26. Ibid., 61.

27. Ibid., 97.

28. Ibid., 83, 84.

29. Ibid., 115–17.

30. Ibid., 79.

31. Ibid., 99–105.

32. Ibid., 105–6.

33. Paul C. Ricoeur, *Lectures on Ideology and Utopia* (New York: Colombia University Press, 1986), 299–300.

34. Posner, "The Ethical Significance of Free Choice: A Reply to Professor West," *Harvard Law Review* 99 (1986): 1431, 1433.

35. Cabet, *Travels in Icaria*, xxviii–xlvii

36. B. F. Skinner, *Walden Two* (Indianapolis, IN: Hackett, 1948); see also, for example, Deborah E. Altus and Edward K. Morris, "B. F. Skinner's Utopian Vision: Behind and Beyond Walden Two," *Contemporary Justice Review* 267 (2004): 272.

37. Northrop Frye, "Varieties of Literary Utopias," in *Utopias and Utopian Thought*, ed. Frank E. Manuel (Boston: Beacon Press, 1965), 25–26.

38. See Wayne A. Rebhorn, "Introduction," in Sir Thomas More, *Utopia*, trans. Ralph Robinson (New York: Barnes & Noble Classics), xxii.

39. See Richard Marius, *Thomas More* (Cambridge, MA: Harvard University Press, 1984), 240–44.

40. Rebhorn, "Introduction," xxviii.

41. Martha C. Nussbaum, *Poetic Justice: The Literary Imagination and Public Life* (Boston: Beacon Press, 1997), xvi.

42. H. G. Wells, *A Modern Utopia* (London: Chapman & Hall, 1905), 9.

43. Lewis Mumford, "Utopia, the City and the Machine," in *Utopias and Utopian Thought*, ed. Frank E. Manuel (Boston: Beacon Press, 1965), 9.

44. Peter Ruppert, *Reader in a Strange Land: The Activity of Reading Literary Utopias* (Athens: University of Georgia Press, 1986), 9.

45. Mumford, "Utopia, the City and the Machine," 10.

46. More, *Utopia*, 61.

47. Ibid., 119.

48. Ibid., 67.

49. Ibid., 95–96.

50. Jonathan Swift, *Gulliver's Travels*, ed. Paul Turner (Oxford: Oxford University Press), 272.

51. More, *Utopia*, 101.

52. Carol Weisbrod, *The Boundaries of Utopia* (New York: Pantheon Books, 1980), 115.

53. Crane Brinton, "Utopia and Democracy," in *Utopias and Utopian Thought*, ed. Frank E. Manuel (Boston: Beacon Press, 1965), 51.

54. John Stuart Mill coined the term "dystopia," which the *OED* defines as "[an] imaginary place or condition in which everything is as bad as possible." *The Oxford English Dictionary*, 2nd ed. (1989), s.v. "Dystopia."

55. In *Brave New World*, this internalization begins with children. A group of students, for example, has been trained to believe that "every one belongs to every one else" in part because "upwards of sixty-two thousand repetitions in the dark had made them accept [it], not merely as true, but as axiomatic, self-evident, utterly indisputable." Aldous Huxley, *Brave New World* (New York: Harper and Row, 1969), 26. See also, for example, George Orwell, *1984* (New York: Signet Classic, 1950), 210–11 ("[A party member] has no freedom of choice in any direction whatever. On the other hand his actions are not regulated by law or by any clearly formulated code of behaviour. In Oceania there is no law.").

56. William Wordsworth, "Nuns fret not at their Convent's narrow room," in *William Wordsworth: The Major Works*, ed. Stephen Gill (New York: Oxford University Press), 286.

57. Frank E. Manuel, "Toward a Psychological History of Utopias," in *Utopias and Utopian Thought*, ed. Frank E. Manuel (Boston: Beacon Press, 1965), 95.

58. Oscar Wilde, "The Soul of Man under Socialism," in *De Profundis and Other Writings* (1891; London: Penguin Books, 1986), 34.

59. Michel Foucault, "Of Other Spaces," *Diacritics* 16 (1986): 22–27.

60. Ibid., 23.

61. Ibid.

62. Ibid., 24.

63. Ibid.

64. Ibid., 27.

65. Ibid.

66. Ibid.

67. Italo Calvino, *Invisible Cities*, trans. William Weaver (1972; New York: Harcourt, 1974).

68. *Stewart Dry Goods Co. v. Lewis*, 294 U.S. 550, 577 (1935) (Cardozo, J., dissenting).

69. *Batson v. Kentucky*, 476 U.S. 79, 131 (1986) (Burger, C. J., dissenting) (internal citation omitted).

70. *Miranda v. Arizona*, 384 U.S. 436, 505 (1966) (Harlan, J., dissenting).

71. Robert M. Cover, "Violence and the Word," *Yale Law Journal* 95 (1986): 1601.

72. Ibid.

73. Ibid., 1617–18.

74. Ibid., 1609.

75. Ibid., 1613.

76. Seamus Heaney, *The Government of the Tongue* (London: Faber and Faber, 1988).

77. Adam Liptak, "Justices Call on Bench's Bard to Limit His Lyricism," *New York Times*, December 15, 2002, 41. *See also* Porreco v. Porreco, 571 Pa. 61, 77 (2002) (Eakin, J. dissenting).

78. Liptak, "Justices Call on Bench's Bard to Limit His Lyricism," 41.

79. Ibid.

80. Ibid.

81. Ibid.

82. Ibid.

83. Ibid.

84. That relationship could be contested in many ways—for instance, by looking at the imaginative shame sanctions that judges have devised for convicts. See, for example, Dan Kahan, *What Do Alternative Sanctions Mean?*, *University of Chicago Law Review* 63 (1996): 591, 631 ("By using these [shame sanctions], either alone or in combination with conventional sanctions such as fines and community service, American jurisdictions can fashion politically acceptable alternative sanctions").

85. Cass R. Sunstein, *Why Societies Need Dissent* (Cambridge: Harvard University Press, 2003), 71.

86. Benjamin N. Cardozo, "Law and Literature," in *Law and Literature and Other Essays and Addresses* (New York: Harcourt, Brace, 1931), 34.

87. Ibid.

88. Ibid.

89. Ibid., 34, 35–36.

90. Robert Flanders, Jr., notes that "dissents often exude an infused passion, an expressive potency, and even a telltale hint or two of not-so-latent literary leanings—together with other dynamic and imaginative qualities—that are typically lacking in more homogenized majority opinions." Robert G. Flanders, Jr., "The Utility of Separate Judicial Opinions in Appellate Courts of Last Resort: Why Dissents Are Valuable," *Roger Williams University Law Review* 4 (1999): 401, 410 (citing Antonin Scalia, *The Dissenting Opinion*, 1994 J. Sup. Ct. Hist. 33, 42). Richard Primus observes that although the claim that dissents are more literary than majority opinions may be overstated (because we only need to read the good ones) it is nonetheless true that dissents are "less guarded, less qualified, and more literary." Richard A. Primus, "Canon, Anti-Canon, and Judicial Dissent," *Duke Law Journal* 48 (1998): 243, note 83.

91. Cardozo, "Law and Literature," 36.

92. William O. Douglas, *America Challenged* (New York: Avon Books, 1960), 4–5.

93. Bernard Schwartz, *A History of the Supreme Court* (New York: Oxford University Press, 1993), 39.

94. Ibid.

95. Donald G. Morgan, *Justice William Johnson, The First Great Dissenter* (South Carolina: University of South Carolina Press, 1954), 168–70. See also Schwartz, *A History of the Supreme Court*, 62–64.

96. Robert Post, "The Supreme Court Opinion as Institutional Practice: Dissent, Legal Scholarship, and Decisionmaking in the Taft Court," *Minnesota Law Review* 85 (2001): 1267, 1274.

97. Ibid., 1354–55 (quoting Douglas, "The Dissent: A Safeguard of Democracy," *American Judicature Society* 32 (1948): 104.

98. Andrew Lynch, "Dissent: The Rewards and Risks of Judicial Disagreement in the High Court of Australia," *Melbourne University Law Review* 27 (2003): 724, 726.

99. Ibid.

100. J. Louis Campbell III, "The Spirit of Dissent," in *Judicial Politics: Readings from Judicature*, ed. Elliot E. Slotnick (Chicago: Burnham Publishers, 1964), 373.

101. Gordon D. Henderson, "Controlling Hyperlexis—The Most Important 'Law and . . . ,'" *Tax Lawyer* 43 (1989): 177, 194 ("Laws that aren't enforced can be worse than no laws at all, because of the disrespect they breed for government"); Ad Hoc Comm. on Foreign Payments of the Ass'n of the Bar of the City of N.Y., Report on Questionable Foreign Payments by Corporations: The Problem and Approaches to a Solution 9 (1977) ("[L]aws which cannot be enforced 'represent poor public policy' because, after the failure in enforcement becomes evident, the credibility of the government enacting them is diminished"); Patrick J. Long, Comment, "The Good Samaritan and Admiralty: A Parable of a Statute Lost at Sea," *Buffalo Law Review* 48 (2000): 591, 627 ("A law that is not enforced is worse than no law at all.").

102. Albert Einstein, "My First Impressions of the U.S.A.," in *Ideas and Opinions*, trans. Sonja Bargmann (New York: Modern Library, 1994), 3, 6.

103. James Garfield, *The Heretic's Handbook of Quotations*, ed. Charles Bufe (Tucson, AZ: Sharp Press, 1988), 26.

104. Compare S. 1861, 91st Cong. (1969) to the Racketeer Influenced and Corrupt Organizations Act, Publ. L. No. 91–452, § 901(a), 84 Stat. 922 (1970).

105. Compare S. 735, 104st Cong. (1996) to the Antiterrorism and Effective Death Penalty Act, Publ. L. No. 104–132, 110 Stat. 1214 (1996).

106. Universal Declaration of Human Rights, G.A. Res. 217A (III), U.N. Doc. A/810, Prmbl. (1948).

107. Mary Ann Glendon, *A World Made New: Eleanor Roosevelt and the Universal Declaration of Human Rights* (New York: Random House, 2001), 235.

108. Hersch Lauterpacht, *International Law and Human Rights* (1950), 450, quoted in Glendon, ibid., 235.

109. Glendon, *A World Made New*, 235.

110. Ibid., 236, quoting Abraham Lincoln, "Seventh and Last Debate with Steven A. Douglas, Alton, IL," in *The Collected Works of Abraham Lincoln*, vol. 3, ed. Roy P. Basler (1853; Rutgers: Rutgers University Press, 1953), 301.

111. Hurst Hannum, "The Status of the Universal Declaration of Human Rights in National and International Law," *Georgia Journal of International and Comparative Law* 25 (1995/1996): 287, 289; see also Edward D. Re, "The Universal Declaration of Human Rights and the Domestic Courts," *St. Thomas Law Review* 14 (2002): 665, 668–69.

112. See, for example, Glendon, *A World Made New*, 228 (listing the constitutions that refer to the Universal Declaration); Glendon, "The Rule of Law in the Universal Declaration of Human Rights," *Northwestern University Journal of International Human Rights* 5 (2004): 26.

113. Glendon, *A World Made New*, 236.

114. Hannum, "The Status of the Universal Declaration of Human Rights," 354.

115. Michael Abramowicz and Maxwell Stearns, "Defining Dicta," *Stanford Law Review* 57 (2005): 953.

116. Anonymous, "Dictum Revisited," *Stanford Law Review* 4 (1952): 509, 512.

117. Ibid.

118. *United States v. Carolene Prod. Co.*, 304 U.S. 144, 152 n.4 (1938).

119. Schwartz, *A History of the Supreme Court*, 231–32.

120. Ibid., 233–34.

121. See, generally, *United States v. Carolene Prod. Co.*, 304 U.S. 144 (1938).

122. Ibid., 152, n.4.

123. See, for example, J. M. Balkin, "The Footnote," *Northwestern University Law Review* (1989): 275, 282.

124. Compare John Hart Ely, *Democracy and Distrust* (Cambridge: Harvard University Press, 1980).

125. Bruce A. Ackerman, "Beyond *Carolene Products*," *Harvard Law Review* 98 (1985): 713, 715.

126. *Plessy v. Ferguson*, 163 U.S. 537 (1896).

127. Tourgée's brief for *Plessy* declared: "Justice is pictured blind and her daughter, the Law, ought at least to be color-blind." Hon. John Minor Wisdom, "Plessy v. Ferguson—100 Years Later," *Washington and Lee Law Review* 53 (1996): 9, 11 (1996).

128. *Plessy*, 163 U.S. at 559 (Harlan, J., dissenting).

129. Alan Barth, *Prophets with Honor: Great Dissents and Great Dissenters in the Supreme Court* (New York: Knopf, 1974), 52.

130. *Brown v. Bd. Educ.*, 347 U.S. 483 (1954).

131. Ibid., 495.

132. Ibid., 349 U.S. 294, 301 (1955).

133. For criticisms of the "all deliberate speed" phrase, see, for example, Sumi Cho, "Redeeming Whiteness in the Shadow of Internment: Earl Warren, *Brown*, and a Theory of Racial Redemption," *Boston College Law Review* 40 (1998): 73, 141 ("*Brown II*'s oxymoronic standard would predictably encourage Southern resistance and permit segregated schooling to continue"); Charles J. Ogletree, Jr., "From *Brown* to Tulsa: Defining Our Own Future," *Howard Law Journal* 47 (2004): 499, 523–26 (discussing disappointment of *Brown* lawyers with the formulation); Jim Chen, "With All Deliberate Speed: *Brown II* and Desegregation's Children," *Law and Inequity: A Journal of Theory and Practice* (2006): 1, 3–4 (similar).

134. *Grutter v. Bollinger*, 539 U.S. 306, 343–44 (2003).

135. Ibid., 342.

136. Ibid., 343.

137. Num. 20:12; Deut. 32:48–52; Deut. 34:4.

138. Percy Bysshe Shelley, *A Defense of Poetry*, ed. Albert S. Cook (Boston: Ginn and Co., Albert S. Cook ed., 1903), 46.

139. George Oppen, *New Collected Poems*, ed. Michael Davidson (New York: New Directions Books, 2002).

Index

Index

The Amherst Series in Law, Jurisprudence, and Social Thought

EDITED BY

Austin Sarat, Lawrence Douglas, and Martha Merrill Umphrey

Law and Catastrophe (2007)
Law and the Sacred (2007)
How Law Knows (2007)
The Limits of Law (2005)
Law on the Screen (2005)